LIVES OF GREAT MEN

Published November 2017 by Team Angelica Publishing,
an imprint of Angelica Entertainments Ltd

Team Angelica Publishing
51 Coningham Road
London W12 8BS

www.teamangelica.com

A CIP catalogue record for this book is available from the British Library

ISBN 978-0-9955162-3-6

Printed and bound by Lightning Source

An earlier version of 'Forgetting Lamido' is included in the 2016 anthology *Safe House: Explorations in Creative Nonfiction* (Dundurn Press and Cassava Republic Press). 'The Shea Prince' was first published in *adda*, 2016, by CommonWealth Writers, the cultural initiative of the CommonWealth Foundation, London, U.K. www.addastories.com.

Lyrics from 'Taxi Driver (I don't care)' by Bobby Benson quoted by permission of Bobby Benson Jr..

Names have been changed to protect the innocent.

LIVES OF GREAT MEN

LIVING AND LOVING AS AN AFRICAN GAY MAN

A MEMOIR

CHIKE FRANKIE EDOZIEN

TEAM
ANGELICA

For Iya Meso

"You write in order to change the world... if you alter, even by a millimeter, the way people look at reality, then you can change it."

– James Baldwin

TABLE OF CONTENTS

"Until the lion has his historian, the hunter will always be a hero."

– Anonymous (Elmina Castle, Ghana)

PRELUDE: FORGETTING LAMIDO

I open my eyes but I'm not moving. This siesta has probably lasted twenty minutes and now I'm staring at the lanky, striking man awakening beside me. It's mid-afternoon, and outside the streets are choked with crawling vehicles. Over the past few days the ubiquitous horn-blaring has been getting on my nerves. When did Ikoyi become so noisy? At least it's serene here inside the Moorhouse. The air conditioner is humming softly, chilling the room. The severe brown wood paneling décor is masculine. Nothing's soft about the furnishings. This small boutique hotel may be tailored for busy businesspeople but it's also an oasis amidst the chaos of Lagos. And it's in this oasis that I'm reconnecting with my childhood love. I stretch and see our naked selves in the mirror, legs intertwined on crisp white sheets. All afternoon we've been canoodling. Then having furtive, furious sex.

It's been ten years plus since we last met. Even after all this time our bodies haven't lost that feral magnetism for each other. At first we tried to tamp down the sexual tension by staying out with others at the bustling Eko Hotel. But in the end we just gave in.

He stirs, spurring me to inch closer, put my arms around his waist and peer over his shoulder. He smiles and I melt.

"You dey okay?" he asks softly.

Years ago, whenever we were alone, his deep voice softening to a whisper made me feel loved, and it does today. He still has dimples, and the whites of his eyes still shine against his groundnut-colored skin. He has no tribal marks but turns to look and see if mine remains. Few people notice it. It is tiny and hidden like a small scar under my right eye. He finds it, smiles, and strokes it with his thumb. Then he kicks off the sheet. And as my Fulani lover's sinewy, naked body stretches out into the 'X' position I touch his 'fro gently, marveling at how thick and soft it still is. What sort of pomade is he using now? I gaze at this body that's remained taut, even though it's now without the chisel of yesteryear.

"You look great," I say, gently fingering his bellybutton. His stomach tenses.

"I no be fine boy again oh," he replies, adding, "Your hair still plenty." He always appreciated the hair that sprouts abundantly all over me. I shave my head and face but I love my hairy chest, legs, and arms, and rarely trim or 'manscape'. I'm happy it still thrills him but I feel trapped. Even his scent, a mix of cigarette smoke and musky cologne, holds me captive. I hug him tighter. That Diana Ross ditty floats in and out of my consciousness: *Touch me in the morning/Then just walk away/We don't have tomorrow/But we had yesterday...*

What am I doing? I've just spent hours having sex with someone else's husband. And now we're in a post-coital afterglow with little to say. I remember him always talking, even after sex, but today he just smiles.

We look into each other's eyes. We both want to be here. Guilt isn't part of the equation. With this man it never has been. Not when I was nineteen, and not now, when we are both in our thirties. Nothing's changed. Yet somehow today everything is different.

Alhaji Lamido Gida and I first meet in the 1980s, when we and our families lived not far from this hotel. My brothers and I are Ikoyi boys, 'Aje butter' children – middle class kids whose parents have multiple cars, homes with domestic help, and who send them abroad on holiday. Lamido is twenty, and to my mind an adult. He's friends with my elder brothers and we meet when he comes to visit them. I'm sixteen and home on holiday from boarding school in Port Harcourt.

During my years at the co-ed Federal Government College I'm introverted, bordering on shy, but come alive when I get involved with the drama troupe and the press club. It takes three years before I finally begin to enjoy boarding, and by the time I meet Lamido I have friends from all over, not just the Lagos kids.

I also discover that the boys' dormitory, where these life-long friendships are formed, and where everyone strategizes about chasing girls, is home to hidden but rampant guy-on-guy desire.

By sheer happenstance I'm seduced by a classmate who I call Smiley. Although he's two years older than me, we're both going into Form Five and gearing up for the West African School Certificate examinations.

After oversleeping one morning I didn't have a pail of water to bathe with. I'd already missed the bread-and-boiled-egg breakfast, and didn't want to risk wasting more time with the trek to the outdoor quadrangle where the twenty-four communal taps were situated. So I ask Smiley, who isn't one of my friends but who is also running late, if he can share his full bucket with me. I expect a 'no' but he says yes with a little smile. And we bathe together, sharing the water, scooping just a little at a time so there is some left for the other. I make it to class on time and we become pals.

One evening when I go to fetch him for night study I'm surprised to find he's not ready. He has a brown cotton wrapper tied around his waist and no shirt on, as if he's about to go to bed. Without a word he pulls me into one of the tiny inner rooms behind the long, bunk-bed-filled main dorm, locks the door quickly, turns out the lights and whispers, "Shhh."

We keep still while the prefects usher everyone else out. I hear the clanging of the chains on the outer gates and know everyone's gone. Smiley sits back on the lower bunk and beckons. The tiny room has only space for one bunk. I lie beside him on the thin foam, and in the darkness he begins giving me little pecks on my lips and then my cheeks, sending sensations I'd never had before shivering down to my toes and up along my spine. I'm contorting each time he licks someplace. Then the furious rubbing of his prick against mine through the fabric of my shorts and his wrapper gives way to us removing our clothes. Smiley whispers, "Turn this way." I'm confused but he gently moves us into a comfortable position. And for the first time I'm having sex. Intercourse feels weird at first, then fantastic. There is pain, but that comes later. When in the deep throes of ecstasy I heave and ejaculate I think I've just peed. Smiley calmly explains: "It's just sperm."

That night kicks off moments with him that I can't even tell Paulie, my best friend back in Lagos, about. At fifteen this kind of sexual play is new to me. But not to Smiley, who tells me of others he's 'gone out' with. Boys having sex with each other surprises me. Until then I didn't realize it was even possible. After I leave I feel great, but later the 'good boy' in me is wracked with guilt. The term is almost over, thankfully, and the first thing I do when I arrive home in Lagos is head to my parish and get on my knees in the wooden pew, where my priest gives me his undivided attention. During these years confession was often heard out on the church verandah, privately but not in a wooden box.

"Bless me father for I have sinned. Since my last confession..." I have lost my innocence.

The Church of the Assumption in Ikoyi is a single-story building next to a marble office-tower and across from the Falomo Shopping Centre. I'm a regular reader at morning Mass and have worshipped here with my family from infancy. The young priest knows me well and names my 'sin' homosexuality. He acknowledges my internal struggle and encourages me to end this liaison. He is sympathetic but warns of consequences, and makes me feel that this is behavior I can vanquish if I just try harder. And am strong.

But I'm never strong when I return to Port Harcourt. No number of Hail Marys work. At some point I move into Smiley's room. We're now seniors prepping for O Levels so I'm not under scrutiny as I was when in the lower classes. Another classmate – Christopher – and I also begin to fondle occasionally, sneaking off when we can, meeting by the twenty-four taps under cover of darkness for moments of frottage. But I know this thing is passing: it's puberty play, purely physical and devoid of real emotion. So I keep going to confession and I pray. I pray for a good girlfriend. I pray to be like my four elder brothers.

Lamido changes all this. I'm now in Lower Six and have more freedom at home. I've aced my O Levels but flunk the yearly Joint Admissions & Matriculation Board (JAMB) exam so can't get into university yet. My options are either to take it again a year later, or complete my A Levels, which will take a further two years of study. As I prepare to retake JAMB I'm studying all day and partying with friends at night.

On Friday evenings Paulie and I usually head to Jazz 38 on Awolowo Road to listen to live music. Sometimes the Afrobeat King, Fela Anikulapo-Kuti, pops in en route to Ikeja, where he plays his standard set at the Shrine.

Paulie and I have been close since primary school, where both of us eschewed football and worshipped Motown divas, particularly Diana Ross. We were blissfully peculiar before we knew what it meant to be so. Taking turns at the microphone on the outdoor stage to belt out Sade Adu's 'Smooth Operator' is becoming our thing.

Lamido appears in the crowd, sees me, waves and comes over to us. Though his parents are in Kano, he lives with his siblings in Ikoyi. He's up for anything in the name of fun. He feels no guilt. "I'm a Muslim," he tells me, "so I don't drink, but I'll smoke anything smokable." I nod admiringly. He oozes charisma. He loves his brothers, reveres his sister and dotes on his nephews. It seems his siblings are in charge of his education. There have never been sparks between us – he's really my brothers' pal not mine – but now, as my friends and I gallivant around Lagos, I start running into him often.

Strolling by the waterside near the 1004 residential complex on Victoria Island to gawk at folk, gist and drink is something Paulie and I do often. In those heady days after high school, seeking out palm wine or barbequed meat has become de rigueur for us. We generally stroll along the lagoon on the road to Maroko, but sometimes we make a detour and stop at the chop bars on Bar Beach, along the ocean side of the island. Victoria Island is upscale residential, and more and more nice joints are popping up all the time. We both love to people watch.

Other times we retreat to the snooker room at Ikoyi Club,

the members-only recreational enclave that has been there ever since it was founded in 1938. Our friends bring their girls along. We all go to the same house parties. Sometimes I have a girl who likes me and I invite her to tag along; at other times I'm solo. I'm fine alone.

It's on one of these unattached nights out that I run into Lamido near 1004. He and I leave the others and go get suya near the Second Gate. I find these piping hot skewers of beef, peppers and onions irresistible. It's a cool evening and Lamido's wearing one of his floor-length caftans, a brown one, with black leather slippers. Chatting with him alone while chopping suya and licking our fingers feels nice. Afterwards he takes me home in a taxi. We get out at the Queens Drive junction and stroll to my gate. Once under the giant tree that provides shade during the day and blocks out the streetlights at night, he leans in and sneaks a kiss. His tongue slides in and out of my mouth very quickly. No one can see. It's unexpected but so enjoyable all I can do is smile. I'm seventeen; he's twenty-one. Before tonight I'd not thought of him romantically. He smiles and says he'll see me tomorrow, and many subsequent evenings he comes to fetch me, for us to hang out alone. "Oya make we waka commot," he says before our moonlight strolls. He's old enough to drive but I've never seen him behind the wheel: we take taxis everywhere. When guys walk hand-in-hand it usually feels brotherly, but I get goosebumps every time he touches my hand. I shudder when his hand meets the small of my back. He's tactile and I like it.

Lamido's a man-about-town, energetic, slim, with a thick head of soft black hair. I love touching his 'fro. I like his dimples. He's always elegant, and his scent – cigarettes and cologne – makes him seem so adult. His body is toned but I've never known him to play basketball, football or any other sport. He talks a lot, switching effortlessly from Hausa to pidgin when sitting barefoot on the floor with the house-helps; but at Ikoyi Club he'll discuss politics in the Queen's English before going dancing.

He's a tough guy, but when we're alone I see only tenderness. He tells me jokes in a soft voice and is, he says, full of gratitude for me. I love that his eyes light up when we meet. He loves that I'm not so butch, and doesn't mind my sometimes swishy gait. Gossip has little effect on him. He lives contentedly in his own space and I enjoy being there with him. He only desires that we meet. Often. In the bedroom reserved for overnight guests in my family's home we're constantly having life-conversations, then having sex when everyone's at work, then more conversation, followed by more lovemaking. We talk of our dreams too. Lamido encourages me to dress traditionally and gifts me a metallic-gray brocade caftan. It has intricate embroidery in thick white thread around the chest area and along the edges of the sleeves and hem, and is obviously expensive. He thinks I can pull it off with the kind of natural savoir-faire that he has as a Fulani man, but all I want to wear are jeans and T-shirts from London. He seldom wears Western clothes, but when he does his outfits are more fashionable than anything I own. He's the first to use the 'L' word. "You're my first love," he says over and over.

I stop going to confession.

But sometimes I wonder: is he just 'toasting' me, as we guys do? I'm not sure how this love happened. Lamido is popular and has options, including the many girls who want him. Meanwhile I've been going through the motions with a Warri girl who has decided that I'm her boyfriend now my brother is done with her. I say okay: it seems the easiest thing to do. Back in Port Harcourt I had a girlfriend. Most of the time we just passed notes and met up to chat. It was fun and simple, but not electric. Now in Lagos I have this girl who, after flirting with my brother, has settled on me. And it's fun to take her places, to hug and hold her tight as we say goodbye; to show her off. But the truth is, I have zero desire for her. When Lamido looks my way, my heart beats faster and my smile grows bigger. It's a jolt and I'm happy.

I find Lamido has a whole circle of friends who are similar to himself – top and bottom, or 'TB' guys, in-house slang for the peculiar. He's far along in his studies at the Ahmadu Bello University in Zaria and has a girlfriend there. I've seen her picture. He rarely mentions her to me, but often shows her photo to others.

After one term in Lower Six I abandon school and focus solely on studying for JAMB. My brothers are already at university so I'm the only one at home. On my second try I pass, and later receive my admission to the University of Port Harcourt's theatre arts department. I'm supposed to be thrilled, and in a way I am, but it means saying goodbye to my love. When we meet up, we talk about how we could disappear and get hitched... if not for the gender thing. "If to say you be girl, I for don marry you carry you go Sokoto," he says.

In my first year at 'Uniport' I'm a young man in love. But not with Janice, the girl I'm now dating, (the Warri girl moved on when I left Lagos). I'm acting, and even get a part in the lavish operatic dance-drama production 'Woyengi' at the Crab Theater. It's demanding and I give myself over to it, but still I yearn for Lamido. I wish he could see the show. I long for his touch, his constant whispering in my ears, telling me that I'm his bobo. I miss the way he pulls me close, his reassurances that all will be well. I ache for him.

I crave Lamido even when my high school romp-mate Christopher appears on the scene. We bump into each other on campus, and every so often he politely asks to visit – dormitory space at Uniport is so tight I've had to rent a room in Choba village. It's in a bungalow that is home to a large polygamous family and my room is next to the shared toilet. It's tiny, with just enough space for a single bed, an ironing/study table and chair; and there's a corner in which to hang clothes. The paint on the walls is blue and peeling.

Though I miss the camaraderie of dorm living, in Choba I have some degree of privacy, and my space is also a refuge for Christopher. He's discreet, visiting only late at night, and, when he stays over, slipping out very early, before the family rises. Once we're in bed, we pick up on the frottage we engaged in during our last year of boarding school. Afterwards we say little, and we never socialize together; we hang out with our girlfriends, and exchange nothing more than a quick hello if we run into each other. These encounters make me hunger for Lamido's full-throttle, passionate lovemaking and big personality. Christopher's fun but unsure, while Lamido's certain and knows how to fuck. And live.

Now, more than a decade later, Lamido and I are luxuriating on the king-size bed at my hotel. I've rediscovered his touch and realize how much I've missed it. But he's been some woman's husband now for more than ten years. He's also a businessman, running an import concern in one of the new office towers near Kingsway Road.

The next evening he brings along a strapping gardener from Suru-Lere who he'd introduced me to the day before as "someone to play with later". The guy's handsome, quiet, noticeable even when he's saying little. His arms are huge, and his body's carved by the work he does. I feign appreciation but yearn for the old days: then Lamido would never have thought to share me.

But now he's declaring we must "chop this yam together". We have a threesome. This is a first for me, and really what we do is take turns having furious intercourse with the gardener – which he enjoys – before turning to each other to make love tenderly.

The gardener's a tall area boy with a shaved head and shaving bumps on his chin, and I enjoy chatting with him once our roll in the hay is over. His voice is soothing and I find I like him. His mother is Yoruba, from Lagos, and his father is also Yoruba but from Benin Republic. Lamido isn't his boyfriend but they have a 'special friendship'. Over cold Star beers I gather that he earns little and has a wife and young son. He helps Lamido out sexually and Lamido helps him out financially.

When he goes to the toilet Lamido derides him as an "ashawo". I laugh, but I know he's no prostitute: he's just told me with pride of the flowers he's planted nearby, and other gardening jobs he's done lately; he just hasn't earned enough to make ends meet. I give little thought to the seediness or morality of their arrangement. People use each other; that's life. I notice the genuine affection he has for Lamido, but in my gut I know Lamido won't ever reciprocate. Love isn't in the air for either of us. It's clear that Lamido can't stay away from me physically – he's still caressing my tribal mark and rubbing my chest hair – but he has zero interest in rekindling the relationship. The gardener can't see it yet but Lamido is moving on from him too. We can all play here a while, then everyone has to return to their lives, their women.

I wondered how Lamido could move on so easily after seeing me. But after all it was me who chose to leave, even though leaving him behind was difficult for me.

After my first year at Uniport, things changed. The labor strikes and student unrest were constant. And home was a powder keg.

Things began to deteriorate when my two immediate elder brothers secretly left the country and emigrated to America. Then Mum left. At nineteen I was so angry my mother had left that I lost my fear of talking back to my father. I no longer put him on a pedestal. In many countries there is the expectation that when a marriage crumbles the children must be maintained at the standard they have grown accustomed to. Not in my case. My main concern was simple: who was going to pay my school fees? The rug was pulled out from under my feet: I could no longer afford to remain in school. And Dad didn't do anything about my expenses. I in turn sneered at the woman he brought home, and openly scoffed at his sister's insistence that I go to confession for being so rude. Normally obedient, I was done with that. I had an attitude and it wasn't one of deference. And then one evening, in front of his new paramour, he told me I was no longer welcome in the home I'd grown up in. "You can't stay here," he said as she looked on.

The thing to do would have been to fall on my knees and beg. But I just looked at them defiantly, shook my head at the usurper so desperate to become the lady of the house, then went upstairs, packed my bags and left.

I have not lived in any of my father's homes since.

A friend of my mother's who lived close by took me in. I returned to my studies but was constantly broke, living off the generosity of my friend Fela, who split his money with me so I could afford to return to Lagos – albeit only by bus. For years I'd taken the forty-five minute flight; now it was a bumpy twelve-hour road trip. I was constantly brooding. I studied but, having no money, didn't hang out. I auditioned for, and got bit parts on TV shows, which was encouraging, even exciting, but the payments never came. Fela kept me sane by regularly pulling me out of my room and sharing everything with me.

My mother was furious when she found out that Dad had withdrawn his financial support and I was all but starving on campus – she had not expected him to go that far. A year earlier I'd been promised a summer holiday abroad, and my mum, despite now having to make a new life for herself, didn't renege. She bought the ticket for me when I returned to Lagos for summer break. I was to go to my aunt's in London as usual. We had one last meal at Ikoyi Club, and Aunty Joy, a friend of Mum's, casually gave me several hundred British pounds for spending money.

During this difficult period Lamido, the one person who knew me inside and out, and loved me, had little time for me. He was now about to marry his girlfriend. We would not be disappearing together. He'd graduated, begun working; marriage and procreation were the next steps. He had been on pilgrimage to Mecca and was going to have a nice wedding. I, on the other hand, had nothing.

So I zapped. I left Port Harcourt. Difficult as it was, I left Lamido to his new wife and went abroad with no intention of returning.

My first stop was, as intended, London. In happier times I'd been there for summer shopping; this time I spent three months cleaning a bakery in Willesden, to earn some money before making my way to America.

America was a struggle at first, though my brothers helped me find a nighttime office-cleaning job and a small room to rent that was just a ten-minute bus ride away from the community college I had enrolled in. Lamido and I had little contact and our communications withered. He showed no inclination to visit, and I was determined not to return to Nigeria until I too had a degree: I wasn't going to be the one who dropped out. So I adjusted to a life of classes by day, twelve-hour shifts by night and sleep deprivation, but I did graduate, and I began working as a journalist. Acting was out. I was twenty-five and unburdened. For the first time I felt free to make my own decisions.

After years of struggle I lived an honest, openly peculiar but low-key gay life. No one in New York cared. My brothers made no fuss; they had gay friends by then. My sister and mother visited – at different times – the tiny apartment I made my home in Brooklyn, and reoriented themselves to my reality. I never hid.

*

In the late 1990s, on my first trip home since I'd left in a hurry, Lamido was the one person I sought out. I began to come home more often, seeking out work in Africa. In those years many friends and classmates who had fled the country, for higher education or to escape the political turmoil, began returning. But it seemed every 'TB' boy who came home followed the Lamido model: Get married. Have babies. Then continue with secret boyfriends. From my childhood best friend Paulie to Smiley and many in between, everyone fell in line.

Was it the price of living hassle-free in Naija that meant all these TB guys had to find wives? Could they not just be discreet, and live without having to marry women they had little interest in?

Of course, the pressure on women is even greater – at a certain stage all they hear are questions about getting hitched, as if all their accomplishments add up to naught if a husband isn't there to be shown off – but I started to believe these men needed wives to succeed professionally. One friend said he would never have gotten that promotion to senior lecturer at the Ambrose Alli University in Ekpoma if he had remained single. "You're considered mature if you are married," he told me. "That's the way it works."

Having found a career where my sexual orientation hadn't been an issue, I wondered if I'd be able to work full-time in Lagos at a high level without this ersatz symbol of maturity. Folks who presented me with opportunities said yes, of course. I wasn't sure this would have been the case if I'd remained at home, and so I empathized with friends who'd had to join the marital bandwagon.

Some insisted I was overthinking it: "Oh, you still spend too much time working in New York – when you move home fully you will marry and have someone on the side. That's the way it is"; "Everyone does it." No one pays any attention to a man's effeminate gait or his preference for the company of other men after he's paid some woman's dowry and put a ring on her finger.

My lecturer friend left Ekpoma, decamping to England to teach. He took his wife with him and his charade continued, though he couldn't find a solid relationship to have on the side.

He isn't unique: from Manchester to Chicago I meet successful Nigerian professionals in this boat. As long as they are perceived to be heterosexual, it's all good to them. Once when I was in London a Delta-Ibo man with a thick beard and shaved head tried to pick me up in a pub on Rupert Street. I enjoyed the attention and found him very attractive. He reminded me of the late Igbo military leader Odumegwu Ojukwu. It was a plus that he had lived in Asaba, my hometown. As I downed my lager shandy I sized up this to my mind potential mate. We flirted all night, even exchanging kisses after last orders had been called. It was fantastic – that is, until he began to give me details of his upcoming nuptials in Lagos. I stared at him.

"Don't you have the same pressure?" he asked, shocked that I found it incredible he was going home to marry. "She'll be there now! I'll do my thing, ah ah!" he said.

Is it just the career, or is it also parents pushing for grandchildren that leads these men to marry women they aren't in love with and don't even desire? Sharing a life with someone you don't love can't be easy, and I'm not sure I could do it.

I'm lucky; my parents have grandchildren already, so I'm not tasked with keeping the lineage going. My father and I, after some years had gone by, put love ahead of pride, and we now have a warm, open father-son relationship. We are proud of each other. I also have uncommon freedom because my siblings love me unconditionally. But every family is different: I know my supportive siblings aren't the norm, and far too many men can't risk being cut off emotionally or financially from their families. I've known for years that Lamido's sisters and brothers wouldn't accept his gayness. Not back then, and not today.

In the years following our initial reunion in Lagos, whenever I'm in Nigeria I make the effort to meet up with Lamido. He's since settled in Kaduna. All he requests of me when I visit is to bring him some poppers from New York. As he's aged he's embraced his softer side – like when he tells me how he just missed being the 'first lady' of one of the northern states when his ex-boyfriend lost the election.

One evening while I'm in Abuja we go to his brother's home in Asokoro for dinner. The meal is an elaborate spread of tuwo shinkafa with goat meat and fish soup. There's no booze, but the conversation flows. I listen as his siblings talk about flying across the country in a private jet with their friends. His now grown-up nephews are preparing to head back to British universities, and gab on about the different business-class options. Lamido, his current boyfriend and I have a swell time. But even in this rarefied and intimate bourgeois circle Lamido refers to his man as a friend.

When our hosts rise from the table and are out of earshot I say to Lamido that his new boyfriend is really nice. He shoots me a look of absolute panic. "Na wetin I do you now?" he says. I'm not to use the 'B' word while in the house. I apologize profusely: I thought it obvious that they are a couple. But if he refuses to acknowledge it to his relatives, then as far as they are concerned his relationship doesn't exist.

Back in Lagos, over some Chapmans at Bogobiri, Paulie isn't surprised. He tells me his own fear is not just of his brothers, but his in-laws. Should they ever find out about his boyfriends, he'll just deny it, he says.

I often wonder if Paulie and Lamido had a thing after I left. They both refer to each other as Lagos sluts and never hang out together. Now both of them are married to women they never spend any time with, pretending to the world they don't love men. Smiley too, who never left Port Harcourt, and eventually became a preacher who punctuates his sentences with "in Jesus' name", would be devastated if his family found out what really stirs his loins. He's been 'happily married' for years.

One school-friend who it had seemed to me wouldn't deign to marry for societal approval eventually did, and it shocked me: Chidi Omalichanwa, after decades in Europe, returned to Lagos and pulled a Lamido. He was a class ahead of me, and I had no idea of his gay adventures until we reconnected in the early 2000s. Chidi told me that back then he was sexually active with some of our schoolmates. All boys, all now married with children.

I felt the electricity that passed between him and another classmate when we all bumped into each other recently. Their hug was long and tight, and then both seemed to get shy and be momentarily at a loss for words. They hadn't seen each other in thirty years.

After high school Chidi got an engineering degree then went to Europe for postgraduate study. His career skyrocketed. I admired his joie de vivre, and seeing his successes I wasn't surprised when he moved home to helm a multinational. Over the years the geek I remember morphed into a macho guy – tall, broad-shouldered, dark-skinned and handsome, chic and bespectacled, an *Oga at the Top* – with a good career, a good home, an upper-middle-class life: a catch. But still I was dumbfounded at how quickly he married a woman he'd met soon after resettling. Children followed.

After two decades of boyfriends Chidi is now forty-five and 'straight'.

It made more sense to me for Paulie, who had never moved away, to get married, and I was able to rationalize Lamido's marriage for similar reasons. But Chidi's remains a head-scratcher. The man returned to Nigeria with accolades and his hiring was a coup. He already had the career and financial muscle so why jump into forced heterosexuality? Over the years he's joked – or at least I thought he was joking – that I was lucky I got away from him in high school; he'd set his sights on me, he claimed, but my sexual awakening only happened later. I'd flirt back lightly and say, "Damn, if not for that oyinbo boy you have, we could have been together."

Nowadays my response is a poker-faced, "Too bad! You've gotten married!"

One very clear evening, when the stars are shining brightly in the Lagos sky, Chidi and I join other school-friends for drinks at a swanky V.I. hotel rooftop bar. I'm swilling wine and having a good time.

After Chidi's downed a few shots of Maker's Mark I pull him away for some real talk. In a low voice he tells me that even though he had male sexual contacts in school, at university he had three serious girlfriends. "Ah. Maybe he's one of those truly bisexual guys," I think. But then, after moving to Europe, he fell in love with a man. There, though he certainly finds black men extremely attractive, he dated English and Irish lads only.

As he talks I'm reminded of a difficult break-up he'd had a few years before he returned to Lagos. Even though it was raw,

I had hoped he'd get over it; I hated to see my friend, a really good guy, so hurt. But now here he is, telling me that that break-up was the straw that broke this camel's back. Loving dudes afterwards was just too hard, he said. His solution to healing was to tell himself, "It's time to settle down and get married."

If he'd married right after he left the University of Nigeria, Nsukka, would he have missed out on his amazing career abroad? Or might he have soared all along in Nigeria, rising higher than he is now? Probably: he's that bright. I stare into his eyes and wonder, how is he doing this?

It's proving difficult: his attraction to black men is strong, so he's avoiding places where he could be hit on. But yes, he has flings. "Each time I travel to Europe. They're not lovers, just 'contacts'. It's not as if I'm looking, but if I travel it happens. I choose not for it to happen here because of the situation here," he whispers, afraid the servers might overhear.

The 'situation' is the criminalization of gays, and the pre-scribed fourteen-year jail-term for same-sex marriages, approved by lawmakers and the president in 2014 as a populist gambit ahead of an election they ended up losing anyway. The stunt unleashed a manhunt of suspected gays among the hoi polloi. Folks of means retreated indoors and carried on. Or went abroad.

Chidi refers to his interactions with his foreign fuck buddies as having a "coffee and a chat". But even these trysts are becoming rare: it's as if he's weaning himself off men.

It's a high price to pay in order to function in Nigeria.

Before we rejoin the others I pull him closer for a hug and mischievously whisper, "So does this mean there is no more hope for us?"

Chidi pulls his head back, takes a good long look into my eyes, and bursts into a fit of laugher. And responds, "There's always hope for you! We'll have a coffee and a chat when we're in London."

Months later we chow down on some goat pepper soup, yam and tender guinea fowl at Ikoyi's Casa D'lydia. A giddy Chidi is explaining that life isn't terrible – he wanted kids and now has three. And he's finally found someone. Someone local. Someone safe. Someone married with children too. His companion is a businessman whose family lives in Sokoto. Weekdays he's on his own in Lagos. He gets Chidi. Chidi gets him. They are happy.

"To be free is not merely to cast off one's chains, but to live in a way that enhances and respects the freedoms of others."

– Nelson Mandela

ONE: LEAVING LAGOS

December 2011

I t's been three years since Dr. Scott and I began dating. We spend the few weekends he has off in my Brooklyn flat. Most of the time he's so fagged out from his overnight shifts at the Montefiore, the gargantuan Bronx hospital where he works in family medicine, that he dozes off on the silver-gray Ethan Allen sofa that also pulls out into a bed. Usually he's in it all weekend. If he's worked the 'night float' there isn't much chance of us doing anything; it's video games on the couch, with my eggplant-colored feline friend cuddled up next to him – Scott's a cat lover, and he dotes on Weber, who's lived with me since I turned twenty-six.

The flat is small and the walls are painted white. My furniture is all silver and gray, and the walls are hung with masks and artifacts from places I've visited around the world. Primarily the artwork is from African cities. But there's also the elaborate brown clock with the intricate black lettering on its face that I picked up in Beirut, and a large photo of the supermodel Naomi Campbell across from it. The photo is a black and white shot of a young Naomi in all her black woman topless glory. Her arms are extended over her head and out, and her manicured fingertips touch the walls. Her breasts are on display, supple and inviting. It was shot by the American photographer Bruce Weber, whose work I've admired for years. I was so enamored of Weber's photographs that at one point I bought a collage of them and hung it on one of the walls. And though she's female, I named my kitten Weber in his honor.

Across from Naomi is a framed black and white image of a man and woman kissing, a print of the iconic 1950 photo by Robert Doisneau, 'Le Baiser de l'Hotel de Ville', shot outside the Paris City Hall. It was a souvenir of my time there as a college student on an exchange program – I could afford to bring home nothing else. On that side of the room I also hung the stone octagonal clock I found in Marrakech. It has a cement base, with the brown and red decorative detailing common to that part of the world. The hour and minute hands are black and the second-counter's bright red. It ticks noiselessly and looks ancient, but in reality is a quartz battery-operated contraption. And a framed sketch by Fred Berger, depicting a Middle Eastern Jesus with a huge smile, welcomes me into the living room every morning. 'The Laughing Christ' is the only depiction of Jesus I've seen with him in full throttle laughter, and I love it.

Mixed in with the photos and masks are colorful oil paintings from Brazil – one large, predominantly blue one hangs above my bed. And my books – novels mainly, but also textbooks – crowd the sagging bookshelves. I have long black wooden male and female Ewe masks from Ghana, with the Adinkra symbol 'Gye Nyame' ('Except God') etched in them in silver. Other masks from Nigeria hang in the bathroom. I've grown fond of African masks even though many would tell me they are carved for purposes other than just simple display. I didn't care and I still don't: I'm Catholic, so not bothered.

From my travels in Ashanti land I've brought home wooden stools, the thrones their chiefs sit on. I threw one of the stools in my suitcase and packed my clothes around it. The ebony piece made it to Brooklyn without a scratch and lives next to the poufs – round leather cushions from northern Nigeria that are sold flat, and the purchasers have to stuff them with shredded paper or old newspapers to give them shape. Once stuffed, they transform into beautiful footrests or things to sit on low to the ground.

Over the years I've realized that I'm a homebody, and I love being quietly transported to places I've been by these artifacts I collect. But when Scott's around I have a burst of energy and want to go take big bites out of the Big Apple. After a long week of work I often find myself ready for a Saturday night out, only to settle for watching Scott and Weber doing the thing they love the most: sleep. They curl up next to each other on the Ethan Allen, eyes tight shut, while Naomi Campbell looks past them. And I have to figure out something else for our weekend.

But this particularly Saturday Scott is wide awake and ready to hit the road. We are far, far away from Brooklyn, having just spent almost a week in Abuja. He's made it to Nigeria, we've been having a delightful time with my sister and cousins, and he's been enjoying the modern city that Abuja is.

Each morning, when we wake up and look out at the lush, rolling greenery of the Katamkpe Hills, Scott says it reminds him of the Arizona landscape. The estate we are holed up in is relatively new, just off the Kubwa highway, twenty minutes or so from the city center. Past the gate, within the walls, all is tidy and orderly. The houses, townhouses, duplexes and apartments are uniformly ochre. The paint is bright and pleasing to the eye. The lawns are tended, and mounds of bougainvillea and hibiscus explode from every patch of herbaceous border. Outside my brother's townhouse, in which we are comfortably ensconced, multiple brand-new cars line the driveways of his neighbors. Guards in smart brown uniforms escort visitors to doorsteps to ensure they aren't robbers, and when the power goes out every now and then, a generator for the entire estate kicks in immediately. John Yusuf, the house caretaker, is excited to see us, and spends all his free time chatting with Scott and me. The Beninois chef, Ibrahim, delights in serving us intricately-presented meals – the French way, he emphasizes. All this opulence has Scott convinced that, despite my modest home in Brooklyn, I must have a secret trust fund and a family that is very comfortable.

"You guys are 'one percenters'," he says.

If we were, I tell him, we wouldn't fly commercial. And my brother is just generous, giving us the use of his home – "but don't get used to all this," I warn.

Each day we leave the estate to visit my sister and cousins in Wuse 11, a comfortable middle-class enclave. We also hang out in the more upscale neighborhoods of Maitama and Asokoro, where the roads are paved and the houses are bigger and then bigger still, and adorned with fountains, and surrounded by flawless lawns and ever-higher walls.

We are trying to take a big bite of Abuja life. So it's fun outings daily. My friends and family join us at the Silverbird Galleria for movies, then drinks at bars. We spend a lot of time at my favorite suya joint, Yahuza, also in Wuse, and we even take time to go check out the zoo next to the Aso Rock presidential villa.

For a city that is gleaming with brand-new high-rises and spectacular office towers, and is bookended by a glorious, gold-domed mosque and a large national interdenominational cathedral, the zoo, despite its lush hilliness and postcard ambience, isn't so thrilling. Many of the animals look like they are starving; others just seem in desperate need of better care. And the paying guests are sparse. Scott keeps taking pictures. I wonder if he is building a case for PETA.

Abuja in December 2011 is very hot, so we go swimming each day at the Transcorp Hilton – or as some of my Nigerian friends call it, 'the village square'. After our afternoon swim we relax at the Piano Bar with jugs of Chapman, the quintessential scarlet-colored Lagos cocktail, while chatting with friends who come to chill with us. Most evenings there is a lounge singer crooning American standards as folk drink and chow down on warmed-up peanuts. Some gay Nigerians drop by, as well as doctors and health workers from New York who Scott's connected to, as the Transcorp is easy to get to.

Before he got his medical degree, Scott worked in HIV prevention. Our mutual friend Kent Klindera, who at the time vetted international grant applications for funding from the American Foundation for AIDS Research (AmFAR), has some colleagues who come to hang out with Scott, and they invite us to their homes for meals. Scott delights everyone when he ditches his T-shirt and jeans and dons one of my traditional caftans for dinner. Now, after what has been a relaxing week, it is time to fly south to Asaba, the Delta State capital and my ancestral home. Scott doesn't oversleep this Saturday: he's raring to go. He is to finally meet Dad and a plethora of my uncles for the first time.

Asaba is much smaller than Abuja, and even with the multitude of people crowding the footpaths that are hewed into the red soil of its mostly unpaved roads, it feels quieter. This town on the banks of the River Niger was once Nigeria's administrative capital, and even all these years later never seems to have had the industrial boom that elevates many a town to 'city' status.

In a few years Asaba will become a hub for movie-making, presumably because of its abundance of picturesque rural landscapes, perfect for depicting village life on the screen, while also boasting airports, hotels and places with studio equipment and editing facilities.

Asaba in the festive season is very colorful – at the Grand Hotel, a spacious luxury hotel on the riverbank, the Christmas lights are bright greens and reds and yellows, and Scott is mesmerized. He's a keen swimmer, and we spend a good deal of time here so he can use the Olympic-size pool.

For the next couple of days we walk and drive around, enjoying more suya and visiting uncles and friends of long standing. We visit Umaru, a northerner by ethnicity and a Muslim, who has lived in Asaba for as long as I can remember and is practically a family member. When he was younger Umaru lived with us and worked for my dad as a security guard. Now he's an Aboki money-changer, particularly of dollars and pounds, and has a huge family of his own. They live some distance away, in Cable Point, which is further away from our home in Umuezei, but he still goes to work just down the street from Dad.

We also go to my grandparents' homes, and I explain my lineage, which goes back to the town's founder, Nnebisi. Scott enjoys meeting my elderly aunts, and I show him the grave of an aunt who lived on Victoria Island who we called 'Orange Mummy' because of her very fair complexion. The grave is next to the house my late grandmother lived in until she died, and the house is next door to the palace of the town's traditional ruler, the Asagba, who is Dad's elder brother. With motorcycles thronging everywhere (okadas have been banned in Abuja at this time) Scott says Asaba reminds him of Lusaka, the Zambian capital where he lived for a year.

Like many towns in Nigeria, houses of worship abound, and churches are on every corner it seems. I show him Saint Joseph's Cathedral on Nnebisi Road, the catholic monsignor's seat where the family worships. As we crisscross the town we regularly pass a ginormous stone and fiberglass statue of a pregnant girl in the center of a roundabout. She is dressed in what seems to me the normal uniform worn by high school students: a light-colored blouse, the sleeves rolled up as is the style with kids, and a darker-colored skirt that stops just at the knee. Her hair is plaited in the local style, and on her feet are sandals of a type common to schoolchildren everywhere. She is meant to depict every schoolgirl here. The statue's swollen stomach is a transparent glass bowl and within it a fully formed fetus is visible. Below her feet, on a raised green platform, is lettering in white. Green and white are our national colors. The sign, which is huge, reads STOP ABORTION. IT IS EVIL AND DANGEROUS. I hadn't noticed it on my prior visit, but later learn it was commissioned by a church group, the Knights of Saint Mulumba, in 2009.

I am horrified.

I particularly love street art, and the numerous sculptures and full-length statues on Asaba's streets always please me and make me proud. There is one of an elephant with its tusks raised high, another of a lion being killed by a townsman, and yet another of Nnebisi, the founder of the town, from whom every Asaba indigene can trace his or her lineage; and even one of the women's leader, the Omu. Almost every entrance to each of the five main villages that make up the town has some cultural artifact that beckons one in, and most are interesting and invite questions about their meaning. Yet this graphic pro-life message delivered as public art stops me cold. In recent times many Nigerians have embraced a rabid religiosity that veers towards conservative and literal interpretations of religious texts. Asaba is no different, but the graphic nature of this more-than-twelve-feet-tall statue shocks me. Scott finds it amusing and proceeds to take pictures of it and with it, acting like a tourist who has just come across a major hidden gem. I join in, posing and smiling in front of a piece of art that makes me queasy. My uncle Douglas finds us amusing and can't comprehend our bewilderment: this is normal, not a big deal. The corner is now known as 'Stop Abortion Roundabout', he tells us. Like everything else it serves as a useful landmark and that's all folk think about it.

When not roaming Asaba's streets we spend much of our time hanging out with my father in his compound, which decades ago he dubbed the House of Gold. It is spacious, with three buildings within, and many bedrooms. Scott spends a bit of time talking with Dad about his health, going over his medications and taking notes on his iPad. At the time Dad's dealing with a back condition and the side effects of the treatment for it. Surgery in Europe has worn him out, and now he is now content to remain at home for long periods, limiting his travel. His reception of Scott is very warm, and I think how far we have both come over the years. Pictures of his children and grandchildren cover the living room walls and are particularly dense around the well-stocked liquor bar – he's never been too much of a drinker but always has enough to entertain.

Many of the photos are formal graduation portraits, but Scott zeroes in on one that isn't, a picture from a 1980s party of me with my sister, my dad and my aunt. I'm wearing a white button-down long-sleeve shirt, partly open to reveal my chest. I also have on what was then the pièce-de-resistance from my closet: shiny gold trousers. It is an outfit that I picked out myself, from Selfridges and Marks & Spencer's on Oxford Street, London's shopping Mecca. The white leather shoes likely came from one of the tiny boutiques on nearby New Bond Street. I have a bag (a 'murse' really) slung across my shoulders. The photographer captures me in mid-strut (apparently I strutted the way the fictional Olivia Pope would make popular decades later) next to my family, all of whom are resolutely dressed in traditional attire. I remember loving those gold trousers.

Scott stares and dissolves into a fit of laughter. "You were sooo gay!" he squeals.

And then the doctor can't resist taking a copy of the photo so that we have it back in New York.

After laughing for what seems like hours he regains his composure and says he wants to post it on Facebook. He hasn't yet. Gazing at this picture, one I had forgotten about and am surprised Daddy framed and kept here in Asaba, sends me down memory lane fast. I stare at the teenage me: how carefree I was then, clutching my murse and taking wide strides while Daddy and Sister smiled. I was gazelle-like in gold pants, rocking an afro and prancing around Lagos.

This carefree, gold-pants-wearing guy was the guy that Smiley was drawn to, the one that Lamido couldn't resist.

The naïve, gentle young man looking into the camera that night would not have imagined morphing into the jaded, defensive New Yorker now looking back at his teenage self and reminiscing about growing up in idyllic Eko – the traditional Yoruba name for Lagos.

Back then, as now, Las Gidis, as Lagos is also known, was the place that many flocked to in hopes of finding fame, fortune, or just themselves.

I was eleven years old when I first left Lagos for boarding school in Port Harcourt, two hundred and seventy-three miles away. This was in 1981. When I wasn't in school I was back at our family home in Ikoyi, a residential part of Lagos filled with civil servants and posh private sector or foreign-service families. In that era residents of Ikoyi and Victoria Island, the community across the lagoon, mainly lived in houses with big yards that were relics of the British colonial era. Street names were of lords and governors such as Cameron, Milverton, Bourdillon Glover and Ruxton.

The first Lagos home I really remember was a detached structure on Lugard Avenue with lots of well-established trees around it. The street was named after the last British Governor-General of Nigeria, Frederick Lugard. In the compound, past a pair of high metal gates, was a U-shaped driveway. On each side of the driveway huge trees provided shade. On one side of the compound were trees that when in season had bright canopies of red flowers, and people called them the flame of the forests; on another were perennials the adults said were Christmas trees, though naturally these were not like the one in the storage room that we brought out to decorate each year at yuletide. There were also mango trees, and the almond tree everyone simply called 'fruit' because of its tasty droppings. The house had a large veranda at the side and was built slightly raised from the ground, as was the style of the time. Dad was then an engineer with the Ministry of Works & Housing, and Mum was a virologist, producing yellow fever vaccine for all of West Africa from her laboratory in Yaba.

These large, rambling houses can still be found across West Africa wherever the English lived. An architect once told me they were raised high because the Europeans were afraid of mosquito bites and the thinking was the higher up the better. Their anxiety was justified: for a time West Africa was 'The White Man's Grave' due to malaria. No matter, in the 1970s and '80s we lived in one of those houses. Beside the house was what was left of a swimming pool put in by occupants past, probably British, though by then only the faded gray concrete that outlined it remained; the pool itself had been covered over years earlier. There could have been room for a tennis court if anyone played. It was that kind of spacious; and the grounds were large enough for us to bike and play soccer in and not bother anyone – though we were careful not to kick the ball in the direction of the gleaming gray Lancer Dad had parked out front. My first dog, a black dachshund puppy with gold streaks on her face, lived with us then. I named her Lucky Queen.

The house didn't have a wall around it like many have come to have since, though it did have a wire fence, and passers-by could see through the trees into the property. To me as a child it was idyllic. We had a petit bourgeois lifestyle, but in Ikoyi this wasn't unique. Our neighbors were of a similar ilk and mostly quiet. My friend Henry's home was equally large, with pawpaw trees in the grounds, and boasted a huge aviary, from which a cacophony of chirping emanated every time one walked by. My brother's friend Emeka, who lived down the road and had many, many sisters, had a similar style home to ours, just with more cars in front of it. And the walled compound across the street belonged to the white embassy folk, and had a generator that kicked in automatically when the power was out: that home was always brightly lit.

As a kid, Paulie, who went on to be one of my closest friends, lived on one of the parallel streets nearby. His family home was similar to mine, the house more or less in the same style. And though most of us weren't private sector millionaires it was a comfortable time; an era when the world spoke of

Nigeria in glowing terms. We'd just hosted the Second World Black Festival of Arts & Culture (FESTAC), a feat so grand that it has never been repeated, and from January 15 through February 12 1977 it seemed Lagos was filled with foreigners and music. Everyone smiled, and the Nigerian naira was almost on par with the U.S. dollar. 'Taxi Driver', the 1950s-era hit by the great highlife musician Bobby Benson, seemed to be our unofficial anthem.

For most of us Christmases were generally spent in the ancestral hometown, a great migration east that continues to this day. Back then, if you were lucky and your parents could afford it – or simply wanted to keep up with the Mbakwes – a summer holiday in London might also be sprinkled in your year. My most prized wardrobe items, like the white button-downs and the gold pants I wore in the picture, came from one such summer trip. For some families the USA might be on the cards, but back then it was mostly to the colonial mistress, the United Kingdom, who at that time didn't require visas of Commonwealth citizens from West Africa, that we went. At other times there were trips within West Africa: to Togo, with its fantastically French capital, Lomé; to Benin Republic right next door; and to Ghana, with its vibrant capital, Accra. Everyone came back with tales of places their parents had taken them in the school breaks.

I am attending the Home Science Association School, a private elementary with extremely small class sizes housed in a four-story building. One day, after school and before my parents return, and while the house-help is preparing lunch, a man comes to the house with an envelope. He was from the ministry and it was official business, he said. I took the envelope and innocently presented it to Mum when she got back from work. She opened it, read it and in seconds went from happy to angry. As often happens, a higher-ranked political appointee had seen our house on Lugard Avenue and decided he wanted it. And just like that, we were given an eviction notice.

Dad was furious. With no wall to keep out prying eyes it was easy to see why someone had noticed our house and the generous expanse of land around it. My father, though a high-ranking and well-respected civil servant, was powerless to stop us from being pushed out. The occupant-to-be was a member of the cabinet of the new civilian president, Shehu Shagari. I gathered at the time that the new occupant was from northern Nigeria and probably had a large family. And so we had to leave this slice of paradise.

We moved to a smaller property, a duplex that might originally have been a single home, but was now divided to house two families – though the sole occupant on the other side, also a northerner, was a civil servant whose family never relocated to Lagos. It was on Adeyemi Lawson Road, just off Queens Drive, and next to the lagoon that separated tony old-money Ikoyi from nouveau riche Victoria Island. One of Dad's younger brothers, Uncle John, lived up the road with his family.

We could not play ball or run around as we used to, but we were also growing up, so the need for play-space was fading. Our dog family was increasing; we acquired a shaggy male creature I called McDuffy, and hairy half-daschund puppies followed. Some we gave away; others, like a shy all-white one, Scouty, we kept. Dad had an extension built onto the side of the house, creating an entire new wing to accommodate us – he's an American-trained engineer, and found shrewd ways to maximize the use of the smaller space – and also erected a covered car park for his growing automobile collection. He had a Mercedes Benz, a Volvo and a Toyota; Mum had two Peugeots – a larger 504 and a smaller 305. At that time Lagos was becoming congested with traffic, so the municipal authorities devised a workday driving schedule where cars with odd-numbered license plates were allowed on the road on some weekdays, and those with even-numbered plates on the others. A noble idea, but families like ours got cars with different plates so as to still be able to drive to work daily.

Our home had two living rooms, one where the kids hung out, and the other a plusher 'big sitting room' for the grown-ups, with a built-in bar complete with bar stools, and gold-colored furnishings. This bar Daddy went on to replicate in his Asaba home. He stocked it with wine and fancy brands of brandy. Dad also added a guesthouse in the back for out-of-town visitors. This he did by dividing up the three-room boys' quarters where the house-help lived so it had two separate entrances.

We all settled into our routines. The one constant was dinner as a family at six p.m., with both my parents and all my siblings at the dining table. Missing dinner or eating separately was not allowed: there were no telephones, no television, just food and conversation.

Now and then we had parties to celebrate something, an adult birthday or just because. Everyone got all dressed up, the records would play, and my parents would dance with their friends. One anthem always sure to get everyone on the dance floor was an ode to motherhood: the highlife hit 'Sweet Mother' by Prince Nico Mbarga would be played at the beginning and end of the evening.

Star beer, Mateus Rosé, (a light Portuguese wine), and all sorts of booze flowed. By this time my eldest brother and sister had graduated college and moved out, but they were still frequently around. It was at one such party that the picture of me strutting in my gold trousers was taken. At that time I already recognized I was different, but with the fragile egotism of youth merely thought I was special.

Paulie was the first queer friend I had, though at the time we shared only a general recognition of our otherness. Paulie gamely channeled his lack of interest in traditional boyish pursuits like soccer into snobbery towards our less sophisticated classmates, which they ignored. We often played together after school, and shared elaborate fantasies of other lives elsewhere, and he did a wicked impersonation of Diana Ross, miming vigorously to Supremes songs on my parents' record player. My father had brought back many records from America, including loads of 1960s Motown classics (I knew and sang the words to 'Love Child' before I had a clue what Ms. Ross was crooning about.) Paulie was different from every other kid in our school but self-assured. He was special.

As a teen, the first 'peculiar' adults I knew in our insular Ikoyi world were the hairdressers from Ghana who worked at the salon down the street, taking care of the 'madams' in the neighborhood. In the 1980s what seemed like millions of Ghanaians of all economic stripes had moved to Nigeria, to escape the political instability at home at that time. For these guys, who worked long hours, twilight was the time to let loose, and once the sun had gone down they would sashay along the street, smoking and chatting with people. Friendly and flamboyant, they turned Adeyemi Lawson into their personal catwalk, prancing up and down, breaking off to talk to the ladies at the junctions who sold sweets, groundnuts and other items from their round metal trays. But unlike the other passing men who sometimes flirted with these ladies – who were mainly married to the drivers, gardeners and domestic help attending to the better-off occupants of the area – the hairdressers appeared to be gabbing to their sisters.

In one of her boys' quarters, their madam had turned a few rooms into a salon, and the hairdressers lived a few rooms further away. A convivial bunch, they were different, and even as teens Paulie and I, though we didn't have the language to describe them – or us – knew we were all, in our way, the same. They were an amiable bunch and I enjoyed talking with them most evenings.

It soon became easier for me to spot the peculiar ones. In every place I lived, or frequented, or even just visited, gay people occupied a space that I saw.

Take Port Harcourt, to which I was sent at age eleven. At the time federal boarding high schools had been set up as 'unity schools', where students from all parts of the federation were housed and educated together for five or six years. This took you out of your comfort zone, as you lived with students from very varied socio-economic backgrounds. Uniforms were worn (ours was white shirts and maroon shorts by day and blue checks in the evening) and schedules had to be adhered to. Our school motto was the Latin phrase 'Pro Unitate' ('for unity'). In your first year you were oppressed by everyone; by your second you could at least dole out errands to freshmen.

I hated the first year. My mother came to see me a couple of times, but it was a flight away, and not feasible for her or anyone from home to come every month on the school's visiting day. We lived in dormitories that had names like Faith, Charity, Loyalty, Honor and Peace, and these were the values it was intended for us to take away and live by for the rest of our lives. After classes we retired to bunk beds with thin mattresses we called foam. Everyone had a small locker where you could keep your snacks and other provisions, and any personal items.

We had chores to do before the day began. Some of us had to sweep the floors, others tidy up outside; and most of us had to trek some distance twice daily to fetch a pail of water to shower with as there was infrequent running water – I don't remember the actual showers ever working.

A drab gray building stood a few meters away from the boys' dormitory. Inside, there were holes in the cement floor. The holes were right next to each other with no privacy. Students had to squat and excrete into them. The building had a permanent putrid smell, and many students missed the holes, took dumps on the floor, and ran off. Which was unfortunate for those who had the task of cleaning these pit toilets in time for Saturday's dormitory inspections. Saturday was the only day you could use the pits without worrying about stepping in shit.

By way of exercise, three times a week there was compulsory morning jogging around the inside of the walled school compound – which we weren't allowed to leave without a permission slip called an exeat. The grounds were extensive, and designed to have everything that students needed right there on campus, so in theory there was no need to venture outside. But the food was downright awful. Even so, many boys and girls rushed for it, grabbing heaps of caked white rice and loading their aluminum plates with watery stew, leaving little for the weaker students, who often referred to this boorish behavior as 'massacre'.

One joy for many of us was the gentle guy who came and sold roasted groundnuts to both students and staff during the afternoon breaks. Okon would flip the nuts he'd just peeled after cooking them in little sheets of paper. We'd hand over our money and he'd hand over twisted newspaper cones filled with hot groundnuts. The cones would remind me of pyramids, and I would think of the gigantic groundnut pyramids the country was once famous for. Sometimes we'd buy roasted corn to go with them. Okon always had a sunny disposition. His son would later attend the school. There was also a student-run 'tuck shop' where biscuits, sweets and the like were on offer. But none of this could make up for the poor quality of the main meals we were served, and many scaled the walls at some point to get food and other illicit stuff in nearby Rumokoro village, where Cool Breeze was a favorite chop bar for those who made the unauthorized trek. At one point someone knocked a huge hole in the wall so there was no need to scale it; just bend down and off you went. Following the footpaths into the village.

There was a small coterie of students who had medical issues and were called 'sicklers' by the staff. They were fed from a smaller pot of stew that was cooked separately, without pepper. Even minus the pepper their stews seemed so much richer in other things that I became a 'sickler' for the sake of better grub, feigning an aversion to spicy food.

By my third year I was fully acclimatized, and going back each term wasn't so traumatic. Part of the reason I had become more comfortable there was I was now in the press club, and regularly put together news bulletins for the Friday assembly, listing all the gist that happened in school, and all the things that needed fixing – like the water tank near the dorm, which in theory should have fed the shower system but in practice never did.

I was also in the drama club, so when there were inter-school events I got to go. But most important to me was the school principal, a great educator named M.C. Ebo, by whom we were guided both morally and academically. He was an Asaba man who my mother later told me taught her chemistry way back when, but even though he knew my parents he doled out no favors. He made all in his charge recite portions of the Henry Wadsworth Longfellow poem 'A Psalm of Life' during the morning assembly, and those of us who were lucky enough to be his students memorized the lines,

Lives of great men all remind us
We can make our lives sublime,
And, departing, leave behind us
Footprints on the sands of time

As students we may not have understood everything he was trying to instill in us, but the words of the poem stuck with us as we grew up, and we still remember his urging us to attempt the great things that would ensure we made our mark in this world and left our own 'footprints on the sands of time'. For those who were fortunate to have his tutelage he remains a pillar that looms large even when we don't consciously think of it. His words, and the friendships many of us made in those years, have been enduring.

His successor, Principal Omotosho, was just as strict but not as awe-inspiring.

In January 1984, a month after the civilian government was overthrown in a bloodless coup by the military junta, Muhammadu Buhari, then an army major-general, was declared the new head of state, ushering in a period of repressive military dictatorships and coups d'état. This dark period would last until 1999. But even with dark clouds hovering over the entire nation, life went on. Workers put their heads down and submitted to a 'War Against Indiscipline' and a severe, belt-tightening 'structural adjustment program'. Money was hard to come by and the currency was devalued. Prices for everyday items ballooned, and in some cases even bread disappeared from dining tables across Nigeria.

Despite the woes and worries of our parents, once we returned to the boarding school we were insulated. And as it was a co-ed institution, in the third, fourth and fifth forms heterosexual romances bloomed for many – including me – though generally amounted to little more than passing love-notes and choosing to spend time with each other between classes, or walking your 'girlfriend' around the grounds and whispering sweet nothings to her at the T-junction – dubbed 'Love Junction' – that led either to the boys' dorm or to the girls' facilities.

In the fifth year a friend bragged to me about how he'd gone one big step further, and had lost his virginity with one of the less popular girls in the back of one of the classrooms.

'Chaaai! Me sef I chop am well well oh!'

His glee was infectious, and I laughed, congratulated him and pressed him for details – Was she willing? How did you lure her to the back of the classroom? – and so on. 'What if somebody saw you?' I asked, pondering what had been going on with Smiley and me, and Christopher, because I too had been having sexual adventures, though mine could not be bragged about.

As the years progressed, even though I remained deeply into Lamido, I became more and more aware of other peculiar folk, especially once high school was over and I was at the university. Even in Asaba I would notice peculiar spaces and people, for peculiar though we may have been, we were hardly an anomaly. Like the dude who swished along Nnebisi Road with a wrapper tied around his waist and gabbed with the market women there – who a pal of mine drove over to chat up, thinking him a woman, and then realized to his supreme annoyance that 'she' was a guy. He drove off laughing at his mistake.

Or my aunt Orange Mummy's utter bewilderment at the actions of a much older great-aunt who had moved in with another, younger woman. "How can a woman marry another woman?" Orange Mummy asked, seemingly totally befuddled by the concept.

This was the time Lamido was making his life decisions, and I too was about to try something different, by dropping out of university and heading to America.

So now I'm here in Asaba, and Scott has managed to find the first photographic evidence that even as a teenager I was growing up queer. After he snaps a picture of the photo on his iPhone we hit the town again so we can visit Orange Mummy's grave and her old home, and so I can introduce him to the lady who's taken care of Grandma's house since her death. We are also having nightly cocktails at The Grand Hotel's Jetty Bar, from which we can look out over the River Niger.

This is the same hotel where a few years ago I first ran into Lamido's 'special friend', his pal the gardener. After our threesome we all stayed in touch for a while, but then he – the gardener – cut off contact, and on my next visit I discovered he'd taken up with the hotel's European general manager. For some reason he wasn't keen on renewing our friendship. Even though it had been a few years since our roll in the hay, I found his coolness towards me surprising. I called Lamido in Kaduna to say I'd just seen Jacques (though he is Yoruba, his franco-phone dad gave him a French name) with the European manager of the hotel. "Er hen. No be ashawo wey e be?" he said. "Abeg make I hear word." Lamido never wavered in his conviction that Jacques was a prostitute, and we moved on to chatting about something else.

In the hotel bar on our last night in Asaba I secretly had

hopes that Jacques would still be there, but he was nowhere to be found, and I later heard that his companion had been replaced by another foreigner.

So Scott and I leave Asaba after a fantastic few days and head to the ancient city of Benin, finally ending up in Lagos. I'm eager to show him the Lagos I've gone on about for years.

"We Must Be the Change We Wish To See."

– Mahatma Gandhi

Two: 'Finding' and Accepting in America

I leave Lagos in July 1989, determined to pursue a university education in America. My first stop is London, where I stay for the summer months, working in the tiny bakery on Willesden Green High Street – the only job I can get without the necessary work papers. I'm cleaning the shelves and mopping the floors a few times a week, and being paid in cash and pastries. The wages are meager, the pastries fattening. By September I have landed in upstate New York, just in time for the beginning of the academic year. I enroll in Onondaga Community College in Syracuse, a college town with – as I am soon to discover – loads of snow. It is where my two brothers live, though one is getting ready to move to Chicago. Downtown Syracuse is crowded with skyscrapers and everyone drives. Unlike London there are no underground railways here, so buses are the only means of mass transit, and to me it feels provincial and village-like.

I rent an upstairs room in a house along the bus route to the college, on the 300 block of Onondaga Avenue, a family home occupied solely by an elderly grandmother who is probably renting it out as much to have a man in the house as to earn some extra money. I never wander outside of my space and rarely even use the kitchen, though she tells me I am welcome to do so. She often gives me newspaper articles if Nigeria is mentioned. I am grateful and she's a delightful landlady, never intrusive, always helpful when I ask for anything. I soon get a job as a janitor, cleaning offices at night downtown.

Snow can come as early as November in Syracuse, and is cute the first time, but soon gets old, and it gets really cold. It is a sad, draining time, very gray, and I never really adjust well. Outside the classroom I am totally uninspired.

For a Lagos boy, Syracuse in 1990 is a tad too sleepy. Everyone seems to be enamored with the new shopping mall or the State Fair; I am unimpressed. Desperate to escape the provincialism, one time my brother Gil and I, and our great friend Francis Egbuson, drive down to New York City to see a concert. It is the king of Afrobeat himself, Fela Anikulapo-Kuti.

I recall all those times I sang at Jazz 38 with Paulie, when Fela would come on later in the evening. Those were not exactly 'open mic' nights, but the band singer would at some point call up people from the audience to come and sing while the musicians accompanied them. Paulie and I were young and bold and probably sounded alright. I often looked at it as an impromptu theater performance, and so long as I remembered the words to the song it was a success. But the main event was after midnight, when Fela passed through. He put me in a trance and was wonderful to see live even if the set always felt a tad short – it was sometimes a warm up for his more elaborate show later on at the Shrine.

His New York show, with many women surrounding him in varying states of scanty dress, is long, ebullient and fantastic. The energy he radiates is incredible, and even after a long evening of driving to get here we shake our heads, tap our feet and sway all night. We sway and shake to long rhythm sections before he finally launches into song. When he sang his hit 'Lady' – about certain African middle-class women refusing to answer to the word 'woman' and embracing full equality of the sexes – we yelled the chorus back at him – 'She go say I be lady oh!' – as we jumped up and down.

He sang about African women who refused to be called 'woman' but stated their preference to be referred to and treated as ladies.

Through his songs the master storyteller gives us many tales, the boisterous and varied audience – many Nigerians yes, but others too, blacks, whites and other Africans – spinning to beats and chanting back in adulation. The modern African ladies wore the pants in the household, he seemed to imply, and lacked the rhythm of the traditional women who danced like fire, who knew their men were the heads of the household and cooked for them. It might have been chauvinistic, but everyone, men and women alike, screamed, danced and chanted back at him during this song and throughout the entire set. It was exhilarating and well worth the trip.

It is only after the show is over, and as we're heading off to find a late-night supper place, that I finally take notice of Manhattan. It's as if I'm seeing it for the first time. The buildings here seem to actually touch the skies; there are lights everywhere, even at three a.m., and people are walking around, walking around! Few did that in Syracuse, especially in winter; and of course in Nigeria this is the hour for sleep – or nefarious activity under cover of darkness. Steam rises from the sidewalk grills movie-ishly. My brother says it has something to do with the trains underground. This place is magical: the skyscrapers, the endlessly busy streets, the yellow taxis, and all the people who are not white and have every sort of accent. This is where I need to be, I decide, not in the room I've rented on Onondaga Avenue: I have to leave that place and come here.

I last a year and a half more in Syracuse. After that trip I begin to make plans to move to the Big Apple, regardless of whether or not I am admitted into any schools. I get into New York University to study journalism and work at night after classes. I have no dating life because there is simply no time. In the evenings I work as a long-distance telephone operator for AT&T, which at the time is the nation's leading phone company. I do this job for years, trudging most evenings to a skyscraper at 33 Thomas Street in Lower Manhattan. It is a brown tube of a building, and entirely windowless. New York fascinates me, with buildings like this that scrape the sky but offer no view of the world outside their walls. My job is to assist folks making long distance calls, and to 'win back' customers who have defected to upstarts like MCI and Sprint. Working from six p.m. till two a.m. after a day of classes at N.Y.U. that often begins at ten a.m. leaves me zero time and energy for socializing, and I barely make friends with my co-workers, who are primarily black, with many hailing from the Caribbean. In Syracuse, where I first learned to be an operator, there was only a smattering of black workers. When I'm not working or in class I am at the colossal Elmer Holmes Bobst library, struggling to get my homework done, or simply to stay awake.

When I do have the rare opportunity to go out I head for a wonderful dive bar I've discovered on Christopher Street, at the outer edge of the gay village, down towards the piers. Dingy, always crowded, and somewhat hidden away, it is called Kellers, and black gay men troop into it nightly. I do too, whenever I can muster the energy to be the African gay boy in a crowded, exotic mix of all sorts of black men, along with a sprinkling of Latinos. I walk in and inhale the testosterone. The mannish energy reinvigorates me.

I have never been a big drinker but the bartenders are friendly enough. I don't converse a lot, but the sensations I feel as I stand there are enough to send me to therapy. Blocking out the emotional fallout from my failed relationship with Lamido, I had thought New York would somehow give me a clean slate, and that I would revert to my plan of graduation, working and getting married to a woman. No more shenanigans. But the pull to what I really desire is intense, and I am both happier and more comfortable trooping down to Kellers than going on dates with the girls in my class who show an interest in me.

I took one such young woman to our university's spring party, dubbed the Violet Ball. I liked her: we were two black kids who were both working our way through N.Y.U., and this was a night to dress up, party and get loose. She was excited; I wasn't, but managed to fake up some enthusiasm so at least she would enjoy herself. But to head to Kellers? I didn't need convincing. It helped that it was tucked away from everything, and no one I knew would be there unless they too were on a manhunt.

The free counseling sessions offered to undergraduate students back then helped. Now that I think about it, the counselor was probably a graduate student, and she spent most of our hours taking copious notes by hand. I babble. She listens. I feel better afterwards. And she does help me understand that being gay isn't really the issue I seem to think it is, and that I'm not alone or even special in that regard.

She tries to steer me in the direction of looking to my own guilt-free happiness. My comfort level slowly grows, and though my free time is increasingly scarce, more and more of it is spent at Kellers; the drag queen favorite Two-Potato; or on the piers that abut Christopher Street, where minority gay teens and adults flock for community, many of them homeless. And it is one Friday night in Kellers, as I stand shyly admiring all this masculinity on display, that Marvin Timmons rolls up to me and says, "Hi." At this time I don't have a gift of the gab, or the clothes, or the muscular physique many of these guys have, or their seemingly full-blown confidence in their sexuality. All I have going for me is that I think I'm actually a nice guy.

Marvin is a bit shorter than me, very light-skinned, and a charmer. I am surprised he wants to chat with me since he seems generally popular, the room is filled with hotties who have the language of the place down pat, and I am a wondering kid pressing his nose to the aquarium-glass. It is the same feeling whenever I work up the courage to come in here; even as I return more frequently, and enjoy myself, I remain the outsider looking in.

My friend Jose Torres, a confident, gregarious Puerto Rican with a huge laugh, baggy jeans and shiny caramel Timberland boots, is less impressed with Marvin than I am. Maybe he knows him from around the way, or maybe he can just spot the unsavory player type.

I will come to learn after a few dates that Marvin is charming but an adult delinquent. He's always full of excuses as to why he is extremely late for a date, or didn't show up at all. But I think he is cute and so I dote on him for months. I make excuses for him and never am so sure why I like him so much. Is it because in a sea of hunky, brawny guys he picked me? Or do I just need the company? Even when he brings over a guest from North Carolina and leaves him in my flat for weeks, finally forcing me to concoct a story about my mother coming to visit to get him out, I still want Marvin around. I am twenty-four and he is twenty-six and a clerk somewhere. He has never been in a college classroom but has street smarts. And in some ways

I admire him. I'm still working nights, he works days, and I am grateful for his company when he is around. He calls almost every night from a payphone near his home (mobile phones were not ubiquitous then) to say goodnight to me, so I figure he is invested in us. But apparently he is also a major player, and Jose, who knows all the bars, clubs and places around the city where gay people of color congregate, lets me know it. He never says he doesn't like Marvin, but he avoids hanging out with us as a couple, and often asks me to join him in a pub-crawl whenever I complain that Marvin has blown me off again.

Eventually Marvin is remanded into custody at Rikers Island for six months. Rikers is a large correctional facility on a four hundred acre island in New York City's East River, where people are jailed before being sent on to 'real' prisons, most often upstate. It is an awful place to be, and humiliating for a visitor: you are searched and bossed around as if you too have committed a crime. He's been charged with grand theft auto, but it is not his thievery that breaks us up; it is the repeated indignity of going to Rikers Island to visit with all these other families that finally opens my eyes. This is not my life; this is not my American dream, to visit my partner in jail, and I had no intention of it becoming so. Prison bars, clanking doors, uniformed and hostile correctional officers – must I scrape the bottom of the barrel quite so hard for companionship?

Jose, when it dawns on him that my adventure of being a doormat is finally over, gives me that *I-told-you-to-leave-that-motherfucker-alone* look and talk. I don't argue back.

"The world is before you and you need not take it or leave it as it was when you came in."
                                                    – James Baldwin

THREE: OUT @ WORK

With no real plans in place, after graduation I begin my journalism career in America. It's 1993. I had intended to go home after graduating but it now seems like a bad idea. The government has changed hands again, and Nigeria, my beloved country, is being ruled by the most brutal dictator in her history. General Sani Abacha's repressive regime sees the execution of environmental activists, the muzzling of the press – particularly by shutting down newspapers – and the persistent jailing of dissidents on trumped-up treason charges.

In 1994, as Nelson Mandela's South African presidency is ushering in hope across the world, the Abacha regime is making Nigeria a pariah nation. Mandela engages with Abacha and visits Nigeria. In July 1995, as the situation get even more dire, Mandela, known to many by his ethnic name Madiba, sends a small but high-powered delegation to Nigeria that includes the man who will be his successor, Thabo Mbeki, to talk with Abacha about releasing political prisoners and environmentalists.

Many believed the political prisoners would be killed. Mbeki and his team had a specific mandate: persuade Abacha to release the Ogoni environmental activist and writer Ken Saro-Wiwa and the eight others imprisoned with him – as well

as generals Olusegun Obasanjo and Shehu Yar'Adua, who had
been detained for allegedly plotting a coup d'état. Mbeki meets
with Abacha at the Aso Rock presidential villa in Abuja at two
a.m. – Abacha's nocturnal. Mbeki has said since that the
dictator listened, said he needed to reflect on what had been
discussed, and promised to give them an answer before they
left Nigeria.

Later on, the South African delegation is invited to lunch by
Abacha's chief of defense, Lieutenant-General Oladipo Diya. He
gives them Abacha's response: that in the matter of the beloved
writer and activist Ken Saro-Wiwa and his co-accused, while he
cannot intervene in a judicial process, if they are found guilty
and given a death sentence, he promises to intervene so that
they are not killed. Saro-Wiwa and others of the Ogoni ethnic
group had been railing against the environmental devastation
of the Niger Delta resulting from the constant extraction of oil
in the area. The local community, many of them fishermen
struggling to make a living in water poisoned by regular spills,
had seen little of the wealth drilled from their backyard that
was making the country an economic giant. Mbeki says Diya
also told the delegation that Abacha believed he couldn't
interfere with a military tribunal, but that if the tribunal didn't
recommend the release of Obasanjo and Yar'Adua, he promised
to intervene and do so. Mbeki leaves Nigeria and relays
Abacha's assurances to Mandela.

In the months that follow Madiba is under great pressure
to publicly condemn Abacha but refuses to do so. The pressure
mounts and mounts, and by the time he sets off for the Commonwealth Heads of Government meeting in New Zealand in
November many nations want economic sanctions imposed on
Nigeria for its continued jailing of dissidents. But Madiba has
assurances that nothing will happen to the jailed environmentalists.

"It was with this knowledge that President Mandela left
South Africa to attend the New Zealand CHOGM meeting,"
Mbeki would recount years later. But on the first day of the
summit the news filters out that Saro-Wiwa and the rest of the
Ogoni Nine have been hanged. Mandela is blindsided; the
world is stunned. "When Ken Saro-Wiwa and the others were
executed, President Mandela was truly surprised and genuinely

outraged that General Abacha could evidently so easily betray his solemn undertaking in this regard. He then immediately joined others strongly to condemn the Abacha government and approved the suspension of Nigeria from the Commonwealth."

Way back in 1986, as a sixteen-year-old in Lagos I was heavily affected by the assassination of the journalist Dele Giwa, who happened to be a friend of my elder sister Annette, and whose death by mail-bomb solidified the idea in my mind that journalism was not only a noble profession, but that doing it right could get a whole lot of powerful people upset at you. During my years in high school I came alive telling stories through the press club, and as a child in Ikoyi I'd learned to read primarily through the newspapers my father brought home each week. It isn't even a decade later, and now another writer, Ken Saro-Wiwa, who pushed the government hard, has been killed in a grotesquely medieval fashion, as if to warn off others. Death by hanging is no joke. The message was clear: you could be hanged. You will die struggling for air in spasming agony if you go against us.

So I've finished my degree and, like Giwa, I've been doing work for a big New York newspaper. But if the internationally-lauded Saro-Wiwa can be hanged, what hope is there for me to go home at this time? The news is constantly dire, and no one I know is hurrying to get back there to work: it is all wait and see. Abacha wields a heavy hand. Many in the country fall in line. Civil servants display false loyalty, pinning pictures of him on their clothes when they go to work. Until the day he dies, which is not until 1998, fear grips Nigeria.

All this time Diaspora activists and communities push governments to isolate him further. One proud moment for Nigerians in New York was when we got the City Council to change a street name right in front of the Nigerian Consulate to the United Nations to Kudirat Abiola Corner – Mrs. Abiola had emerged as a fierce advocate for democracy after her husband was jailed, and contact with his family cut off, following elections on June 12 1993 that most Nigerians believe he won fair and square. She was assassinated in 1996, and many discreetly pointed the finger at Abacha. Nigerians in the Diaspora couldn't bring about too much change from the outside, but it was a small victory to have Abacha's representatives in New York walk into work daily facing a sign with Abiola's name on it. Today, every time I walk into Nigeria House, a gargantuan skyscraper at 828 Second Avenue in Midtown Manhattan, I smile and swell with pride, not so much at the flapping green-white-green flag on its pole above, nor even at the Nigerian food cart selling delicacies from my youth such as fried plantain and moi-moi, but at the street designation: KUDIRAT ABIOLA CORNER – a sign the Nigerian government has nothing to do with, and cannot remove.

This one street sign represents to me a triumph for both committed Nigerian activists, and regular folks whose voices are more often than not drowned out by their own government. In New York City pro-democracy voices were heard and we have our lasting proof.

During these years I've been working in the newsroom of the *New York Post*. In late 1993 I began as a copy boy – a clerk-cum-news-assistant who on occasion got to report on or write up metro news stories. Once trained, after a few years I was promoted to staff writer and would remain there till 2008. Over the next decade and a half I work covering government, politics and healthcare, always trying to make a difference.

It is in New York, at a professional gathering for gay journalists, that I have a life-changing moment: I meet Marcus Mabry, then an editor at *Newsweek* magazine. He is not only an out-and-proud African-American journalist but handsome, kind and charming to boot. He is integrity personified, and I am strongly drawn to him. I visit him weekly at his Upper West Side apartment on 86th Street in Manhattan. We talk and watch TV together. Unsurprisingly we both love the political drama *The West Wing* and rarely miss an episode.

I soon realize that I have a brother in New York City: the family void is filled. I decide that I too can be, following Marcus' example, an out and proud gay man in the workplace. It helps that I have discovered a Jesuit parish in Manhattan, Saint Francis Xavier, where I can worship and be both gay and Catholic freely and without guilt. One year I attend a mass where the priest, addressing the gay congregants there, had a simple message: 'Come closer.'

The parish wanted us there and encouraged our attendance, reminding its congregants that God doesn't make mistakes and His home is for everyone. It even supported its parishioners at New York's annual Gay Pride Parade.

These Jesuit priests made it clear that in their houses all were welcome, no ifs, ands or buts. I marveled when, in the summer of 2017, the archdiocese of Newark New Jersey, under the leadership of Cardinal Joseph Tobin, threw open the doors of the Cathedral Basilica of the Sacred Heart to welcome gay Catholics, telling all who attended he was their brother. That gesture made international news, but for me it was what the tiny parish of S^t. Francis Xavier had been doing for decades, even when Church leadership discouraged it.

It wasn't until the late 1990s, when a friend from my boarding school days invited me to attend his wedding there, that I returned home to Nigeria.

Over the years I'd been scraping by; now as a journalist, before then getting through university working nights for AT&T. During that time I'd stayed away from any Nigerians I didn't know. Once I got spooked by a dude who wanted me to grab data I had access to from the office and bring it to him. "We could make money," he said, his eyes bright and hungry. I stopped returning his calls. I was broke, but could live with myself.

Like me, my high school buddy had moved to the U.S., and he insisted that he wanted no gifts but merely my presence – along with that of another pal of ours who had also moved to the States – at his wedding back home.

So we fly down to Nigeria and my brother Don picks me up from the airport and I stay with him for a couple of days before going on to Ibadan for the ceremony. Don used the time I was with him to remind me that life is short and time is moving on, and that the family is still a family despite it all.

I hadn't seen Dad since I left so abruptly, and outside of the two who lived in the States, even my other siblings rarely saw or heard from me. The years were going by, Don said. Since by then I had a life I mostly liked, and a career I could be fairly proud of, I had no desire to cause any anguish, and so a détente was reached: I forgave, and, after a quick trip to Asaba, re-sumed a relationship with Dad. It was like the ending to the Nigerian Civil War: after all the bloodshed, and all the lives lost, no one got an apology. It was simply 'No Victor, No Vanquished'. We moved on as if we'd never fought.

The wedding was lavish. At one point there was 'rain' – showers of blessings. At another the groom's crew – his friends and brothers – danced with him, accompanying him through the crowd to wait for the bride. And when it was her turn, her entourage of girlfriends and family easily dwarfed the groom's! It was a boisterous celebration, and a great time was had by all. And for me it was a beginning. Perhaps I could replant myself in Lagos.

I didn't fully move back then, but spent a lot of time exploring my city, later renewing or making acquaintance with other parts of the country and the continent; and I kept finding ways to write about Africans and the contemporary African's way of life. But of course my main responsibility at the *New York Post* was to do journalism in America about Americans on American-centered issues.

One of the great professional gifts I got from working in America at this time was membership of the National Association of Black Journalists (NABJ), where I found family in the years I could not go home. From the first convention I attended, in Washington D.C., with my late friend and then boss, the *Post*'s associate metro editor, Lisa G. Baird, I was hooked. Lisa was for a time the only African-American editor at the newspaper, and for many years was the only person of color at the table where both metro and national stories were conceived, edited and run. She took a keen interest in the younger reporters and was extremely kind to us. She always insisted that on big American holidays like Thanksgiving and the Fourth of July American Independence Day celebrations, when most people had their families to go to, I come to her home. This was a spacious high-rise apartment in Fort Greene, overlooking a thirty-acre park designed by Frederick Law Olmsted and Calvert Vaux, best known for Central Park, and I'd always find a proper hot meal waiting for me. Others came by for some grub as well; Lisa never wanted those of us without family in New York to feel we had to work on the holidays; or if we did, that there was always some joy to be had.

My first NABJ convention – a week-long event – was a revelation. Upwards of three thousand journalists – black journalists – met up each year to share strategies not just for doing good stories, but for dealing with newsroom stresses and the challenges to moving on up, and for making our careers in a predominantly Caucasian industry easier to navigate. The mentoring that was absent from the newsroom one worked in could be found here. It was a psychologically helpful gathering, of course, but it was also filled with skill acquisition workshops and seminars that I found inspiring and extremely useful, and I made many friends and found many mentors there. There weren't – and still aren't – many minorities in newsrooms, and there were things I couldn't discuss with the people in mine, so reaching out was a necessity. NABJ was an offered hand.

In our down time Lisa played bid-whist and introduced me to other editors and writers. I was in heaven.

NABJ also gave me the opportunity to meet Thomas Morgan III, who was to become both a mentor and a dear friend. Tall, broad-shouldered and with beautiful brown skin, he had the biggest, highest-wattage smile I'd ever seen, and when I happened to sit next to him at an NABJ event, I knew I had to get to know him. So I did what in years past I'd have been too shy to do: I made jokes and flirted with him openly. In my mind I was certain it would come to nothing, but in the meantime I would enjoy this hot guy's presence. It was bold to flirt with a black man who I presumed to be straight in a room full of other black journalists, but I didn't care. I smiled and he smiled back.

It turned out he was a past president of the organization, and was actually openly gay. That was exciting, though I was mortified to learn that I been flirting with one of the pillars of the industry, and a beacon of light to many, without even realizing it. But he laughed so hard at my feeble attempts to chat him up that my embarrassment soon fell away. Even though, as the kids in the clubs would say, my pick-up lines were 'wack'.

Tom lived in Brooklyn as I did, and I grew to love him; and he and his partner, also named Tom, became great friends to me. He encouraged me in my career, and believed in my talents even when I was unsure of them. Endearingly, he always made a point of showing up for my birthday parties, at the holiday home I rented each summer in Fire Island Pines.

Not far from New York City, and wedged between the Great South Bay and the Atlantic Ocean, the small barrier island, which is next to Long Island, is home to two historically gay villages, Cherry Grove and Fire Island Pines. I started off by renting rooms in a house in the Grove, and after my thirtieth birthday went on to rent a very modest place without a pool in the more upscale Pines.

Tom routinely showed up for dinner at my Brooklyn flat, and always made himself available to me in my moments of self-doubt. Later in life he got into pottery, and a green vase he made and gifted me is one of my prized possessions today. He was a big brother to me until the day he died, in December 2007, from AIDS-related complications. I still miss him very much. Through him I got to understand how gay men could have family outside of blood that ran so deep.

Lightning had struck twice for me, first with Marcus, then with Tom. I only wish he could have met my partner Scott – his partner Tom Ciano has, and I'm grateful for that.

Through NABJ I met many other black gay journalists, and no matter what city we were in, we always set aside one night during the convention for a pink pub-crawl. In the 1990s and 2000s the National Association of Lesbian & Gay Journalists would send a representative or two to the NABJ convention, and often they gave us ribbons that we would pin to our lapels to show solidarity with each other: a public display of pride. A good number of us were members of NLGJA too, and attended their conventions and events, but some in NLGJA didn't belong to NABJ. It was always awkward asking those brothers in the gay journalists' association to come to NABJ conferences: when they said they didn't feel welcome, it was hard to argue. Still, for us brothers at NABJ it was home, and we were there to stay.

By late 2003, the same sex marriage debate was heating up across the United States. George Curry, an influential black journalist who at the time was the editor of the widely-read-among-black-folks *BlackPressUSA*, weighed in with a column titled 'Mixed Feelings About Same-Sex Marriages'. In the nationally-syndicated column he said his religious beliefs left him torn between feeling that homosexuals should not be discriminated against because of their sexual orientation, and believing that same-sex marriages should not be sanctioned by the government or the church. Fair enough. But then he threw in this bit:

> Sure, there are some things that are common to both movements, but except in limited individual cases, gays and lesbians have never suffered anything approaching the oppression of African-Americans. They were not lynched because they were gay, they were not brought here in chains because of their sexual orientation, they were not deprived of the right to vote because they like people of the same gender, and no White girl in the United States has ever been killed for whistling at a White woman.

He, like many African-Americans at the time, seemed incensed that the push for gay equality was being equated with, and used rhetorical tropes from, the civil rights struggle. He was, and remained, an influential voice, as for decades he had used his journalism to champion civil rights and the black press in general. Curry was lauded that year as the NABJ Journalist of the Year, so was listened to by many when he spoke. And at the time, his reasoning stung. Not only did his opposing 'black' to 'gay' erase black gay men and lesbians from the conversation, but his column came out a time when black gays and lesbian *were* being killed solely for their sexuality, including a young woman in New Jersey named Sakia Gunn, who at age fifteen was stabbed to death in the street for refusing the advances of a – black – man who approached her.

Curry had at that point been such a stalwart fighter in the war against AIDS in the Black community that his broadside was shocking to me – he'd worked with the Black AIDS Institute on several programs, and had interacted with black gay men and women, and yet still held this view. Marcus and another close friend of mine, Kai Wright (who had worked with Curry), and I decided to write a public response to Curry's article. I put down a first draft I hoped many of us would sign, and Marcus, both wiser and smarter than me, polished off the anger and honed it to the points we most strongly wanted to make. Kai threw in some concise arguments that helped effectively rebut Curry's claims, and eventually we had a document we could send out.

I then began to call on all our friends who were black gay journalists, many of whom we had done the annual pub-crawls with; and the others reached out to their friends too. A core group of us signed the document, including my dear friend Patrick L. Riley, an NABJ stalwart who had served the organization forever. Others waffled, however. One dude who worked hard for the organization waited until the very last moment to tell me he had 'problems' with the language. Bear in mind we'd circulated this letter among ourselves for about ten days beforehand, and had had many conversations and made numerous revisions. Yet he just couldn't bring himself to sign it. NABJ was his world and he could not rock the boat.

I understood where he and some others were coming from: one would be outing oneself unequivocally to the broader NABJ community. It would have been for many a first public declaration of their sexuality, and that was very scary. Homophobia in the African-American community was very real then. It still is. Also, the letter was likely to be seen as a public rebuke to not just Curry but the entire black press establishment, which up until then had been able to easily shrug off criticisms from predominantly white gay organizations such as the Gay & Lesbian Alliance Against Defamation (GLAAD). But we firmly believed that change had to come from within.

We finally sent off the letter with just ten signatories, and we stressed the following points:

> ...As for lynchings, we remind Mr. Curry, one of the most powerful Black journalists in America, of the scores of anti-gay murders that occur annually. This year, five Black and Latina transgender women were murdered in Washington, D.C. This summer, a 15-year-old Black woman from New Jersey was stabbed to death at a train station after identifying herself as a lesbian to a man who tried to pick her up. This gruesome list goes on, and it only includes those that the police actually classified as being motivated by the victim's sexual orientation. All of this, of course, excludes the fact that the HIV infection rates among gay and bisexual Black men in their 20s is on par with that of the most ravaged

countries of sub-Saharan Africa... Moreover, we cannot help but note that had mainstream Black institutions and opinion shapers been able to put their homophobia aside as this epidemic emerged, we may have saved countless Black lives with the sort of early intervention other communities mobilized at its outbreak....

The widely-read blogger on journalistic matters, Richard Prince, reported the response on his *Journal-isms* blog, and mentioned that some who signed the letter had never revealed their sexuality in public before. Curry told Richard the incident represented a difference of opinion, not homophobia on his part. In a later column he addressed his critics, who he claimed were spurred on by a letter-writing campaign by 'predominantly white GLAAD', but rather tellingly didn't refer to our letter. No matter: the point had been made, and it seemed like a good moment to put into practice an idea one of our members, Mashaun D. Simon, had mentioned over the years – to have official recognition at NABJ in the form of an LGBT task force.

But how? Others had talked about it in the past, but when they had broached the subject with the NABJ leadership they'd been rebuffed. A past president claimed not to know of any gay people within the organization. Shocking. We began to strategize informally, and our tribesman Jerry McCormick, who was on the NABJ board at the time, worked so, so very hard to get us our moment before them.

It finally happened in Queens in January 2005, on a windy, snowy day. We sat and listened as Marcus, by then the chief-of-correspondents at *Newsweek*, made a fifteen-minute presentation, then for about ninety minutes answered questions from the eighteen board members present. Tom Morgan showed up for us and I was immensely grateful; he'd always been supportive, and as a former president carried a lot of weight with the board. Many listened silently. Only one, Sarah Glover, spoke about the caliber of the members who had come forward to ask for this task force, and how we had demonstrated our commitment to NABJ over the years. (Glover herself would go on to become NABJ president in 2014.)

We had hoped the board would put aside skepticism and, indeed, prejudice, and embrace us. A day later we were informed that, after some deliberation, they had voted thirteen-five in our favor. We hadn't swayed everyone but I was happy. I told Richard Prince for *Journal-isms* that this was a historic moment:

> In the last year, one of the biggest stories in the nation has revolved around marriages for gays and lesbians. Another has been black sexual identity in America – the diversity of the Black LGBT community and the increase in HIV/AIDS in our community. NABJ should lead or play a vital role in how these issues are covered. Now the organization has a formal organized structure to deal with these issues.

Curry, who died of a heart attack many years later, in 2016, left behind him a legacy of raising up black journalists, the black press and civil rights in general. And back in 2003 he was, in his own way, a catalyst spurring black gay journalists to action.

After this I was publicly gay in my career and out in my New York circles. There really was no going back into any form of a closet now. Not that I'd ever wanted to; my years in New York had taught me to cherish myself as I am.

Marcus and I were the initial co-chairs, and the Task Force had at its inception forty-six members. It didn't, as some had feared it might, fall apart – America was having a prolonged gay conversation, and it was right that gay ethnic journalists be an identifiable part of it. NABJ's vote spurred the National Association of Hispanic Journalists (NAHJ) to form its own official caucus barely a month later, and without the sort of protracted discussions we had had. Progress, it seemed.

But we still had to perform.

For our first convention, which was to be held in Atlanta later that summer, we needed to raise money for a reception and for workshops for the NABJ membership on how to cover LGBT issues and related matters. Raising cash isn't the strong suit of many journalists, including me, and I was thrilled when friends in New York – the head honchos at the New York Dermatology Group – stepped in and covered those expenses.

For our coming out party at the convention we planned to sponsor a workshop discussion featuring J.L. King, who had written the controversial and much talked-about tome *On the Down Low: A journey into the lives of Straight Black Men who Sleep With Men*, as well as hold a reception to honor our trailblazer, Tom. Everyone on the Task Force worked really hard to get all this to happen, and before the event I confidently told the convention newspaper that our work would be the foundation for things to come: "We're journalists. All different kinds of NABJ people trying to make black journalists better and stronger."

Inside, however, I was very nervous. Would anybody even turn up? I need not have worried. The 'Low Down on the Down Low' panel was standing-room only, and King was his typically funny and provocative self, pushing the many women in the audience to look for 'signs' their men might be having gay relationships on the side. The attendees spilled out into the hallway, and after it was over they lingered.

King's talk raised a lot of questions. How should these issues be covered? What was our role as black reporters? How do you now cover the HIV issue in our community? Were men with HIV, and bisexual men, being demonized and seen as perpetrators while straight women were positioned as victims deserving of compassion? There were no easy answers, but folk were thinking and talking.

The reception for Tom was a great success too. His former colleagues, including his *New York Times* publisher, Arthur Schulzberger Jr., all showed up, as did board members past and present. It too was standing room only. It turned out to be the last convention Tom attended, and even though I had loads of one-on-one time with him in Brooklyn, it was special being by his side in front of an admiring audience of his peers; and then, back in our Atlanta hotel room, listening to stories about the organization the event had reminded him of was wonderful too.

Despite all the good that was happening, attitudes were slow to change. When I bumped into the recruiter for the Associated Press, Robert Naylor – another pal from New York – in the hallway after a successful day of programming, I gave him a hug and kissed him. He smiled broadly. He's older, had been an editor and bigwig in the Associated Press news wire service and the NABJ for years, and for years had pushed for diversity among the staff at A.P. Some of his convention buddies had never had any confirmation of his gayness up until then, and he told me later that my kiss had been conversation fodder for them. That generation was one of 'Don't Ask, Don't Tell'; among them only Tom was openly gay in the organization. Robert had never confirmed or denied his sexuality; now my kissing him in public had opened him up to chatter. To my relief he reveled in it.

Generally being gay is no big deal for many New Yorkers. But sometimes a whiff of it, or even an accusation, can have deadly consequences.

For many years I am stationed at City Hall, working primarily as part of the team responsible for government and politics coverage for the paper. On a particularly hot July day in 2003 I see firsthand how the shame of being tagged as gay can destroy lives.

For some time now the councilman for Fort Greene, my local legislative representative, has been James Davis. Though I keep a professional distance from the lawmakers, I am in varying degrees friendly with all fifty-one city council members, and James and I in particular have a cozy rapport. I see him regularly in Fort Greene, and in my mind he's a good neighbor and active lawmaker who always shows up for things.

A month earlier, in the wee hours of the morning, he spots me on my way to City Hall, trudging to the subway, and pulls over to give me a ride over the Brooklyn Bridge to the office. He is gregarious and has a wide, cherubic smile – I don't know if I've ever seen him not in a good mood.

Today is the twice-monthly meeting of the City Council, and a number of press conferences are given beforehand on the wide gray steps of City Hall. After one of those, as folks are milling about, I see James waving and beckoning me to join him: he wants to introduce me to a fellow he has been chatting with. I shake hands with a man wearing a nicely tailored, form-fitting summer suit. He tells me his name is Othniel Reginald Askew. I'm into suits, and have recently acquired a bespoke aquamarine single-breasted one from Alexandre on Savile Row in London, so I look for telltale signs of quality. His suit isn't great quality, but Othniel wears it well, and pairs it with a royal-blue shirt, a gold tie and a metal collar pin.

He looks really good but makes little sense when he speaks, and fumbles over basic questions like who he is, what he does for a living, and even where in our neighborhood he lives. He dresses like a lobbyist of the kind that hang around the halls of government regularly but he isn't one, and I am not clear why James is introducing me to someone who seems to be just a constituent.

After our brief chit-chat they head up the grand spiral staircase to the ornate Council Chamber. I do too, but use the side staircase to take my seat at a desk at the front that has a view of the entire chamber and is reserved for the media. The vast room has red carpets; and fifty-one individual desks, one for each lawmaker, face an altar-like area where the presiding officer sits, and from which he or she runs the meetings. The presiding officer is usually the public advocate of the city, an elected representative with a vague but extensive portfolio. The council speaker's desk is next to a podium in the center aisle. Members of the public sit in a visitors' viewing balcony.

It's too early for the meat and potatoes portion of the meeting, so I go over the agenda, trying to figure out what is likely to be the best story to pitch to my editor – generally I can only get one story from these sorts of meetings into the following day's paper – while being open to writing up others if they turn out to be unexpectedly interesting or controversial.

Folks are milling around waiting to collect their citations for civic service, which are given out in the opening ceremonial portion. A group of Islamic sisters are going to be honored, and they and others are assembling on one side of the hall. Most haven't climbed upstairs yet but there is already a buzz in the room. I'm the only one from the media at our desk because the ceremonial portion rarely gets coverage and even I don't plan to write about it; I'm just early so I can scour the agenda. But nothing is juicy. Nothing is calling my name.

And then.

POP!

POP!

POP!

Loud sounds come from the viewing balcony overlooking the floor – pops like firecrackers. And then screams. I look up and see a man in a formfitting suit standing there wielding a handgun, and six more POPs crack out as I dive under the desk. A sergeant-at-arms follows me, and she clings onto me as the shots crack out. Then there is silence.

I peek out. I'm still holding my notebook and pen and tape recorder. Clouds of cordite smoke haze the air. And then pandemonium breaks out: shrieks, screaming and crying. Those under the balcony have no idea what is going on.

The Speaker of the City Council, A. Gifford Miller, is crouched down by his podium just a few feet away from me, looking startled. One of his bodyguards, who is kneeling beside him, draws his weapon as a voice screams, "He's on the balcony!" and fires from the floor directly at the lone, rigid figure standing in the front row of the visitors' balcony who is now aiming his gun at a body at his feet. The impact of the bullet knocks him down.

A moment later Miller is hustled out of the chamber by the rest of his New York Police Department security detail. An immediate security lock-down follows. Since the meeting hadn't actually started, the other reporters hadn't come upstairs yet from the Room Nine press room down below; meanwhile I am trapped with the rest of the council staff in a side committee room we've all been rushed into. I'm trying not to be too stunned by what has happened, and am wondering who the person the killer shot was; wondering if he or she and others have died; wondering why. There is whimpering. The Public Advocate, Betsy Gotbaum, a motherly figure, takes charge, hugging and comforting shocked members of staff. I quickly start fidgeting: even if we're not let out for hours, I'll still have to file to deadline. I scribble down some notes, telling details that otherwise may evaporate from my mind. We gather at the window and watch as a body on a stretcher is loaded into an ambulance. It's not the gunman. Many groan and their tears flow as an officer tells me it is James Davis.

When we are finally allowed to leave I rush to the main newsroom on 47th Street in Midtown Manhattan – quite a way from downtown, where City Hall is located – to write up my account, and help the graphic artist who is trying to recreate the scene. As I work feverishly, NYPD detectives show up in the newsroom to interview me about what I know and what I saw. I leave nothing out, including my peculiar conversation with the killer and James outside City Hall. What I tell them is essentially what will be in the paper the next morning.

As far as anyone could remember it was the first shooting there had been in City Hall, and James had been killed by Othniel, his own guest there. Othniel had been waved through security by James without being searched, and had sauntered in with a hidden firearm. Plainclothes officer Richard Burt, a mild-mannered, married father-of-three, and the gentleman who shot Askew dead, is promoted to detective and given a golden shield for bravery by the mayor, Michael Bloomberg.

It turns out that just hours before gunning down James, Othniel called the Federal Bureau of Investigation to complain that Davis had threatened to out him as gay. He further alleged that Davis had bribed him in a bid to get Othniel to agree not to run against him for office – he was, he said, planning to run against Davis for the Fort Greene council seat. I live in Fort Greene, and as a political reporter I know or have at least heard of most of the people in my neighborhood involved in party politics, but I had never heard of Othniel before meeting him. It is also part of my job to keep track of campaign financing for the city. The New York City Campaign Finance Board oversees a program that allows candidates to get four dollars' subsidy for every one dollar they raise, so as to level the playing field in politics. If Othniel wasn't raising money – and records showed he wasn't – then he wasn't a serious contender.

Yet he had cropped up in the record: James had been quoted in a Brooklyn newsletter saying of Othniel that he'd "never heard of him. Or her." – a dig that some saw as possibly anti-gay. This didn't make sense because James had been a staunch supporter of LGBT rights, including voting enthusiastically for one of the earliest transgender bills on record. And so his quote was dismissed as just a jibe at a potential rival with an unusual name rather than a put-down for his sexuality.

How in 2003 could labeling someone gay be so damaging to a political candidate that he would kill over it? Like others I have concluded that the well-dressed and surely paranoid killer committed his crime out of passion and perhaps gave it little coherent thought. Did the combined pressures of racism and homophobia push him over some edge? And yet it was a black man and an ally he killed.

James, Othniel, and Richard Burt are all black men, and the violent killings have me pondering about our community. I'm glad that I've been working every night on a side-project, the *AFRican* magazine, intended to promote positive images of Africans; and am also more generally pushing stories of our own that would not usually get coverage in mainstream newspapers or magazines.

While the Big Apple has a liberal bent and gay people are generally accepted there, it isn't the same around the country, let alone in my own African Diaspora community, and it's still a special pleasure for me to see out and proudly gay Africans represented. I highlight a few of them in a feature for *The Advocate*, the nation's premier newsmagazine for gay readers. It is headlined 'Out of Africa, out in America: With the Help of a Group Called Uhuru-Wazobia, Gay Men and Lesbians from Africa Have Built New Lives in New York City after Leaving Their Native Countries'.

My article explores how people from several African countries – Kenya, Côte d'Ivoire, Nigeria, Sierra Leone, South Africa and Mali – folks who can't simply hide their authentic gay selves – have formed a family in the Big Apple. They still hold onto their mother cultures, and have found strength in knowing that they are, as Africans, not alone there. My buddy Lawrence Harding, who is one of the men I profile in this piece, holds functions and often hosts gay Africans in his uptown Manhattan apartment, not far from Central Park. He is Sierra Leonean, and over the years I have grown to admire his uncompromising stance on being out and proud, and his fostering of that feeling among many others.

It is important for me to write these kinds of stories and find the right outlets for them because of what I am faced with every day – in life, and at the newspaper where I work.

Just a few years earlier, in 1999, another West African transplant, a go-getter who had made his home in the Bronx, upended my world. He had settled in New York with hopes of going to college to study computer science. This dude was a quiet guy with a gentle smile. He had stammered growing up – he called his mother Maam because his stammer stopped him from saying Momma. He was born in Liberia but grew up in Guinea's capital Conakry, a small seaside city of close to two million residents. His mother's business had taken him first to Togo and then to Asia, where he spent his formative years in Japan and Malaysia, and developed his love of reading. After attending the International School in Thailand this shy, studious guy had moved to New York. Sometimes he'd wear his baseball cap turned backwards as was the style of the time.

Before Thailand he'd been in Singapore, to learn about computing. He was his mother's first-born, and had two younger brothers and one sister. His well-heeled family ensured he was global in his thinking, and his international education had allowed him to pick up Spanish and Thai; and though Francophone he was also fully fluent in English – his native Fullah and French were a given. He was five years younger than me.

He loved New York and he loved America. When he left Guinea in 1996 to make it in the Big Apple he left a note for his mother that said simply, "The solution is U.S.A.: Don't leave my brothers and sister here." He was going to do whatever it took to earn an American university degree, and while like most children of successful parents he was keen to make it on his own, he wanted his mother to make sure his younger siblings would also get that opportunity – an opportunity and a solution that many Francophone West Africans don't often see as an option.

He was a handsome Muslim man who sported a thick 1970s-style mustache, a full head of hair and a winning smile. He ended up moving into a tiny apartment on Wheeler Avenue in Soundview. This neighborhood of low-rise houses occupied by working-class families is in the South Bronx, a borough of the Big Apple that has over the years developed into a West African enclave.

In January 1999 he was on the cusp of achieving his dream: finally, after all those hours, weeks, months of working out-doors selling clothing and accessories on the sidewalks, he'd gotten enough stability to do what he came to America to do – study. His excitement bubbling over, he called home. On the 31st of the month he called the one woman he loved above all others to share his news. "I'm so happy right now, Maam! I am going to do it!"

"Do what?" his mother asked from the Conakry compound where she was raising his younger siblings.

"Enroll in college!"

She could feel his smile without seeing his face. Her firstborn son leaving Guinea so abruptly and unexpectedly with just one thousand dollars in his pocket had been jarring for her, but now it was all going to be worth it: he would become a computer scientist.

Mama was prepared to send some money for tuition or other expenses but her son felt he was an adult now and continued to resist. "No," he replied. "I only need your prayers." He was a practicing Muslim. A harsh life in New York had not made him jaded, and his faith was unwavering.

A few days later, at around 11:30 p.m., he returns home as usual, following a twelve-hour selling stint downtown. It is Wednesday, February 3. Normally it is TV and then sleep, but he sometimes goes out for a juice or some other beverage. Shortly after getting home and changing his clothes, he steps out onto the stoop. But he doesn't get very far. He is on his doorstep when a car pulls up in front of him. It contains four white men. They get out and words are exchanged. What words? Only they know.

It is dark, and these burly American guys yell, and he reacts. He reaches into his pocket and pulls out his wallet, which contains his pieces of identification. He also has a pager. Upon seeing something in his hand – the dark wallet – the men pull out their weapons and open fire, raining down bullets on the man trapped in the tiny doorway of the building. Scared neighbors duck for cover. Obscenities fly from the mouth of one of the shooters, and two of the men don't stop firing until the sixteen cartridges in their 9mm handguns are empty. One of the men trips on the shallow steps leading up to the doorway and his partners continue firing, believing he's been shot. In fact no shots are fired in their direction.

It is now 12:45 a.m. on February 4 and a total of forty-one shots have been fired. Nineteen of those bullets pierced the body of the twenty-three-year-old Amadou Diallo, killing him instantly.

The four white men turn out to be New York City police

officers assigned to what is described as an elite Street Crimes Unit. They are on the prowl for a rapist in the area and were, they claim, 'intimidated' by the black African man standing in his doorway.

As they were dressed in street clothes Amadou would not have known that they were police officers. But he likely complied with their authoritative request to identify himself, and so reached into his pocket for the wallet that contained his ID. This gentle African guy was dead in an instant, his wallet lying on the floor next to his bullet-riddled body. All four officers maintain they mistook that wallet for a gun.

When they heard the news his family were traumatized, and his cousin, one of the many Guineans who lived nearby, told me his mother back in Conakry couldn't comprehend it. She'd just talked to him, she said; wasn't he going to enroll in college? How did he even enter police crosshairs? "She doesn't understand how somebody so calm, who cannot even kill a rat, could be killed like an animal."

In the days that followed I remember my editor Stuart Marques, who had promoted me from copy boy to fully-fledged reporter, thinking out loud that this awful case could result in a riot in Soundview, but I was sure it would not. We are Africans. We would react, but not that way. We had to mourn. And find the family. Still, Stuart dispatched me to the Bronx to gauge local feelings, while the reporters at the *Post*'s police bureau worked the cop angle.

Everything was so familiar in his neighborhood. Talking to his friends and neighbors and roommates I kept thinking, this could have been me. We both left home to pursue the same American college dream. And just as I had done, he got a room and worked round the clock to achieve that dream. But now, through no fault of his own, he'd been slaughtered by the police in front of his own home.

From the first time I went to Soundview I tried to own the story. I pushed my editors and was allowed to cover it extensively. Amadou was initially described by an NYPD spokesman as a street peddler, and framed in a negative light as an illegal immigrant who, though he had no police record, was probably engaged in serious criminal activity.

Many immigrants have moments when they may be 'between papers', or working 'under the table', or even illegally selling videotapes, socks and gloves on a Fourteenth Street sidewalk (itself only a misdemeanor) while they sort themselves out. As I was trying to find my way in London, having no work permit I myself briefly worked illegally for cash payments. It's just a thing that happens, and no indication that the immigrant will be a career criminal, or won't get his or her papers eventually.

And sometimes we immigrants lie to survive, as who does not? Amadou sought asylum when the truth was he had family back home. But that doesn't a hardcore criminal make.

His room, in the first floor apartment of that Wheeler Avenue building, was cramped, and he slept on a twin metal-frame bed. His reading material consisted of computer manuals and a copy of *The Signs Before the Last Day of Judgment.*

Amadou worked six days a week, doing twelve-hour shifts selling on the streets, but I knew from my experience as an African in New York that we are more than the sum of our current jobs. I cleaned toilets and cleaned offices at night after arriving in America with two hundred dollars in my wallet, and a few years later here I was, writing for one of America's largest dailies. It was not an unheard-of scenario for an African to make that jump from undocumented and/or working poor to educated middle-class within a strikingly short time. I was sure that, had he lived, Amadou would have ended up prospering in some technology firm. His uncle, Oury Diallo, an engineer, told me Amadou was so proud when he qualified for a credit card. He'd hoped to use it to open an America Online (AOL) account so he could email his family. "He was really impressed with the way things were organized in New York," Oury told me. "He always said, if you do things right in this city, things will work out."

When his mother Kadiatou Diallo landed in New York to claim her son's body, city officials collected her at JFK airport and put her up in a deluxe Midtown hotel, the Rihga Royal, (now the London NYC), on Fifty-Fourth Street. She went straight to her son's Bronx home. I'd been staking it out along with other reporters. As she walked slowly and deliberately through the waiting throng with her head held high, I could see the sorrow etched on her face. And also confusion. It was as if she didn't believe what was happening; as if she was in an episode of *The Twilight Zone*. But even then I knew she was a woman of substance. The NYPD would have New Yorkers believe that this young man was an abject immigrant and petty criminal, but everything about his mother told me it could not be so. And as reporters peppered her with questions and cameras mobbed her I ran up to her, got in front of her and kept repeating to her, "I'm Frankie. Remember me. I'm Frankie from Nigeria. Remember me." We locked eyes, and she said nothing, but I knew she'd understood that I was going to make it my mission to find the stories with which to reclaim Amadou's narrative.

Fortunately – in those better-funded times – the bosses decided to send me, along with photographer Wilbur Funches, to Conakry to cover the funeral. There I got to know Amadou's family, and to send many dispatches to the U.S. about this middle-class, multilingual kid whose parents were rich, who came to New York to make it on his own, without the family name, a name which is huge in Guinea. The powers-that-be may have derided him as a peddler, but every opportunity I got to talk about his family life in Guinea I seized. Armed with my information, New Yorkers could make up their own minds about Amadou.

Everywhere I went in Conakry everyone knew the Diallos. Kadiatou was a successful trader in precious stones, and before she returned with Amadou's body – I went on ahead of her – I met his sister and younger brother in their well-appointed Conakry home. Most of my media colleagues had elected to fly in with Madam Diallo, the civil rights crusader the Reverend Al Sharpton (who was acting as family adviser), and Amadou's corpse, but because I had gone to Conakry immediately I had days to really get to know his family, and when it was time to go to the airport to collect their mother and Amadou, I truly understood how important the Diallo name was there.

Thousands of people showed up at Conakry's Gbessia International Airport to greet Madam Diallo, including the foreign minister. Government officials boarded the Air France jet to carry the coffin down onto home soil.

Amadou's sister Lauratou, a stoic young woman who had

been holding the family together in her mother's absence, and greeting the multitude of well-wishers who had been arriving since sunup, broke down at the sight of the coffin. She had told me how much of a loving big brother he was, regularly calling from the States to grill her about her romantic and career choices. She'd recently got engaged and Amadou, she told me, kept asking her if she knew what she was doing. How would it affect her career at a local mining company, he wanted to know. She told me how he kept her secrets and those of others; and how he secretly bought gifts for family members without telling other family members about it. He was, it seemed, the quintessential good African big brother.

Up until he was buried in their hometown, Hollande Bourou, at the feet of the Fouta Djallon mountains, an eight-hour drive away along dusty, winding roads, folks gathered for Madam Kadiatou Diallo, doing all they could to give her strength by being close. Even during his internment, seemingly so far away from everything, crowds poured in to mourn.

After returning to New York I would see Madam Diallo everywhere, and I kept writing stories on this issue that I could not let go of. I got to know her well, and got to know the family lawyers too; and once they realized they couldn't shake me off, and that I had the Diallos' best interests at heart, they were helpful to my reporting. They filed a $61,000,000 lawsuit against the city – $20,000,000 plus $1,000,000 for every shot fired.

In New York the situation was getting ever more tense. Thousands of people participated in acts of civil disobedience at New York's police headquarters, One Police Plaza, and were getting arrested daily, including the former mayor, David Dinkins, the only African-American ever elected to the post. Eventually the four police shooters, two of whom, it was revealed, had been involved with killing black men before, were indicted by a Bronx grand jury. But the venue for the trial was moved one hundred and fifty-two miles away, from New York to Albany, the state capital.

All this time I kept in contact with Madam Diallo. She had initially been represented by the late Johnnie Cochran, the Los Angeles-based attorney best known for securing the acquittal of

O.J. Simpson, the American football star and actor accused of murdering his ex-wife and her friend, but at some point in the summer of 1999 she told me during one of our chats that she was not enamored of Cochran. Yes, he might be a star, but all she wanted was justice for her son, so she informed me she'd settled on an exclusive white shoe law firm downtown, Gair, Gair & Conason. I smiled. They were a quiet firm but their reputation was stellar.

I called the managing partner, Bob Conason, and we talked briefly. While he didn't tell me what strategy he would be using, he confirmed that he would now be representing Madam Diallo and her children, and would give her all the time she needed. I quickly worked up a piece detailing what had just transpired. It became a *New York Post* front page story with the cheeky headline (not my own), 'Johnnie Be Gone'.

Some in the activist black American community were unhappy Madam Diallo had ditched the black star legal team for a quiet white guy downtown, but I think she was just tired of the backstage bickering and extraneous media showboating. She wanted justice but she wanted to heal too. Conason and his team remained by her side till the end. The month-long criminal trial was arduous, and upstate New York was painfully cold. Then the shooters, Edward McMellon and Sean Carroll – the two who didn't stop firing until their chambers were empty – and their co-accused, Kenneth Boss and Richard Murphy, were acquitted. Not even a charge of reckless endangerment stuck. Years later a civil litigation suit was settled out of court for three million dollars.

In the meantime I kept writing. I simply could not let go of the story, and remain in touch with Amadou's mother and the lawyers involved even today.

Since then the list of black men and boys who had no weapons on them but died at the hands of police officers keeps growing, including at time of writing: Freddie Gray, Eric Garner, Michael Brown, Laquan McDonald, Tamir Rice, Akai Gurley and and and and...

Sixteen years after Amadou's death the Black Lives Matter movement would be born, at a time when cellphone cameras enable regular people to document police actions, and put them in the public domain before law enforcement can control the narrative the way they did with Amadou.

Kadiatou Diallo has set up a foundation in her son's memory. It continues to work hard at giving others the American university education that was snatched away from him.

The Diallo case forced me to look at how I could use my work to try and reclaim the narrative of Africans in the West. It took repeated efforts on my part, but eventually the *Post* would refer to Amadou as a vendor rather than a peddler. A small victory, but something.

After this heart-wrenching series of events – an odyssey that lasted several years – I found I couldn't continue to use my journalism simply to chronicle governmental goings on: I needed to do more for my own community; for all my communities. I was an African immigrant and a gay man living in New York City, and so I devoted myself to writing and reporting on Africans, on their healthcare needs in New York, on the immigrant experience, on black communities and on gay issues. This was my 'enterprise' work, and it had to be done alongside the work I was assigned – and paid – to do, and that my employers wanted. Back then, as continues to be the case today, there were few reporters of color in mainstream news organizations, so it wasn't (and isn't) uncommon to have to straddle the personal need to cover the stories most reporters and editors overlook while at the same time avoiding being marginalized as one who only reports on 'minority' issues.

Still, my commitment to telling our stories was unwavering, and so I created the *AFRican* magazine, joining forces with another Nigerian resident of Fort Greene, Edinam Oton, who had publishing experience, to create something for us. It was done with love, sweat, and our savings. I was co-founder, and edited it for eight years. It was a niche magazine that focused on the African-in-Diaspora experience. While I continued to write for many mainstream publications, and made every effort to get stories about Africans into the *New York Post*, I put a gargantuan effort into the *AFRican* too. It meant a whole lot to us, and to our readers, even though we struggled to get advertising.

"There is no African Culture. There are African cultures."

– Wole Soyinka

FOUR: BIG APPLE DATING WHEN YOU ARE NIGERIAN SEEKING THE SAME

By the late 1990s and the early noughties I am comfortable in my own skin, and comfortable enough to not see myself as doomed to a life of solitude. Part of this comfort comes from living in cosmopolitan New York City, but a big part of it comes from meeting African gay men who are out and very much at ease. I happen on a space for folk like me. Not a crowded gay bar like Kellers, filled with preening hunks, and not a club like the Octagon, with pounding dance music and sweaty, sculpted bodies, but a community of LGBT African men and women who meet up and let everyone simply be. It is called Uhuru-Wazobia and is championed by two men who end up being great friends of mine, Lawrence Harding and Nguru Karugu, and they foster a community of love and support.

I still recall the unbridled joy I felt the first time I went to one of their events. It was a hot summer evening in a small ballroom in Harlem. There were men and women and the gender-nonconforming from Nigeria, Côte d'Ivoire, Cameroon, Mali, Sierra Leone, Uganda and more, francophone and anglophone. Some had driven in from out of town especially, and everyone had paid a nominal gate fee to party all evening. Every now and then the DJ would make way for a musical interlude from a female impersonator decked out in traditional regalia complete with elaborate headscarves, who would jazz up the crowd even more. It was a fun night for African gays and lesbians and those who loved them, a space to be free and safe until it was time to head back out into the streets. Some were couples, some were friends; others were seeking the solace of community, or hoping to meet some desiring other. And everyone was welcome: I met Columbian and Mexican immigrants dancing side by side with their African friends.

Uhuru-Wazobia isn't all about parties, I soon find out. Sometimes it is about shoulders to lean on, and I look forward to going to Lawrence's home when he opens it to all for drinks, conversation and whatever is on our minds, accepting and encouraging us to refer to one another as we wish. He tells me that many of us from the African continent have issues with labels, and that the varied ways sexual minorities describe themselves don't always neatly translate to 'gay' or 'lesbian' or 'trans', and also that in many of our communities we've always had a name and space for difference. For instance, he has what the West would call gay male buddies from Senegal who call themselves 'goojigen', a Wolof term they say could mean 'man-woman' but – while not meaning a hermaphrodite, yet still suggesting gender non- conformity – cannot be translated as the Western concept of LGBT either. "It doesn't translate as 'gay' and it can't; it doesn't translate into any other term," Lawrence says. In his Manhattan home everyone is welcome, whether or not a wife is about to be shipped over from the continent, or one is being pressured to procreate.

Years later I will look back at these times and think that those wonderful folk just needed space to be themselves. The group started off as 'Wazobia', from the Hausa, Igbo and Yoruba words for 'come'. As it grew in numbers the forceful Swahili word for freedom, uhuru, was added.

Lawrence's salons bring all sorts – writers, artists, dancers and more – together for libations and conversation. I never know who I'll meet in his tightly-packed living room after climbing the two flights of stairs, but am always happy to see this physiotherapist from Sierra Leone not just give of himself as a host, but simply be so happy to be himself. There seem to be no internal struggles.

I want that level of comfort for myself. I will go on to achieve it, but it takes years.

Nguru too is very comfortable with himself, and whenever we hang out he shares with me parts of his journey. He grew up the son of diplomats in Kenya, and I enjoy listening to the tale of how he reached his light-bulb moment.

For years he struggled to accept his sexuality, even though he was kissing boys at the Nairobi prep school he attended before being sent to university in America.

"My image of gay in Kenya was white men. I remember thinking this was something for expatriates," he says. But when he returned home to work in health care in rural Kenya he found men like himself there, as well as in what were known as 'tea-rooms' (public toilets) in Nairobi. As these men had never left Kenya, and many had had no contact with white people whatsoever, it dawned on him that it wasn't worldly foreign influences that had dictated his attraction: it was simply who he was.

"Oh. My. God. There are others like me. I used to say, 'All I need is to find the right girl and I'll be okay.' But then I [changed] the conversation of 'I'm crazy and bi' and all that to 'I'm gay and I'm okay'. I felt so strong and I could see my ancestors saying, 'When are you going to get it? Now let's move on; get away from your drama.'"

While the Uhuru-Wazobia group is relatively informal, they often raise money to help those escaping persecution in their home countries; and in the summer of 2005 many of its members marched openly under their own banner in New York's Gay Pride March, a first for an African group. Lawrence remains in New York and continues to build communities there; Nguru ultimately continued his activism in Nairobi, where he relocated after a few years of going back and forth.

I work on 'dating with ease'. For straight men, dating in New York isn't so difficult: there's a large pool. And for gay men it isn't difficult either; if you are conventionally attractive and outgoing there seems if anything an even larger pool to choose from. But a gay Nigerian seeking the same faces a particular set of challenges. The pool is of indeterminate depth, and the size keeps changing. At least two men I thought might be suitable mates turned out when I met them to be Good On

Paper only. They are both doctors, and lovely except for that one crucial thing: they are in the closet. There is plenty of Good On Paper in New York.

Even here in America, thousands of miles from home, these men are still bound by families determined for them to marry, even if they are being 'slow' about it. This can't work for me. It's not as if I have some sort of righteous indignation. It's just that it seems to me no different from dating or hooking up with semi-straight men in Brooklyn – which I have done many times, much to the amusement of my buddy Kai, who snickers at my hypocrisy. Yet somehow I hold my Nigerian people to a higher standard and, confronted by closetry, find myself just saying no.

At weddings and other functions I meet Nigerian men I know are gay but have gotten married and are fathers too. Then they have affairs with guys on the side. I can accept that in Nigeria, but in America it seems like a tragedy. Encountering these guys made me begin to all the more utterly admire those of my African gay friends who live in New York and refuse the charade. Slowly my friendships with these married men drift apart. I see no reason for anyone African who has made his life in America to be in the closet, maybe one day marry some unfortunate African lady to please family back home, and continue to perpetuate what African-Americans call the Down Low syndrome. Eventually I will get of my high horse, but in the 2000s I am full of judgment of these men. And I keep running across them: doctors, lawyers, pharmacists, engineers, lecturers – highly skilled and accomplished Nigerian men who are gay, but even living in the West can't handle the thought of people knowing.

Take one New York cardiologist I know. Funny, charming and broad-shouldered, he grew up in Abeokuta, a Nigerian city I've come to love, and has a nice home in New Jersey. He's lovely, so tender, and so attentive to his circle of gay male friends – except when his sisters or parents come around. Then he disappears, and we have no contact until they have returned to Nigeria. To date he hasn't gotten married, though I often wonder when that will happen. Instead he works very hard and, as his career soars, he dates quietly, secretly, afraid of holding on to anyone who might spill the beans and not understand his need for the utmost discretion. And it's odd because for all that he'll go to Black Gay Pride events and circuit parties and sweatily hope there will be zero Nigerians there.

He's still officially single, despite the many pictures of ladies on his Facebook page, but in reality has fallen for a closeted Gambian accountant in the same boat as he is. Yet even though it is difficult for me to get into his headspace, (oh-so-gay among friends, extremely sweet and kind for the most part, and then a perfect stranger when family appears), he isn't a rare case. Another gay Nigerian, an investment banker who I'd hoped for a long term relationship with, and who lives in Brooklyn, told me point-blank that his two worlds don't mix and they never will: "Lai-Lai! I can't introduce any gay person to my family whether I'm dating them or they are my friends. It will bring suspicion on me. So, no way."

So that fizzled out too, despite the many intimate dinners at home, and the dancing close, and the long walks in the parks of the city, during which so many small confidences were shared. Once relatives are nearby, we are reduced to strangers.

One Boston-based lawyer I meet at a relative's wedding in America is gay and married (to a woman) and has children. He's happy to carry on multiple sexual affairs with other Nigerian men so long as they remain no more than 'friends', and he wants us to meet privately, to hook up. And so here we are at a wedding in Chicago, I, an openly gay Nigerian, chatting amiably with a closet case from home who slyly makes sure I have his number and that he gets my card before I leave.

Once the wedding is over, and we have returned to our respective homes, the full-throttle chase is on. And when I do acquiesce and sleep with him it is tender, passionate and very exciting. Of course I shouldn't have, I'm breaking my own rule, but I do it anyway. We carry on for months, having – protected – sex, never discussing his wife but often his children. It's not like I'm worried about her – I figure they must have set their own boundaries; anyway it suits me to believe so.

And then after a while it really isn't tenable: I am not able to date in secret. Saying to myself I'm just in it to get laid and his wife can take care of him is no longer enough. I'm too into him to keep it under wraps in the way he insists. We can't go anywhere where other friends might be, so it is mainly being at home, or taking in movies and museums in the afternoons; on a rare occasion there might be dinner out. After another weekend away at a 'conference' I slowly begin to withdraw. I don't know if he understands why. Sometimes I am angry about it all, but I say nothing, just slowly wean myself off our encounters. For a time he is really concerned – not about me, but that I will tell my family about him. I try to calm him down: "They don't really care what you do, and I think they've bought into your charade."

In these years I do also manage to date men who are out. In the extremely cosmopolitan Big Apple that could be anyone from anywhere. Some are nice, some not. Perhaps it is the fear of being alone that makes me linger in relationships that I shouldn't have got into in the first place. One such, that lasted years past its expiration date, was with Rafaele, a European guy with a shaved head and big muscles. We meet at the Octagon, a large nightclub on Manhattan's West Side where I am a regular on Friday nights. In those days I work the late shift at the *Post's* midtown headquarters, and then, after one a.m., head over there to dance my cares away for a few hours before the trek home to Brooklyn.

The Octagon is dance music heaven, with hip-hop and house sprinkled in. Black men and those who love them are everywhere, in tight T-shirts and caramel Timberlands, baseball caps turned backwards or doo-rags adorning their heads. It's the 1990s, and even though New York is theoretically welcoming to gay men and women, it is still the era of 'don't ask, don't tell'. So walking into the Octagon each week and being confronted with hundreds of black gay men dancing without a care in the world is simply fantastic to me. I cannot imagine this scenario anywhere else. Outside the club the men (and the few women who join in) are whatever they need to be to survive. But inside is a space where the most macho men can turn catty once inebriated, or just because they feel the need to release the bitchy energy that is constrained in the heterosexual world outside.

I love it there because, unlike in the bars, I never have to muster up the nerve, or fortify myself with liquid courage in order to speak to someone. The dance floor is an equalizer, and dance I do, each Friday, with whoever I want to or simply by myself. There is never a need to be anything other than my authentic self. And one night, after a hard week at work, as I am twirling, lost in a trance as the music blares, a blur of white appears in front of me. And doesn't move on. White T-shirt, white sneakers, and a big white toothy smile. Big smile and shaved head turn out to belong to an Italian immigrant, Rafaele. We bond and begin dating.

Prior to this I'd dated Albert, a Persian Jew who was also an immigrant. I seem to connect with outsiders in America, men who see the world differently because they've lived somewhere else, and have had to go through the same immigration hoops many in my world have.

Rafaele is a head-turner. His obsession with working out has yielded large arms and a torso that T-shirts seem made to hug. He is an only child who escaped his small village to go first to Milan, then Paris, and now lives here in the Big Apple. In the clubs and the queer hotspots he exudes confidence. He talks to anyone, and many of the guys want to talk to him too. He works in fashion and is a natty dresser, not exactly a peacock but always immaculately turned out. He craves attention and needs to have whatever the 'in' thing of the moment is. I am proud to have him on my arm. I take him everywhere, and we spend romantic moments together in the Fire Island rental where I spend many summer nights.

At Fire Island Pines the masculine body is flaunted and idolized, and there he gets the attention he craves, much as he does at the Octagon. I don't mind too much. Fire Island is as much a revelation of the space that can be created for difference as it is freedom. You can be anything you want here, it's a wonderland. Muscle queens have their corner, as do skinny effeminate twinks and everything in between. My family and many heterosexual friends visit me there each birthday, when I have my bash by the ocean, and it's always touching to see them dancing in a sea of gay men: an image of a possible world.

At home, Rafaele shows off his cooking skills when we have guests, but when we are alone his confidence dissipates and he becomes very needy. I constantly have to reassure him that he has talent as a designer. He hasn't been to any tertiary schools, and that makes him feel inadequate. I tell him I admire the way that by sheer force of will he has carved out a good place for himself in that cutthroat industry.

Sex is odd. He is possessive, and becomes very tactile in private. The hair that sprouts all over me turns him on easily and quickly. I learn that I can make him ejaculate fast with a few strategic strokes of my beard on certain parts of his body. Intercourse terrifies him – perhaps it is the possibility of HIV – so more often than not it is full-on frottage on the expensive king-sized bed in his tiny Manhattan flat. I love intercourse, and it is a sacrifice not to have it when I am full of desire for it – a sacrifice I later regret making, since the needy man I see in private turns out to also be the needy one he offers to many others. There is a rotation of us. All black men. He is nice sometimes, but not nice enough for me to put up with that. It takes a while to learn that his need for me isn't about me but the confidence he gets from my cheering him on, no matter what.

And so, after more than seven years of giving unconditional support, it is quite easy to extricate myself from the fiery one: when I stop being the attentive listener to his ever-growing list of problems we don't even have to break up. Once I stop making any effort to find solutions to Rafaele's myriad problems at work, or with his cat, or his visa issues, it is over.

I move on to another Italian and dabble with some Americans but in truth what I crave is the familiar: the African.

"If you are not living a life bigger than yourself, then you are not living at all."

– Viola Davis

Five: Mon Grand, L'amoreux Africain

F inding a loving, compatible Nigerian man in New York who is available and openly gay is a tough ask, so I soften my stance. I try to be less judgmental, and more open to the various kinds of brothers who only manage to teeter on the edge of openness. It is not easy finding someone to date who gets you culturally and is available: most who do either already have partners or are simply not interested. The episode with the Boston lawyer isn't unique to Nigerian men, of course. Recalling that saga reminds me of a very handsome Congolese man who has been tied to me for decades.

It was in the late 1990s, on an extended trip to France, that I first ran across Etienne, the dapper one. As a New York University undergraduate, in 1992 I'd done a Study Abroad program in Paris and had become enamored with the city, returning many times over the years that followed for weeks and long weekends whenever I could find cheap airfares. And on one of those escapes Etienne suddenly appeared.

I am eating breakfast in the center of Paris, at a small café tucked away on the Rue de la Ferronnerie. It is in the Premier Arrondissement and has outdoor seating and gold-painted walls. There is a bright red awning over the sidewalk seating

area and it's called the Banana Café. There are potted palms
outside and also some ersatz banana trees up on the roof. It's
just steps away from the busy Châtelet fountain, where boys
and girls go to flirt and find hook-up partners.

This faux tropical paradise I have stumbled upon is the last
place I expect to meet other Africans in Paris, but there he is,
jauntily bouncing in my direction as the waiter sets down my
daily dose of croissants and chocolat chaud. It is summer but
he is wearing a long-sleeve button-down shirt, partly undone to
reveal a large gold chain with silver pendants on his chest.
Gaudy, I think, but I also admire his other bling – he has a
large gold watch to go with the chain and huge gold rings on
each of his middle fingers.

He has a very dark complexion and his skin is glistening in
the morning sun. Perhaps he has doused himself with baby oil.
Silver Ray-Ban sunglasses balance on his forehead. His head is
completely shaved and he sports a thick, full, immaculately
trimmed beard. There is a light, multicolored cotton summer
scarf draped just so around his neck, to protect it from the
wind. Etienne smells of musk, a fragrance that I could not
identify but knew was expensive. He is rather skinny, and when
he walks he takes very deliberate steps, giving the impression
that he is gliding. His gait oozes confidence.

Quel Sapeur, I think, as I stare and smile a little smile.

He makes a beeline for me the moment our eyes meet. I
smile bigger. We chat; simple pleasantries, and then the
inevitable 'where are you from?' inquisition begins. I am
receptive to his flirtation, inviting him to "s'il vous plaît" sit
with me and have a coffee. Initially I'm not sure if I only want
him to hang around because I'd like someone friendly to
practice my French with. I also need a black barbershop, and
this dude would probably have some recommendations. But
then I begin to enjoy his aura and want to keep him chatting for
hours. I have nothing to do but stroll the tiny streets and go to
museums, and suggest we spend a couple of hours together
being flâneurs. He has to work, he says. So we make plans to
meet up again soon. And we do: we spend the next evening
wandering the Marais, a quaint central Parisian neighborhood
known for its Jewish quarter, gay bars, and owner-run boutiques. We are holding hands and stealing kisses. When we stop

at his favorite gay bar I down panachés, the French equivalent of a lager shandy. I am slightly tipsy when Etienne gets around to telling me he is married to a white Frenchwoman, and that they have a young son, a three-year-old.

"Mais tu es un pédé!" I say, stomping my feet and using the French expletive for faggot. This vulgarity is one I wouldn't normally employ but I am genuinely caught off guard. We are in a gay bar. We've been kissing! It has been so far a very romantic evening. And the fantasy of knowing an out and proud gay African in Paris was beginning to take root in me, to become a reality. But in an instant, it has become fantasy again.

"Oui," he agrees, he is "un pédé"; most particularly during the week. But he has a wife and kid in Le Mans, about one hundred and twenty miles away, and this is why he leaves Paris every weekend. He also has another woman who he speaks to daily. Etienne says she is his mistress. She too lives in Le Mans. When visiting the wife and child, he takes time to see his other lady as well. And he is in a position to say to his women quite truthfully that he has no female companionship here in Paris.

I'm stunned: it seems like overkill to be married and have a mistress on the side when one is actually a gay man in the closet. Maybe he's actually bi. So I ask him why does he have so many women if he is drawn to men? His response is simple: "Je suis Zairois." That he is from Zaire, or is Congolese, and that's just the way it is. Men from his community are 'virile' or at least expected to be. And the Frenchman with whom he shares a large, airy, loft-like flat on the Rue Saint Denis during the week, a flamboyant make-up artist, never questions this arrangement. That this roommate, Poops, is also his lover is a further revelation to me. Etienne tells me that since his assorted other dalliances have come to accept all this, I should too. He's always upfront, he says, and is telling me before things get too deep.

As we sit downing panachés and cocktails in gay Paris I stare at this Kinshasa transplant and wonder how rough it was for him there, before he left for Europe. While same sex activity has never been explicitly illegal in the Democratic Republic of Congo, stigma is very much an issue. More recently, due to evangelical interventions bankrolled by Christian extremists in the West, it has gotten to be dicey there, and though they gain little traction, in the years to come politicians will introduce bills to criminalize sexual minorities. After Uganda introduces the first version of its 'Kill the Gays' bill in 2009, a similar bill will be floated by a lawmaker in the D.R.C. parliament. But regardless of legality, for Etienne in the 1990s the fear of being ostracized by the Congolese community in France seems to be too strong for him to risk being out.

When in Le Mans he lives among his own Lingala-speaking people. They provide great cultural support for his biracial son, and the picture he paints for his community is one of a virile heterosexual with women everywhere. When in Paris he chooses to live not near the African enclaves in the 18th and 20th arrondissements but in the middle of town, just steps away from a red light district, on a street where the women are always scantily dressed, even in the middle of the afternoon, in order to entice male passers-by. This picture is not to be messed with; this is how he copes. The fear of someone from Kinshasa finding out the truth of his life is his nightmare scenario.

Despite all this, I enjoy being with Etienne. He's a great conversationalist who enjoys theater and in particular the opera. He's adept at finding jazz clubs and cool things to do, and is an all-round fun guy.

He is Good On Paper.

I always look forward to seeing him but his reality is a bit too much for me to handle. So 'L'affaire Etienne' is brief – though we remain in close touch after I return to New York.

It is proving too tough for me to have a committed relationship with a man from the African continent since most of those I meet are happily in a similar boat to Etienne's. And it's easy to see why. Openly gay men aren't really safe anywhere; they rarely have been, not even in America, and on the African continent it is only getting ghastlier as the years go by.

When my high school friend Ukonu, who lives in Nigeria and is a straight lothario, jokingly uses me as conversation fodder with other friends it bothers me a little bit, though not enough to make a big deal out of it: it is all in fun and is just gossipy banter. He tells me of mutual friends who had same-sex dalliances during our boarding school days in Port Harcourt who are now happily married to women they met later in life. How he knows all this I don't know, but everyone seems to spill their secrets to him. We were both in the press club during boarding school, and over the years remained in touch, he in Abuja or Lagos, and I in New York. He's visited me several times in Brooklyn, and once accompanied me to America's grand slam tennis tournament, the U.S. Open, in Flushing Meadows. I've stayed in his Lagos flat, and I know his wife and daughters in Abuja. The gay conversation always seems like fun except when the salacious gist is at my expense.

Ukonu can also be a prolific poster on social media. He loves a good debate and does his part to stir up the pot. One day he started a conversation about gay equality that went downhill fast. He has enlightened friends in Lagos who speak out forcefully for equality, but many others used the occasion to toss out words and phrases like 'abomination', 'evil', and 'hellfire' when making their argument that they would never befriend a gay person, and that, moreover, gay people should be locked up. Many wondered openly why he'd even entertain having a gay friend.

But then one poster goes on to say he'd personally pound gays to a pulp and would kill them if he knew any, and encourages others to do so. Ukonu, who is moderating the conversation, doesn't condemn this; others agree with it. I don't know this poster and I don't engage him. But I am livid with my friend and unleash my fury on him. I tell him I find his fault worse: he doesn't even back up his friend Eme, who is speaking out in support of gay people. "It's your very public wall and you chose to advocate this point of view very publicly. What did you think would happen? Of course people can say anything and you've given them the platform. Keep in mind that having gay friends means you can either have the courage – like your friend Eme – to be a straight ally or, if you are not comfortable with that, at least don't give people your platform to talk about stoning people like me and leave it unchallenged."

How can it be okay in his mind, I wonder, to say, "Look at me, I'm so evolved I even have gay friends," but be silent when the mob wants to kill us?

Ukonu is shocked by my fury, as I rarely get so visibly angry. He seems surprised that I appear to have no idea it is a commonly-held view among our people even in 2013 that to be gay is an abomination. So he said he would take down the entire page "out of respect for you." Of course that reasoning made me even more incensed. Take it down because it is bad on its own, take it down because you don't condone it, take it down and check your pals because it's the right thing to do. But don't do it 'out of respect' for me. That's crap. Chastise someone who would openly advocate murder on your Facebook page not because you have one gay friend (in his case actually a few, but not all are out), but because you won't stand for that.

So I tell him, "Do what makes you comfortable, but consider changing your mindset. If people who know you understand this is not how you think, they might be encouraged to think – and act – differently. At this point your public stand is 'against' not 'for', or even 'neutral'. Consider that." He finally gets it, and our relationship has been on a stronger footing since.

As for Etienne, as the years go by he gets divorced from his wife, and a couple of years later he drops the mistress. Then he comes out. I remain supportive every time he rings with news, but never joyous: he has to find his way without my judgment. This macho Congolese eventually settles down with a Frenchman and they make a home together in Paris. He couldn't leave Le Mans behind because his son is being raised there, but the big city is his home, away from the Congolese community.

The years have been very kind to him. I marvel every time I see him in New York or in France at how slender he still is: at forty-eight the gut that appears on many middle-aged men seems to skipped him, even though he insists on bread and wine with every lunch and dinner. He favors formfitting Abercrombie & Fitch T-shirts and still wears his gold jewelry, swanky watches, and expensive rings. His thick beard now has splashes of gray in it, and funky prescription glasses have replaced the ubiquitous Ray-Bans. Two decades after our first meeting he still glides as he walks, and is even more of a head-turner – for both sexes – than he was back then. He's what my Americans friends call a DILF, a 'Daddy I'd Like to Fuck'.

It's been gratifying and rather exciting to see his now grown-up son, the very handsome Jean-Pierre, bring his girlfriend to and dance wildly at Paris' Gay Pride parades in support of Etienne. J-P loves his papa, and doesn't feel shy introducing his father's partner to his friends as his other dad.

The world may not have come crashing down when Etienne came out but he still paid a heavy price. Over the years I begin to notice that friends and cousins who used to be around all the time are no longer there. After one particularly close cousin who 'got' him and made no judgments died, he seemed to have fewer of the Congolese community around him. I knew this was by choice.

Even in his dating life, before settling down with his current lover, he stops making a play for African men in Paris. It's been French men mainly, with occasionally a dark Spaniard thrown in the mix. He often has a sidekick, a lover on the side, also French of course. When I visit him in 2007, curious to meet his current companion, he insists I stay at their new flat rather than the charming Tunisian-owned guesthouse I'd used for years in the 20th arrondissement. They have a three-bedroom place on the fifth floor in the 19th and it is very cozy. One bedroom is a guest room and another is for Jean-Pierre when he visits. There is a terrace where on summer nights they drink wine and look out over the sprawling City of Lights.

Etienne is happily ensconced in domestic bliss with Didier, a tall, bespectacled teacher with a swimmer's build. Didier's arms are big and he is well-defined but he insists he never works out, says he just swims daily. He is polite and welcoming when I arrive in the early afternoon, but afterwards seems to be brooding, and says little the rest of the day.

Their bathroom is large, and in it they keep a washer, dryer, and an ironing table. I am in there shaving when Didier comes in to get some clothes out of the dryer. I try to make some small talk, apologizing for my rusty French. Though still taciturn, he tells me my use of his language is better than the New Yorkers he meets in the Marais, who won't deign to speak French and only blab on in English. I can't read his expression.

I ask Etienne at some point over dinner when Didier is out of earshot if everything is OK, and if perhaps I should have stayed at the hotel. He says everything is fine and his companion is actually besotted with me. Etienne says his 'mec' reckons I look better than my photographs. Well, brooding's an odd way of showing delight, I think, but no problem.

Later in the evening I say my goodnights, shower, and am

under the sheets in my favorite powder-blue pajamas, about to
doze off, when two gentle knocks come at the door. I mumble
something. Didier comes in. He is totally nude and completely
erect. I stare at his body and, as he tugs at his sizable uncut
member, think, 'Wow, for a fifty-something he's taken really
good care of his body.' When I first met him he was in jeans
and baggy button downs, and I thought him a serious businessman type, not exactly a looker. But now, as he is standing
towering over me, I remember the adage about not judging a
book by its cover. I gawk at his brawny, toned, physique, which
I now find to be totally appealing. There is not an ounce of fat
on him. No paunch, and a broad, hairy chest making an Adonis
V. Perhaps I should start swimming, I think.

My reverie is interrupted when Didier ever so politely asks
that I please come spend the night in their room. I stammer my
response, which really is a question: "Etienne. Il est ou?" Didier
calmly and with a smile replies that his 'mec' is already in bed
waiting for us.

Etienne is indeed waiting for us to make a passionate
sandwich, with Didier, then myself, at the center. And after an
exuberant romp we all fall asleep. As I recount later to my close
buddy Nectarios, a European transplant in New York and my
go-to cultural interpreter, "I was a guest in their home so I did
the only polite thing. I obeyed; went in the room and we
fucked." He laughed enviously and shook his head.

At the breakfast table the next morning Etienne cannot
understand any reservations or queasiness I feel. Now my
friendship with his man will be on a strong footing, he rational-
izes; there will no longer be any awkwardness as the sexual
tension has been dispersed. It must be a French thing, I think,
reaching for the apricot jam.

In recent years Etienne has evolved into a world traveler.
He regales me with tales of his exploits, and is always
WhatsApping me photos from far-flung excursions. He routine-
ly returns to West Africa. He has developed a real fondness for
Senegal, and he and Didier are quickly making it their base
when not in Paris. They have built a small bungalow there.

On occasion I've turned over my Brooklyn apartment to
Etienne and his friends – when not with Didier, he likes to
travel with a small entourage. Invariably there is a side ro-

mance going on with someone in his travel group. Even though he lives in the multicultural City of Lights and travels so much, his friends and romances remain very Eurocentric.

On one of his visits I take him to an event in Fort Greene Park in Brooklyn. The Soul Summit Music Festival is an all-day party held on occasional Saturdays in the summer, and though it is not a specifically gay event, we find tons of gay black men there, dancing in the sun. As they twirl the afternoon away, more and more hipster heterosexuals join in. (The demographics of Fort Greene have begun to change: gentrification is taking hold, and what was for years a predominantly black artistic enclave is now more mixed.) Even seniors and other regular park users gravitate towards the music. Soul Summit is a Brooklyn party with a carnival ambience, and there are barbecue pits and food stalls just steps away from the dancing area. The sun is blazing and many men are shirtless, serving up a buffet of buff with nary a whiff of self-consciousness. House music is pumping, and when folks aren't dancing they stand on the sidelines chatting, smoking, and flirting. The scent of marijuana wafts across the afternoon and everyone looks happy. It reminds me of the glory days of the by-now-defunct Octagon nightclub.

Etienne gazes at these uninhibited black men with such an intensity one would think he'd been caged up for years and had just been released. Yet he makes no move to chat anyone up; instead he remains at my side, dancing with me for hours. If I don't introduce him to someone he just stares. His normally macho tendency to go and get what he wants is not on display today. It's not about language – in New York his French accent is always an icebreaker when we are out – and he's never shy, but today he says little and is subdued. Yet he seems pleased to be there, and is certainly enjoying dancing. He looks ravishing in his tight blue muscle T-shirt, low-slung jeans and Adidas whites.

Suddenly, as I am shaking my hips on the dance floor, my hands up in the air, my head bobbing and my ass wriggling to the beat, Etienne pulls me close and, with his arms around my waist, whispers, "Mon grand..."

The music is blasting, the tempo is fast, and in the middle of the crowd he is attempting to slow dance with me. His lips close to my ear, he laments what he calls "the fact" that we could have been like these couples all around us if we had only gotten over our hang-ups and I had moved to Paris all those years ago when he was still married. Or if he had left everything behind and moved to New York.

I'm thinking to myself, does he really want to have this conversation now, as we're dancing in the middle of thousands of people? And he's messing up my rhythm by getting all lovey-dovey on the floor when I just want to shake it. But I smile brightly, and joke that he refused to move here because he is too haughty to sell things on the streets like other francophone immigrants who don't yet have a strong command of the language. It's a running joke between us but he is not smiling this time. Rather he seems to be seriously pondering what could have been. And so here we are, tightly embracing each other as if slow dancing to Marvin Gaye while everyone around us is flailing their arms in a house music-induced ecstasy.

I understand how he feels. Even though he came out years ago, Etienne can't bring himself to delve into Paris' gay black community, or even consider romance with another black man. Most days he doesn't think about it, but here, amidst so many potentially available, uninhibitedly out black gay men, he's feeling the sting of regret. All these years the loss, or potential loss, of his community has hung over him, threatening a violent downpour at any moment. A hurricane that never manifested, and if it happened he could have dealt with. Hindsight vision is 20/20, they say.

Trying to wrangle a smile out of him I say there are now many out gay Africans guys in Paris: he doesn't need me. He looks me in the eye. "Non Cheri: t'es l'amour Africain," he says, insisting I was, and remain, his sole African love. And that is it. He'd rather date and fuck non-Africans than deal with the baggage he is still carrying. And after all these years, even though he's been all over the globe, he's never returned to the Democratic Republic of Congo. And has no plans to.

"If you sit silent about your pain, they will kill you and say you enjoyed it."

– Zora Neale Hurston

Six: Having the Talk!

Not many Nigerian parents of my father's generation talk with their heterosexual children about their sexuality or their love interests. So I never felt I was being deprived of anything relative to my straight siblings. If I was introducing them to a potential life-partner, a situation that would require families joining in marriage, that would be the time for a more intimate conversation.

Over the years my brothers got married and had children. I kept shuttling between continents, working in New York and spending all my free time in Nigeria. But we never really had a conversation about my sexuality or relationship status.

In 2006 my brother Victor invites much of the family for the first time to his brand new home amongst the lush Katamkpe Hills, for New Year's Eve.

We've all just spent a joyous Christmas in Asaba, and are heading north in a convoy of cars to Abuja. Victor, who I have since dubbed 'Big Vic' on account of his success in turning failing businesses around, pulls me aside at some point along the way and mentions that Dad has asked him about something he'd heard from folks in New York – something about me being gay. Vic says he hopes I would not get mad at Dad if he broaches the subject – he knows I have a temper that can be volcanic when it erupts. I assure him that I've worked very hard over the years to keep it in check, and that nothing could possibly ruin our good time.

For me at this point being gay is not news, and it shouldn't be salacious gist, and if Dad wants a conversation about it we can have one. News reports about the NABJ gay caucus have mentioned me by name, and no doubt Dad's nosey-parker friends in America have forwarded those reports to him. If a conversation is to be had, I am happy to have one. I feel good. I'm fully aware of who I am, and fully aware of God's unequivocal love for me. I was born gay and it is no error.

But the way the evening unfolds floors me.

As the clock nears midnight we all drop to our knees in the living room, and each of us prays out loud, saying what we hope for and want from the New Year. Prayer is important in my family, and like many Nigerian families we try to begin each New Year with it.

When it comes to Dad's turn, he prays loudly, in full view of everyone – a niece, a nephew, in-laws, brothers, sister, and his wife – that God should help and forgive all of those who are living in the closet that they may repent, change their ways and get closer to God and yada yada yada. As he goes on and on about it I go from being stunned to silently fuming, and only catch a few of the words he's muttering now like 'forgiveness', 'coming into the light', 'turning over a new leaf' and blah blah blah.

To avoid losing my temper I tune out. I start to return text messages mid-prayer on my smartphone while he rambles on and the kneeling family murmurs amens. Though so many years have passed, in his mind I remain the child in Ikoyi who he can at any moment reduce to tears, or the youth he can always take down a few pegs. I look at my father as he concludes his praying and think, Well sir, not today. Not this New Year. And never again will I allow myself to be hurt and humiliated like this by you.

When the prayers are over and we get off our knees, I calmly ask Dad to step into the bedroom I'm using, which is next to the living room where we've just been praying. I am mindful of my promise to Big Vic, but still I am angry as we go in and I close the door. Without allowing him to speak I make it clear that I am in no closet. I am proud of who I am. I don't need forgiveness. I don't need to change. And, most importantly, that I am simply giving him information so he hears it directly from me, and I am not seeking his approval, or anyone else's. I demand that going forward he respect me as I am, and insist I have no problem returning to New York and remaining outside of his life or that of anyone else in the family who has issues.

By this point I'm not angry. I'm not emotional. I am clinical. I am cold. I don't let him speak until I am finished. My feelings are clear, and this time I have no problems expressing them concisely. After all I have not lived in any of his homes since I was nineteen; and during all the years I worked as a janitor, telephone operator, and hotel room cleaner to make a life in America, he was absent.

At this point, even though I'd been raised to never challenge elders or authority figures, particularly him, I am firm in my belief that no one has the right to, in my mind, belittle me. The hard years abroad and alone have shaped this worldview. Respect cannot be assumed; sometimes it has to be earned.

And he listens. It's as if Dad is hearing me for the very first time. In all these years I've never so much as challenged him. This is the first time I am demanding respect. Perhaps on some level he's even pleased. I feel no guilt about giving him an ultimatum. And it isn't a bluff. He can accept the situation or we can go back to not seeing each other, a situation I know he doesn't want. It's as if I've put a gun to his head and he won't dare me to pull the trigger because the look in my eyes, the flatness of my voice, tells him I would.

Dad then says okay, but also that he doesn't really understand. I promise I will try to be more understanding of his viewpoint, but say that I won't be more patient. I also promise to send him information on human sexuality and marriage equality so he will be better informed (which I do), but I wasn't going to be – in my opinion – put down during prayers or at any other time by anyone in our family.

This day marks a turning point in our relationship, and Dad's very warm reception for Scott when I finally bring him home to Asaba could never have come about without that New Year's Eve drama. But I've often wondered, did I really have to (figuratively) put a gun to his head for him to truly see and respect me as a person?

Sadly this outcome is not the norm for many, and even with my unwaveringly loving immediate family, sometimes someone they are close to will bring me down with the reality of the ingrained homophobia and ignorance that is widespread among the Nigerian population.

It is the summer of 2015 and my big sister is turning sixty. She plans to have a simple church service in thanksgiving and then an elaborate lunch afterwards. As she is doing this in London, where she now spends the bulk of her time, there is to be no gigantic Nigerian-style Owambe, or three-day extravaganza where the streets are closed. Annette simply wants her family and close friends around her. It is hard to get all her siblings in the same place at the same time, given we all live in different countries, but we make it there. My cousins, nieces, nephews, and even my mum make the trip.

We have a long, very jolly afternoon. We reminisce about the year before – January 2014, when our cousin Joe brought a large group of our family together in Cape Town, South Africa to celebrate his fiftieth birthday. I shrieked for joy when I saw my cousin Henry, who I had not seen in years. Growing up, Henry, who is my father's nephew, spent loads of time in our home in Lagos. He was another big brother who I loved, and today he is a smart, charming silver fox. My sister has a photo from those years with me in my gold pants and little 'fro, Henry and Big Vic, all sitting around in Dad's living room. I knew Henry was living in the UK somewhere and had long been married with children, but it had been more than a decade since I'd actually laid eyes on him. And there he was, looking dapper with his young daughter in tow. She was a gem, and I was eager to meet the rest of his family.

As I guide my mum from the Catholic church in Central London, where we have just had Mass for my sister, to the waiting car, she squints, then tugs at me and asks, "Is that Henry?"

I look up and yes, it is indeed him. I wave and he notices Mum and the reunion is joyous, and they chat on and on as we make our way to the center where the lunch is to happen, in a pleasant room with white tables and chairs festooned with lilac balloons. Every table has a large purple and white floral arrangement on it, and party music welcomes us in.

As everyone is finding their seats I say to Henry, "You know, I've never met your wife. Can you introduce me?" He is mildly surprised and walks me over to her. She is full-figured with plump cheeks and a very straight perm. She wears striking red lipstick, and has on a black dress paired with a white sequined jacket. At the table are her children, who seem to be having a good time. After the introduction her first words to me are, "I've heard about you."

I respond with a huge smile and say, "Good things, I hope!"

She responds with a tight smile: "Not really."

"Oh," I say. "Okay, then."

She presses on aggressively. "Where is your family?" she says, gesticulating with her left arm.

Confused, I turn to the table where my brothers, my sister and my mother are sitting and look round at assorted nephews, nieces and cousins, and I say, "Everyone there is my family. Almost everyone in this room is my family. These are all my relatives."

"Where is your wife?! Where are your children?!" Her tone is accusatory.

Then I have the 'ah-ha' moment. She is trying to embarrass and shame me in front of a table of people, including her children. She's daring me to acknowledge publicly that I'm gay. I now realize I'm dealing with some kind of homophobic 'prayer warrior'. If she was a more polite person she could simply have greeted me and moved on, or asked me directly without trying to make a spectacle as we stand awkwardly at the table. I might even have thought her inquisition was genuine curiosity. This is the thing she has heard about me that to her pedestrian thinking is not good.

I look this very provincial person in the eye. I see that she is the kind with the mindset that a woman must marry to be of any value, and men by a certain age should have tied the knot otherwise they too are underachievers. And since she'd heard that I'm gay why not be salacious and push me to deny it? As I stare at this plump woman I smile and ponder my response. In some ways it is my fault, I think, for putting myself in this situation: I actually asked Henry to introduce me to her when he showed no impulse to do so, and now here I am, looking into the face of a woman who is trying to take joy in embarrassing a person she doesn't know in front of his own family.

She fails.

I left the closet decades ago, and would not be slinking back into one, particularly not at a function that was a family party. I smile brighter and I say, "My partner Scott is at home in New York. It was nice meeting you."

I turn and walk back to my table before she can respond. I think about Henry, awkwardly silent beside us. He will always be my cousin, and my sister will always be my sister, but from now his wife will be nothing to me. Soon after, as we settle down to eat, the plump woman begins dramatically singing praises to God for the food and for my sister.

As the years have passed, my frequent visits to Lagos and Asaba, or anywhere where there has been a Nigerian space, provide occasion for me to be asked 'the question': "When are you getting married?"

I don't always know how to answer with integrity. Do I open up a can of worms with total strangers and say, "I'll get married when marriage equality is the law of the federation"? Sometimes, if there are people there who know me and I feel comfortable with, I'll say something like that and leave it alone. More often than not the question is, do I continue with my boilerplate response, "When I find the right one I'll let you know", or do I say something more self-exposing? Some of my pals use the phrase "God's time is the best" to shut up the nosy parker inquisitors.

One of my Nigerian pals, Dike, is over forty and gay. He now lives in London and it's unlikely he will ever move home for good. But on his last visit to his hometown Owerri he tells me how an aunt worried so much that he hadn't brought home a bride that she couldn't let it go. He thought he'd escaped the dreaded question – until he went over to her house to give her money before departing, and she fell to her knees wailing, "Please, *please* find a wife. Please, I am begging you in the name of God, please."

Dike replied, "Please Aunty, get up. I have heard you. I will see what I can do."

Suddenly hopeful she said, "Oh, are you looking for one

over there in England?"

"Ah-ah Aunty, does it matter where she comes from?" Dike said.

"That's true, but it is better if she hails from these parts," she replied.

"But Aunty, at my age I don't think I want to get married anymore."

"Eh?!" she screamed. "Don't say that oh! There is a seventy-year-old man in the next kindred who is looking for a young wife. You are a man. You can even marry at seventy. I have been praying for you. I prayed for you this morning that a good woman will come your way, in Jesus' name."

There is always an older man in the village who needs a young wife.

I feel Dike's pain. Recently a man who was a close friend from secondary school called me up to ask that I donate to a fund to refurbish the school's kitchen. Expecting a more substantial donation than I've offered, he says, "You are not married and you have no kids." His reasoning is I ought to have more to give since I'm only responsible for myself.

I am annoyed. We left Nigeria about the same time, and he knows that at this point Scott and I had been living together for years. And yet I still have to gently remind him that my male partner of close to a decade is my family. And no, I may not be conventionally married like he is, but I'm not single.

While I can excuse his not equating my relationship with his own heterosexual marriage, I couldn't excuse my cousin's wife and her mean-spirited attempt at humiliation. Months after my sister had finished basking in the euphoria of having her family around her, I told her about the plump woman's encounter with me, and how I found her inappropriate and rude, but of course wouldn't have brought it up during the event.

I didn't gloss over her bigotry, particularly since so soon after the encounter she had taken to singing and praising God in that showy, 'charismatic' way Nigerian Pentecostal Christians sometimes do: hands raised to the heavens, eyes closed and belting out something about Jesus' love. What a fraud! I've come too far to be put down by these who cloak their shade in Jesus, and I told everyone in the family so.

I thought about her ostentatious display of piety when I read of a man from Eastern Nigeria who had erected a thirty-foot marble statue of a white Jesus Christ in his hometown. This forty-ton sculpture is the largest of its kind in Africa, and was carved and built by the Chinese – even though unemployment is sky-high in Nigeria and his state is full of talented craftsmen – and then placed in the grounds of a church he'd built.

A year later I am at a memorial service in London for my stepmother. This time my father has made the trip, all the way from Asaba. After Mass and before refreshments are served I am chatting with my dad as his grandchildren, nieces and nephews make their way up to the front pew and encircle us to greet him one by one.

Henry and his wife approach, and as usual Henry is kind, charming and gracious. The wife says hello, and I respond curtly, without the warmth I have for her husband, and then turn my attention back to Dad and the others. As she says her greeting to him I have my arm draped around his shoulders. And my father, an Asaba chief, a retired engineer who in his time scaled the highest rungs of the civil service, and who lives a life steeped in our traditions; a man highly respected by the multitudes of people to whom he's given a hand up over the years, responds to her greeting while holding onto me and not letting me leave his side for a moment. He is basking in the love of his openly gay son. We'd come a long way over the years, and I smiled and looked at this woman, realizing then that in the grand scheme of things she doesn't matter one whit.

Still, I can't help but remember how challenging it is for the majority of sexual minorities who live their day-to-day lives on the continent. A continent where at this time the prevailing sentiment is that this is a taboo, and gays need not be seen, or heard. Or, for some, even exist.

"The purpose of religion is to control yourself, not criticize others."

– Dalai Lama

SEVEN: THE CALM BEFORE THE AFRICAN GAY STORM

By the spring of 2008 I am weary of my job at the *New York Post*. It has been almost fifteen years, any challenge is long gone, and it is a grind. As a City Hall reporter I work in the tiny, cramped Room Nine press room, and sometimes in the even less appealing basement Room 4A (designated as the overflow room) from morning till late evening, and often on weekends too. I need a change. But there isn't really anything else at the paper I want to do, and what I might have desired – being a bureau chief, or covering presidential campaigns on the road – I would not get. It's a feeling that many journalists of color have had: working hard but seeing your career stagnate in the newsroom while non-ethnic journalists are handed great opportunities, and as a result of them pronounced stars. I have hit a ceiling and it is plain to see.

Years earlier, when I was feeling burned out I got sent on an exchange program to London, and I worked there at the *Times* for nearly four months. The current editor is not big on exchanges, and hasn't sent anyone away to any of our sister newspapers in the U.K. or Australia in over a year. I briefly flirt with the idea of corporate communications and make some inquiries but my heart isn't really in it.

I realize I am not quite done being a journalist; I am just done working City Hall for the *New York Post*, even on a high-profile team. I want to head back to Africa and report from there, or find the money to continue producing the *AFRican* – I get so much more joy out of my work when I am doing international stories or pieces that have to do with Africa.

Thanks to my dear, dear friend Kai I got included in a group of journalists sponsored by the Kaiser Family Foundation to cover two successive International AIDS Conferences. The first was held in Thailand in the summer of 2004, the second two years later in Canada. While at those gatherings I'm able to do stories about the impact of HIV/AIDS in various African countries, and on the black world at large, for the Black AIDS Institute's publication and website. Of course I also cover any New York stories for the paper I work for– particularly those concerning the New York City Public Health Department – that wouldn't normally get publicized. But by now I'd prefer to report on issues that focus on Africa's growing pains.

So I apply for, and get, a fellowship from the Kaiser Foundation to write about healthcare in East Africa as a freelancer. But I don't resign just yet; I say nothing about the fellowship and continue to work really hard at confirming a story of legislative malfeasance at City Hall. I know it will be fantastic for me if I can leave the job with one last exposé under my belt that is all mine, and a front page story.

I tell no one about this piece, not even my editors or the bureau chief, until I am ready; until the bulk of my reporting is done, and I have uncovered the evidence I need. I am determined this won't be one of those pieces that start out as my work and then get subsumed into a large 'collaborative' piece with whoever is the current flavor-of-the-month reporter the editors want to push. I've seen this happen too many times, and it only seems to happen to the few reporters of color on the job.

The story I broke came to be dubbed the Slush Fund Scandal, where the higher-ups in the city council wing of City Hall allocated money to fake but appropriate-sounding groups during the budget process, and then, much later on, once the budget was approved, and away from the scrutiny of the media and other watchdogs, reallocated millions of dollars to real groups of their choice. It seems outlandish, but given a budget that hovered in the billions, lawmakers were able to play fast and loose with millions, and consolidate their hold on power by dishing out cash midstream to those they felt like rewarding.

It is a very hard story to pin down, so I work on it through smaller stories that build up bit by bit, and with the help of sources I have known for years – including one Brooklyn lawmaker and his staff, who give me access to documents that allow me to ask the right people the right questions – and a strong anonymous tip which I end up being able to verify, I finally have my story. And I'm thrilled when I call it in and have all the answers the editors ask for in my back pocket. It is headlined 'This is her$ for the Faking', and has an illustration of Council Speaker Christine Quinn with her hand in a cookie jar. She runs the council, with only the mayor above her. I don't think, or have any evidence, that she directed this mess personally, but she's in charge and the buck stops with her. It is a bombshell in New York City government and leads to an F.B.I. probe, and subsequent conviction and prison time for several lawmakers who turned out to be lawbreakers. My bosses are thrilled, and their verbal pats on the back are welcome. After a few follow-up pieces I am offered and accept a faculty position at New York University and tell the higher-ups at the newspaper that my time with them is done. They seem surprised, but I'm happy to leave on a high note, with a huge story that has repercussions in the way the city of New York does business going forward.

After this I go on an extended reporting trip to Uganda and, after an evening in Entebbe, make my way to Kampala, where I'm to write about healthcare and all the innovative things that are happening to push back on HIV, particularly among poorer citizens. At this juncture Uganda had almost one million people under the age of fifty infected with HIV, and seventy-seven thousand people had recently died. The AIDS orphans alone numbered 1.2 million, and everyone knew someone infected with HIV. I spend a fair amount of time observing medical teams at the Infectious Disease Institute (IDI) there.

The place is model facility, and I meet many people fighting against stigma and battling their diagnosis with a tremendous amount of dignity. The unassuming two-story building is host to a mostly African staff who are treating thousands of people – at least ten thousand annually, one doctor tells me – and then taking treatments and therapies out to the rural areas.

The patients here are called 'friends'. The waiting rooms and common areas are filled with joyous singing, and works of art are spread out on the floors and walls in little communal areas that have been carved out for the friends.

"When this clinic started in a small room, a HIV clinic was a specter of a lot of depression and sadness, people laying on the floors. Now as you will see it's a vibrant population," said Andrew Kambugu, the head of clinical services, as he showed me around.

While friends wait to see the doctors they smile and chat. Many tell me it used to be a somber environment, with folks covering their heads and faces in shame, and a major effort had to be made to bring in joy so that patients – or rather 'friends on treatment' – would return. Today all I see in the waiting rooms are friends playing games or making music; and many who had lost loved ones and been on the brink of death themselves before coming here are now getting powerful anti-retroviral therapies. "People are well, they are going back to work, they are looking for spouses if they've lost their loved ones, and they are looking to live life again. For me as a young African professional I think there are fewer places that give more satisfaction," Kambugu added.

Another doctor tells me of challenges I'd not thought about before: "What do you do when you ask a patient why he didn't take his medicine and he shows you the label and it says 'take with food' and he asks, 'Where will I get the food?'"

I tag along with teams of doctors and nurses who travel far into rural areas to take medication to patients who can't get to the institute. Lack of brick-and-mortar infrastructure is not a reason for people not to be treated, they tell me.

Everyone is doing more with less. But what really impresses me is the number of African doctors and scientists from all over the continent who come to learn from the successes here. I chat with physicians from Zambia and Nigeria, and it turns out that some twenty-seven countries have sent over a thousand people here to be trained in the latest advances in HIV care.

At its core this is a clinical research facility, and scientists are all over the place conducting clinical trials in the labs, including a fair number of Western doctors. But "we're not here to train Europeans or North Americans to have their African experience," the head of research, Philippa Easterbrook, insists. She's a medical professor who took time off from teaching at prestigious King's College, London to come here. "We are here to train the next generation of clinicians, teachers, researchers in sub-Saharan Africa. The era of scientific projects emanating from the West, with Africa being the receptacle, is over. It will be us in sub-Saharan Africa saying, these are the questions we want to ask together. We will write the grants, we will do the programs, we will do the analyses, we will write the papers."

When I'm not at IDI I spend time at nearby Mulago Hospital. It is the largest in the country, and a teaching hospital, but there I'm struck by the efforts at care being made by the medical teams in the face of an utter lack of equipment and medication. I'm saddened by the wards, particularly one I wander into that has reed-thin mattresses, and beds with just springs and no coverings. It is heartbreaking that at this hospital patients who have no other hope end up here with even less hope.

I'm reporting a lot but also loving Kampala. Uganda's capital, the city on hills, has given me a new appreciation for good coffee and good conversation. Many of my evenings are spent at Café Pap, which bills itself as Uganda's best coffee shop, and the baristas remember my name after one visit. My home away from home is a club called the American Recreation Association, which has a large swimming pool and a red clay tennis court, and rooms to rent that are affordable compared to hotels in town. My four-poster bed has a large mosquito net over it and is very comfortable in a colonial sort of way. Some evenings movies are shown at the clubhouse and it's an easy way to relax and entertain new friends. On weekends my cousin Moha and I trudge up to Jinja to see the source of the River Nile, or cross the equator line, or hang out on the shores of the mighty Lake Victoria. On Sundays after services we go to brunch at the ornate Kampala Serena Hotel. That is a splurge.

My big brother's buddy Francis, who long ago drove me from Syracuse to New York City to see Fela Kuti in concert, has, like many African professionals, decamped from America, and is now raising his family here. He chose not to return to Nigeria but is living happily in Kampala, and it is a treat to spend time with his family.

On the streets there is a major billboard campaign to stop cross-generational sex as a means to combat HIV. A picture of a middle-aged looking man is captioned 'Would you let this man be with your teenage daughter?' And the answer, one line below: 'Then why are you with his?'

After weeks of reporting, and as I am about to wrap things up, I have tea with a local journalist, Simon Kasyate, who I first met years ago at the International AIDS Conference in Toronto. I gush about how thrilled I am with all the positive stories I have been finding; how lovely the people of Uganda are; and how I am looking forward to going to see bank officials at Standard Chartered, good corporate citizens who are investing in attacking river blindness for the poor – I've heard they've been paying for cataract surgeries in some communities to the tune of $227 a person; and that the bank has also been drilling boreholes in far-flung areas, spending about eighty thousand dollars to provide clean water for rural dwellers. Simon, now a broadcaster, looks at me and smiles. "Why don't you ask them about the gay woman they won't let open a bank account?" he says. "Could they do that where you live?"

What? Are we talking about the same bank? Standard Chartered, a multinational, UK-based bank that has outlets in more than seventy countries? Indeed we are. And he talks and my tea, untouched, grows cold.

Later I get to speak with Victor Mukasa, a female-to-male transgender Ugandan who not only had the nerve to be open about his sexuality and gender identity, and co-found the advocacy group Sexual Minorities Uganda (SMUG), but also works as an analyst for the International Gay & Lesbian Human Rights Commission (IGLHRC). In 2005 Mukasa's home was raided and his friends arrested, and Mukasa went into hiding. He emerged defiant, sued the government for unlawful search and seizure, and became more vocal as an advocate. But then, after opening a bank account and listing IGLHRC as his employer, Standard Chartered Bank froze his account. Their reasoning was simple: gay organizations and being gay are illegal in Uganda.

"She indicated the money was coming from a gay and lesbian human rights organization. It is illegal here," Herbert Zake, the bank's corporate affairs manager, tells me when I visit his office. Wrongfooted – he was expecting a puff-piece about the bank's good works for the poor – he seems genuinely shocked by my questions, and indicates that his hands are tied. Imagine having no access to your paycheck and not being able to pay your rent or bills simply because you are gay or different and do not hide it – as if the bank in which you place your wages is an arm of the state, or the church. I am appalled, and I detail Mukasa's nightmare in a story for *The Advocate* once I'm back in New York.

Shortly thereafter Mukusa moves to South Africa, subsequently ending up in New York, and then, years later, Washington D.C. It will take six years before he is reunited with his loved ones, his partner and their children.

Uganda is at that time starting to gain notoriety for its treatment of its LGBT citizens. Its parliament will go on to pass a bill that calls for the death penalty for gay people that the international community dubs the 'Kill the Gays' bill; and David Kato, a prominent sexual minority rights advocate and Mukasa's colleague, is murdered. In 2011 the now-defunct *Rolling Stone* newspaper (no connection with the famed American pop culture publication) publishes a front-page story titled '100 Pictures of Uganda's Top Homos Leak'. The article lists the names, addresses, and photographs of a hundred people next to a yellow banner that reads, 'Hang Them'.

Some of those listed weren't gay, but the climate was getting tougher for LGBT Ugandans. Many activists pointed the finger of blame at American evangelical pastors, in particular the Massachusetts-based Scott Lively, who, like his cohorts, was reeling from having lost the culture wars in an America that was becoming increasingly tolerant of gay people. These well-financed evangelicals now turned their attention to Africa, bankrolling antigay campaigns in Uganda.

In early 2009 Lively is invited to give a seminar called 'Exposing the Homosexuals' Agenda'. He uses the opportunity to tell those attending that they need to protect the young population against the threat of the gays. Uganda's population is heavily skewed towards the young; and, as in most sub-Saharan African countries, family is valued above all, and is understood in conservative terms. Lively told his audience that gays were coming to recruit their children and to tear apart their families, if they were not stopped.

"They have taken over the United States, the United States government, and the European Union," he declared. "Nobody has been able to stop them so far. I'm hoping Uganda can."

The American online magazine *Slate* reported that Lively would later boast that his actions had the effect of "a nuclear bomb", and that one Ugandan legislator said afterwards, "We must exterminate homosexuals before they exterminate society."

Soon afterwards, David Bahati, a lawmaker who had been present at the seminar, introduces his odious bill. It is October 14, 2009. International pressure from Uganda's donors and other human rights defenders force the issue onto the back burner, but it is revived with vigor in 2012, and this time it passes, on December 20, 2013. This version of the Anti-Homosexuality Act, with a penalty of life imprisonment for gays (rather than the death penalty initially called for) is what Uganda's president, Yoweri Museveni, signs into law and defends enthusiastically, calling offenders "homosexual mercenary prostitutes". Museveni has been Uganda's president since 1986, and the law he approves is so severe that gays and lesbians can be jailed simply for touching.

Following an international outcry and American sanctions, some months later the courts would strike down the law on a technicality. But the damage is done, and violence against gays in Uganda escalates.

As a journalist living in New York City I've always made an effort to keep tabs on Africans in America, and the numbers of asylum seekers who have been beaten or tortured for being open about their sexuality in their home countries keeps swelling.

Despite the recent uprush of homophobic prejudice, often clothed in notions that homosexuality is unAfrican, folks with different sexual orientations have always existed in sub-Saharan African communities, whether they were known as 'goorjigen' (man-woman) in Senegal, or 'kombla besia' in Ghana, or 'dan/yan daudu' – the headscarf-wearing, feminine men of northern Nigeria. The frequent complaint from homophobes in African countries that "it's not in our culture" has always surprised me because it is simply wrong. Most often they 'explain' their reasoning by turning to biblical or Koranic texts, but the Bible and the Koran aren't native to Africa, nor are they factual documents.

In Nigeria we have a history of celebrating differences, and accepting circumstances that may seem unusual. Case in point is the Yoruba deity Shango, god of thunder and lightning, and an Alaafin (king) of Oyo. A macho personage who had at least three wives, legend has it that he once borrowed clothes from one of his wives to escape his enemies, and today he's sometimes depicted with his hair long and plaited, and wearing a skirt. No one would think of branding him a cross-dresser, but in this era labeling yourself as gay, or being different, is a marker for trouble.

In the 1970s my homeland had her own gender-bending musical star, a singer who went by the moniker Area Scatter. Scatter, who wore make-up, plaited his hair, and dressed as a glamorous lady, played the thumb piano for Igbo royalty far and wide. It's been said he told people that, after living through the brutal Nigerian civil war of 1967-1970, a conflict that saw over 100,000 military casualties and an estimated two million civilians dead from starvation, he went into the forest. When Scatter emerged seven months and seven days later, it was as a 'woman'.

Was he a gay man?

Was he a transgender woman?

Does it even matter?

The singer with the melodious voice, who was born a man but performed as a woman, was celebrated, and not subject to the ridicule and violence that transgender people – or anyone with a scintilla of difference in our society – faces today. He also continued to spend time in the forests, and was described by some as a 'witch doctor' or shaman. Did that play a role in his being allowed to be? I'm not sure, but there is ample evidence of him walking the streets freely in women's garb, and film footage of him performing for hoity-toity crowds who applaud his talents.

Today that seems unthinkable, given the normalization of violence perpetrated against anyone who dares to live their truth. And it is not just in Nigeria. Across Africa there is a rising discomfort with anyone claiming and owning their sexuality if it doesn't conform to the way of life of the majority and fall in line with whatever Abrahamic religion is predominant.

When I travel through Zimbabwe in 2011, first to do some reporting, then to spend some quality time with Peter, a fellow journalist I'd been friends with for many years, I wonder how charged the atmosphere will be.

Peter and I got to know each other when we were both fellows of the Kaiser Family Foundation and attended the International AIDS Conference in Toronto. He's also pals with Simon Kasyate, the Ugandan broadcaster who pointed me to the Standard Charter bank situation with Victor Mukasa. Peter's been to America a few times since then, and I was finally making good on my promise to get to Harare, his hometown.

While in Harare I get to know another wonderful journalist, Columbus – a stellar radio reporter who hosts me in the home he shares with his girlfriend and children, and makes sure I am occupied whenever Peter isn't available.

When I first met Peter I instantly knew he was gay even if he hadn't quite come to terms with it himself. Over the years he has, but his tales of same-sex romance seem mainly to take place abroad, and when he picks me up from Columbus' flat he tells me of a girl he is dating who is likely to become his fiancée. She adorns his Facebook page, and they look like any happy young couple. I look forward to meeting her, I tell him politely. And I silently wonder how gay people are faring here. After all, it has been widely reported that President Robert Mugabe has declared gays to be lower than animals. "If dogs and pigs don't do it, why must human beings? Can human beings be human beings if they do worse than pigs?" he is said to have told his audience at a Harare book fair back in 1997.

He also refused to allow the Gay and Lesbian Association of Zimbabwe (GALZ) to exhibit at the fair, dismissing them as an "association of sodomists and sexual perverts."

In the weeks I spend in 'Zim', Peter shows me much of his beautiful city. We also fly up to the magnificent Victoria Falls, and he takes me on a tour of Mosi-oa-Tunya ('the clouds that thunder'), as the indigenes refer to the largest curtain of falling water in the world. The falls, fed by the Zambezi River, are 1700 meters wide, and consist of five grandiose drops. There are more than seven huge gorges that spread out between Zimbabwe and Zambia. And the clouds really are thunderous where the Zambezi spills over a cliff and cascades into a narrow chasm between 233 and 360 feet below. An incomparable natural spectacle, it is over a mile wide, and the entire area has been designated a UNESCO World Heritage site since 1989. It is inevitable that we will get drenched, so the bright yellow raincoats we procure from the ticket office are essential. Afterwards we spend hours strolling through the national park.

Whenever we go out for drinks or tea, Peter has a companion join us. A handsome lad barely out of university flies with us to Victoria Falls and accompanies us on our foray into the park. When we check into the deluxe Stanley & Livingstone resort, the lush gardens, around which small cottages are dotted, make for a very romantic locale, the perfect place to renew your commitment, or, better yet, have a honeymoon. The Stanley & Livingstone is set on the very exclusive 6000-acre Victoria Falls Private Game Reserve, and is a boutique hotel that is tranquil, with maids and butlers who cater to and fuss over every guest. Though tending to the opulent, the cottages are tastefully furnished, with gigantic, sparkling white baths, and each is surrounded by densely-planted flowerbeds. My eye is caught by explosions of red and yellow flame lilies and what look like pink orchids. Exotic plants abound, and when I step onto my balcony to sniff the fragrant air I am greeted by the sight of buffalo going down to a watering hole just beyond the near-invisible fence.

Peter and his current sweetheart's suite is near my cottage. We all go to dinner at the Boma, a traditional open-sky eatery on the edge of the forest. On offer are all the local delicacies, including crocodile meat, warthog, and worms or caterpillars. I skip very little, tasting much that is on offer, and find everything delicious. There are also more typical meat, fish, and tons of vegetarian dishes; and our dinner experience includes being entertained by indigenous musicians and dancers. Diners are given traditional cloth to tie over their clothes if they don't have African garb, a gesture of connection that makes me smile. There are fortunetellers who I ignore, and storytellers; we take drum lessons and dance between courses, and have our faces painted to reflect our animal spirit. I'm given a lion paw on my right cheek. Peter is given a scorpion and his companion two spiders, one on his forehead and the other on his right cheek. It is a superb evening to cap a wonderful few days in a place I would want to return to for a honeymoon if I get married.

We return to Harare relaxed and happy. Peter is infatuated, and his relationship with this lad makes him very, very happy.

I never did get to meet the lady who was nearing fiancée status.

I meet other gay people in Harare, but once one is away from insulated upmarket tourist locales there it is, homophobia, always bubbling under the surface. No one would risk being open here.

Even so, I wonder whether President Mugabe is quite the homophobe he is claimed to be. Consider the case of the first president of Zimbabwe, the late Canaan Banana. His post – he became president in 1980, directly after independence – was ceremonial, and a befitting end to a career as a freedom fighter. Mugabe was initially his prime minister, but by 1987 had muscled him out of office, becoming the executive president in his place. Banana was apparently a gay man – indeed an exceptionally predatory one; he was later convicted of raping many young men who worked for him in the State House, plying them with alcohol, spiking their drinks and forcing himself on them. It now appears that Mugabe knew all the while that Banana was gay, and that he and his officials covered up for him when he had sex with members of staff who didn't consent. This argues pragmatic indifference on Mugabe's part, rather than fanatical prejudice.

All this spilled out into the open when a former bodyguard killed a police colleague who taunted him for being 'Banana's wife'. Banana, by now an ex-president, was charged with sodomy, and the subsequent lurid trial gripped the country. Banana fled before sentencing but was persuaded to return by

Nelson Mandela, and served ten months behind bars. Having stood by him during the trial, his wife sought asylum in Britain because she feared a vengeful Mugabe might kill her. She said she had known of, and come to terms with her husband's sexuality: "Before we moved out of the State House, my husband's bodyguard gave me some startling news. He told me, 'Canaan is gay.' I was shocked," Janet Banana said to the *Guardian* (UK) newspaper in 2002, after she had escaped Harare with one suitcase and little money. "For a long time, I questioned myself: why, why? Eventually, after searching my soul, I began to think, it's his life – maybe I should accept it."

Banana's post-State House life had been as a respected and high-profile spokesman for the Organization of African Unity. Barely a year after Mugabe declared gay people to be un-African, Canaan found himself standing trial for abusing his position and sexually assaulting members of his male staff. He denied the charges: it was all politically motivated, he said. Janet concurred, up to a point: "Mugabe used the issue of my husband's sexuality as a way of mobilizing opinion against Canaan. Mugabe was jealous of Canaan's role in the OAU, which offered him an international platform not available to Mugabe," she said. "Canaan was also regarded as the most likely contender to Mugabe's position. The attack on Canaan was an attempt to eliminate any hint of opposition."

I often wonder, if Canaan Banana had been allowed to be his true self, might he not have felt he had to use his power to get male intimacy and companionship? As I travelled through Zimbabwe in 2011, nine years after the Banana saga, I saw gay men in forced relationships with women, gay men living in fear, and felt saddened.

After Banana died in 2003 Mugabe called him "a gift to the nation" in a radio tribute. But as the *Guardian* noted, Banana's trial 'exposed Mugabe's virulent anti-gay stance – untypical of wider Zimbabwean public opinion – as a façade, because it included testimony that his own officials had covered up for Banana and refused to help victims of his sexual demands. It became apparent during the evidence that Mugabe had known about Banana's sexual misconduct, but done nothing to stop it.'

Today gay folk who live in African cities have very full lives –

challenging, yes, but full nonetheless, as I was to discover on an extended work trip to Accra in the summer of 2008.

Accra has always been a vibrant city. In recent times its population has exploded, and there has been a huge amount of construction in what was once a quiet seaside capital. The discovery of oil in Ghana brought in a ton of foreigners and drilling companies, but in 2008 it seems too early to tell if the 'black gold' has been good for the country.

At the time it would have been easy to miss the lively gay life that was there simply because it wasn't in your face. As in most other countries that were once British colonial subjects, anti-sodomy laws criminalized gay people. But couples would meet up in friendly watering holes like Henry's in the city's Adabraka neighborhood, or Chester's, a fun, spacious bar-cum-club in the residential and middle-class Nyaniba Estates.

Both are always wall-to-wall with guys, preening, sipping cocktails, chatting. Chester's is on the posh side, and perhaps the more popular of the two, and its eponymous owner appears to know everyone who walks in, greeting them by name and ensuring they feel at home in his lounge, which is also his home (he lives upstairs). But it is in the spacious garden, out of view of passers-by, where most of his customers sit.

Chester's was open to all, and the only requirement was being up for fun, and being prepared to dance. Often there was a band with live music, and outside of the preponderance of men it was like any other bar or lounge in the city. It is here I make my first set of friends in Accra. Going to Chester's helps me acclimatize and begin to make the connections that will turn this city into my second home. It is here I have my first date with a Ghanaian.

"If you're not careful the newspapers will have you hating the people who are being oppressed and loving the people who are doing the oppressing."

– Malcolm X

EIGHT: THE TIDE TURNS (INTO A SUMMER OF HATE)

I n the two years following my first extended trip to Accra not much seems to change. I notice more gay men out and about on subsequent visits, and there seems to be very little public discourse on issues of sexuality.

But seemingly overnight the script is flipped. After my visit to Zimbabwe in 2011 I return to an Accra where everything seems to have turned one hundred and eighty degrees around. The public is vocally and virulently homophobic. Gay bashings increase. Every day the media is consumed with the debate on how awful and 'filthy' homosexuals are. Radio – Ghana's most popular mass medium – is condemning gays all day, all the time. And everyone, from government bureaucrats to fishermen, listens in. Radio is the pipeline for information in many rural communities: if it is on the radio then it is believed; and in the towns and cities newspapers sell more copies with alarmist front-page headlines like 'Homos are Filthy', '8000 Homos In Two Regions', 'Lesbian Teacher Strikes' and 'Gays Can be Tried but the Law is Silent on Lesbians'. These stories, very few of them what one could call quality journalism, are read out verbatim on the radio, in salacious tones.

Each week in June brings a slew of new headlines, with one

national legislator, David Tetteh, declaring, "You cannot trace this act to any of the settings in Ghana. So this is foreign and I am saying that Ghanaians cherish our culture a lot, so for anybody to adulterate the cultural setting in Ghana... I have the fear that people could take the law into their hands in future and deal with this people drastically."

And so open season is declared. Gay people who are discreet become more so, and some seem to be getting married – or at least engaged – in a hurry. The vibrant, gay-friendly, live-and-let-live attitude I observed earlier in Accra rapidly begins to evaporate. Gays close the closet doors on themselves. And for those who dare to venture out the safe havens are disappearing. Chester's has closed and reopened elsewhere as a regular bar in Accra's Trade Fair area. Verbal gay-bashing becomes a national sport in the public sphere, and the very few defenders of gay Ghanaians are castigated publicly.

Besides Tetteh, another highly influential lawmaker, Paul Evans Aidoo, delights in firing cannons at this very vulnerable population. The married Catholic, a father of eight, goes on the air at Joy-FM, probably Accra's most popular radio station, to brag that, "All efforts are being made to get rid of these people in society." He urges the country's feared security service, the Bureau of National Intelligence, to round up the gays. And he calls for citizens – landlords, tenants, everyone – to report suspected gays. "Once they have been arrested, they will be brought before the law."

It proves not quite so easy to turn a people into a nation of police informers, and one could still spot gay people everywhere, in bakeries, markets, banks, you name it. However there appears to be no one strong enough, or with a high enough profile, to risk taking on these bullies. That is until an extremely well-liked radio journalist, Ato Kwamena Dadzie, decides that, since no one else will, he will. Using his platform on the air and online, he is one of the few who goes against the grain. He begins to speak out. Often. Ato even devotes two online articles to supporting Ghana's gay community.

"One of the jobs of the journalist is to give voice to the voiceless, and one of the most deprived people in this country – in terms of voice – is the gay community, and I'm more than delighted to speak for them," he tells me when I visit him in his studio.

But the response from many is not, "Okay let me rethink this" or "I respectfully disagree"; it is vitriolic. He is called gay himself, and many write that this is the reason he has gone through a divorce. The callers and online posters are downright nasty.

The intensity of the hatred takes me aback. Since I've always found Ghanaians to be generally nice people, particularly among each other, I have gone to see this much-needed straight ally to make sense of all this madness. Ato blames the mayhem that summer on Ghana's economic woes. Despite the oil-drilling, the revenues haven't begun to pour in; the country is going through an economic slowdown; jobs have been harder to get. Ghana has high unemployment, and nearly thirty percent of the populace is living below the poverty line, according to figures from the C.I.A. World Factbook.

"If I struggle to get one meal a day, and I have a band of homosexuals coming into my community, and I've been told that this band of homosexuals causes God to come and take away the single plate of food that I have, I would fight," Ato explains.

Few dispute the prevailing narrative this wacky summer that gays in Ghana are a foreign import, even though in their hearts they know these so-called 'bands of homosexuals' have always been here.

One who certainly knows this is the noted historian Nat Nunoo Amarteifio. A longtime resident of Accra, where he was born, and sixty-seven years old, he also served as its mayor from 1994 to 1998 (Accra's mayoralty, unlike those in the United States, is by appointment by the president). Nat is a father, grandfather and former New Yorker who has also spent time living in Nigeria. We met professionally years ago, and I immediately took a liking to him as he understood my Nigeri-an-New Yorker sensibilities.

Today he warns me wherever we run into each other that in Accra he's the only 'Daddy' I'll ever truly have, "Sugar or otherwise." It's a joke that always sends me into fits of laugher, but what is true is that whenever I don't understand something that is happening in Ghana, he's the first one I call. And just as I make time to seek out a befitting gift for my father when I go to Nigeria, I spend the same amount of time figuring out what I should gift 'Uncle Nat' on each trip I make 'home' to Accra. Generally I end up settling on quality booze, and books of contemporary popular fiction.

Uncle Nat tells me that there have been out gay men in his society from time immemorial, and that they are sometimes referred to as 'Komla Besia' or 'Kodjo Besia'. "Every community could point out a few and they never bothered anyone. And they were never bothered. And they are not seen as a threat to anybody. They obviously have their own little circles in which they move but it's not seen as a threat as such. So there are no big social proscriptions against them." Until now. As we sit imbibing hard liquor in his office he too suggests that the economy plays a large role. "The country is facing a rather uncertain future. On one hand they have all this promise of oil with the untold bounties, but that was also coming with an awful lot of anxiety. What would be the impact? What sort of inequalities would spring up?"

There were to be elections in two years, and African elections bring up hysteria. But even so, how did this result in gays being bashed in what used to be fairly tolerant Accra?

"It is sort of tangentially linked, but it all points to a state of uncertainty," Uncle Nat says. "Gay bashing had never been a feature of the Ghanaian social landscape until, oh, I would say the last ten to fifteen years. And it came with the evangelical Christians. And the Christianity had never been hysterical about it. That is, the *traditional* Christian churches," he emphasizes. "If you confronted them they would give you the party line, but they don't go out of their way to bash homosexuality because it was not seen as a toxic social element. It's these evangelicals who are looking for Satan everywhere, in everybody's drawers, who have created this specter of an expanding gay universe. This evangelical Christianity has really pervaded the society, and a lot of people are worried about it – they are intolerant, they are dismissive of everything that is not old-testament Christian; even African traditions are rapidly wilting under the force of their attacks. And many of the graduates of our universities are co-opted into these churches."

Indeed, across much of the continent evangelism has taken hold, and some of the most frequent targets are gays and lesbians. This is a phenomenon that can be both subtle, as in the case of my cousin Henry's wife, who sought to shame me at a family gathering, or blatant, as in the case of the many who openly call for gays to be killed, their justification verses from the Bible.

"You have to live here to appreciate that madness; you don't see it in America. In all fairness, maybe they see things that those of us who are not involved cannot see. But they are the ones who are driving this hysteria." Like many Africans, Uncle Nat allowed for the possibility of unknown spiritual insights and powers, and did not wholly dismiss the evangelicals' worldview, though was progressive on gay issues himself.

I wonder if Scott Lively's 'family' seminar has been unleashed in Ghana too. (In 2014, language from the Ugandan 'Kill the Gays' bill that Lively inspired was included in a bid to jail gay Gambians for life, so it is certainly possible.) The churches here are fanning the flames, and whatever is said in pulpits across the country is magnified by the newspapers – particularly the *Daily Graphic*, Ghana's largest-circulation paper. Every week brings another front-page story screaming 'HOMOS' in the headline. I go to them for an explanation.

Breda Atta-Quayson, a genial reporter with a seemingly permanent smile, is the deputy editor at the time. He's spent thirty-two years at the paper, and at fifty-nine is looking forward to retirement the following year. He's the one who has written most of the headlines with 'HOMOS' in bold type for the *Graphic*'s front pages.

"We want headlines that will create a debate," he says. "We want people to be attracted and buy the paper. First it's about commercial [sales.] Secondly 'Homos' fits the space we have... I don't know, but people tend to know 'homos' rather than 'gay'. It's a cultural thing. In Ghana when you say 'gay' most of the people do not have the understanding."

Breda says he did put a pro-gay advocate on the front page one recent Saturday, but for the most part the stories his reporters cover are the 'negative' ones, so he and his team have to report on those. But they have not written an editorial supporting either side. "No," he insists, "we are not pushing an antigay agenda. We are not! Of late it's becoming a topic in the society. For a long time gay issues have been, you know, like everybody is trying to hide it. They don't want to talk about it. The main reason is, we wanted it to be in the public domain. For discussion. This topic is going to lead to a liberal society. Now that it is coming to the fore a lot of people will like to figure out what it is. Even though the religious right is so antigay."

It is hard to believe this, given the stories he's been publishing. The friend and colleague who introduced me to Breda, Nana-Banyin Dadson, says to me afterwards that naturally any editor would want to sell copies and I am surely well aware of that, and he gently chides me for thinking his paper has an agenda. "Editors are supposed to have [the] pulse of [the] readership. It is what is strange that sells," he says.

Nana is the Arts & Entertainment editor at the *Graphic* and edits the weekly *Graphic Showbiz* spin-off. He will go on to retire in 2015. He knows everyone in entertainment, and has often been my guide when I want some culture. "It's strange because this is the first time that it has come up as a subject of open discussion," he says, adding that interest from readers is high.

Still, with the economic situation in Ghana worsening, gays have become an easy target for scapegoating. This goes on for years. When the British Prime Minister, Tony Blair, warns that his government could hold up aid to countries that penalize their gay citizens, and when U.S. President Barack Obama calls for decriminalization and compassion, it energizes local homophobes. They insist homosexuality is a Western import; one that – despite all evidence to the contrary, and despite the fact that all their anti-gay laws are themselves Western imports – former colonial masters and imperialists want to shove down the throats of sovereign African nations.

Gay voices, particularly African ones, are not included in the conversation at all.

Ghana's then-president, John Atta Mills, a law professor, goes on television and declares that he will never initiate or support any attempt to legalize homosexuality in Ghana. It is pure puffery, as while he gained tremendous support for taking such a 'tough' stance, it wasn't as if there was a big clamor across Ghana for any such liberalization.

Mills died in 2012. His successor, John Dramani Mahama,

was unable to lower the volume on antigay rhetoric, even at considerable personal cost.

In his acclaimed memoir, *My First Coup d'Etat*, Mahama thanks the New York-based writer Andrew Solomon for hosting him in the Big Apple and providing him with literary resources. After reading the manuscript, Solomon introduced Mahama to agents and editors, and also welcomed him into his home, where Solomon and his husband hosted a dinner for the then vice-president.

Upon the book's release, Solomon moderates a high-profile New York Public Library discussion with Mahama that is well-attended by the Ghanaian community there; and some of Mahama's brothers join him onstage. It is a proud moment for Ghanaians and other Africans in the Diaspora who live in New York. Yet in 2013, when some Ghanaian newspapers claim – wholly falsely – that Solomon raised money for Mahama to push 'the gay agenda' in Ghana, his presidential spokesman denies that Mahama even knew Solomon. This despite all the evidence to the contrary that was already in the public realm, including photos and videos of the event where the two of them celebrate the book. Mahama has to backtrack and apologize to his friend Solomon, but the antigay climate in Ghana only intensifies, and the few steps gays might have taken into a semi-public domain are erased.

On particular midweek nights, at a few particular clubs, throngs of men and women used to dance the night away. With reckless abandon the men would dance provocatively close to each other; the few women around would do the same; even kisses would be exchanged. At seaside dance parties in Accra, where beer and reggae flowed for all and sundry, it wasn't uncommon for men and women to test the waters and try to pick up companions of the same sex.

All that reckless abandon goes away, and one of the clubs that hosted those midweek soirées abruptly pulls the plug: being exposed as having a gay night would be bad for its reputation, and if someone is attacked outside then the whole business would suffer. The patrons on the gay-friendly night don't compare in spending power to the heterosexual throngs on the weekend.

One western diplomat, a buddy of mine, landed in Accra in 2014 concerned to understand this new reality. He sent in his credentials and was well-received and formally accredited. He's an openly gay ambassador, his partner is also a diplomat, and they represent a large Western European nation that is a big financial donor to Ghana. He tells me that the gay community in Ghana is more fragmented than it is in other African countries such as Nigeria and Kenya. He throws soirées for all sorts of different groups in Accra, and every now and then would host one for all the gays he could cobble together. One that I attend is fun, and I am surprised by the number of people he's gotten to show up – after all, he hasn't been in Accra for years like my very dear friend Ian, a businessman whose house-parties are frequent and often raucous.

When Ian hosts a gay party at his two-story home, which is covered with greenery and located in the quiet Asylum Down neighborhood, there are wall-to-wall men, all carrying on and being unrestrainedly camp in a way that I've not seen on the streets. The guests are ninety percent local, and Ian says that sometimes, much later on, it turns into an orgy of the kind I've been told are organized every now then by gays in the nearby port city, Tema.

One of Ian's friends, Roderick Opobo, a bartender at a local hotel, tells me that those parties – or similar parties at friends of friends' places – are the only places to go now, because everywhere else is not safe. But Roderick, who is forty, tall and skinny, and embraces his feminine side without guilt, says he would never look for a 'husband' at these parties, even though the offerings are plentiful. "Uncountable. People will be coming and they will be leaving. Others are hanging out outside," he says. But the encounters, like those at most sex parties, are fleeting. "The person might want to have something to do with you over and over and that's that." There would be little or no contact afterwards. And so while the body may be satisfied, the heart is starved.

While the parties may be fun, there is very little going out anymore to clubs or bars and openly displaying any kind of affection, for fear of the backlash. This tense situation isn't helped by Ghana's bigger neighbor, Nigeria, as Ghanaians generally follow Nigeria's lead – though they would claim it is the other way around. Antigay rhetoric has flared up with some regularity in the media there, and draconian proposals by the nation's legislators are made but ultimately never seem to go anywhere.

This all changes in January 2014, when workers in Nigeria resume their jobs after the Christmas and New Year break and find that their president, Goodluck Jonathan, in the midst of dealing with an insurgency by Islamist fundamentalist group Boko Haram – which has been detonating bombs in cities and killing scores of students, market-women and citizens in the northeast of the country – has decided to sign into law an antigay bill that no one is clamoring for.

The Same Sex Marriage (Prohibition) Act (SSMPA) has provisions to imprison gays and their allies for up to fourteen years. It threatens jail-time for same-sex couples expressing affection in public. It bolsters the Ugandan lawmakers who, having passed their 'Kill the Gays' bill to worldwide scorn, then saw it revoked on a technicality, and is the kick-off to Jonathon's reelection campaign. Still it is a head-scratcher. It reminds me of what Uncle Nat told me when he couldn't figure out why homophobia flares up in Ghana: "In Nigeria the lines are drawn because of the Muslim north and Christian south. Some are saying that one of the accusations hurled by the Muslim north [at the south] is that they are tolerant of homosexuality, so in order to show that they are not they have to go overboard to condemn it, that's the argument I've heard."

Jonathan is from the south and purports to be a Christian. Up for reelection in 2015, he loses badly. But the damage has been done. Scores are beaten up on suspicion of being gay, and now the state has given its hetero citizens not just the ammunition but also, in their minds, the moral authority to fire on homosexuals. Police officers harass many, blackmail is commonplace, and the victims have no one to turn to.

Even in small-town Asaba scores of women are arrested and charged with being lesbian. Police officers brag about the arrest and news outlets treat it comically, alleging that the women were servicing lesbian politicians. In northern Kano, the State Department of the United States reveals that in January 2015 the sharia police arrested twelve men, accusing them of attempting to celebrate a gay marriage – the typical justification given for raiding any gathering of seemingly gay men. Authorities release ten of them to the custody of their parents, after their mothers and fathers pledge in written statements that they will keep their children away from such activities. By December there is still no information on the other two; no one knows what became of them. Floggings and lashings of suspected gay men become *de rigeur* in that part of the country.

In one case, just weeks after the law is passed, in northern Bauchi gay men are pelted with bottles and stones outside the courtroom, with the sharia judge telling a reporter that his sentencing– death by stoning – was a good one, but that the civil authorities were blocking it. Activists report that those jailed were mocked mercilessly while in prison by both inmates and jailers, and were often derided as 'pregnant women'. Bear in mind that some of these 'women' are married men with children, and that there was no solid proof that they are gay: as with so many witch-hunts it is often just an accusation.

Hundreds of such violations are compiled by the non-governmental organization, The Initiative for Equal Rights (TIERS), and the NGO acknowledges that many more don't bother reporting what they suffer. Beating up on the gay and lesbian community, for sport, or as a diversion from other issues, becomes a tactic in the media, who know that few if any will rush to defend the gays.

Even when police officers are not rounding up suspected gays, government officials still try to shame gays without giving a whit of concern. Even while abroad.

Nigeria House on Second Avenue in Manhattan is viewed by many as a difficult place from which to get documents. Complaints from Nigerians seeking passport renewals or other consular services there only keep growing over the years, and it's no longer a surprise to see news reports about it. Sometimes the excuses leading to roadblocks can be disconcerting, one of the most notorious being, "The air-conditioners aren't working in the summer so no passports will be issued."

It's my most recent passport renewal. I steel myself. I have made the payments online and bought the additional postal money orders. I have all my documents in tow, and have cleared out my schedule, anticipating an entire working day will be spent here. I am ready.

As I join some eighty-plus folks in the small waiting room I keep to myself, avoiding getting caught up in the usual conversation about the country's inefficiencies. I smile and nod in greeting to some while I wait for my number to be called, then bury my head in Taiye Selasi's novel *Ghana Must Go*.

My attention is distracted, however, as I find myself wondering what an American man, apparently going to his wife's country with their kids for the first time, thinks about all this. Used to a Western veneer of slickness, he seems nonplussed. No doubt his wife will have told him about our sometimes cumbersome processes. At the counter a woman is pleading vociferously with the officials because she couldn't get online to pay, and has spent all her money getting here. There are among us some who have come from as far away as Chicago in the Midwest to get the new e-passport. This is the one where consular officials on site take photos of, and scan in fingerprints from, applicants before handing over the green booklet emblazoned with the golden Economic Community of West African States (ECOWAS) coat of arms. Some of those waiting – the optimists – are hoping to travel to Lagos that night, from New York's John F. Kennedy airport.

After the first batch of us have our documents reviewed and hand over our money orders, we are moved to an even more cramped and crowded waiting room to wait for our digital images and biometrics to be captured. The television is set to a satellite channel that shows the Nigerian Television Authority news.

After a while a senior consular officer comes in and introduces herself and invites us to feel at home. She tells us in a rapid-fire speech that even though Nigerians complain about the staff at the consulate, they know exactly what their work is and are here to serve us. To make sure we all go home as often as possible, she tells us that the more we go, the more we bring dollars for our families, and that is good for the nation. She's right, I think, as the tense crowd loosens up and warms to her. I say nothing as they give her verbal high fives and sighs of agreement. She says she will do everything in her power to see that we all get our e-passports today, but that we too must do our part and ensure that the data on our forms are correct because once the passport is made it will be tough to change. And we would have no recourse if the fault was ours.

She goes on to tell us that even she makes mistakes, and recounts how recently she attended to a Nigerian with long hair, manicured nails, dangly earrings and a softly-spoken demeanor. As she was processing the passport she noticed that the gender read 'male' in the forms, and briskly changed it to 'female' on the passport. But what she thought was the form-filler's error was actually hers, she confessed. And the passport holder went ballistic upon receiving it: the 'shim' she said made quite a racket. Each time the madam referred to the passport applicant derisively as a 'shim' I cringed. Many laughed; others kept quiet. She went on to say loudly and proudly that she was a Nigerian woman, raised in her village, and didn't understand 'shims' and 'gays' and 'trans', but what she does now is go by whatever is filled on the form. This was her warning to us all: that her staff would not correct anything we wrote on the forms, however ridiculous they thought it; however cata-strophic the consequences.

And I want to say something, to tell her that while her concerns are duly noted, her example and scapegoating is not funny. But as the Americans would say, I choke. I need to get my passport now and without drama, so, shamefully, I say nothing.

It has taken almost a whole business day, but I leave with my e-passport, and with a profound sense of disappointment in myself; and I am also very disappointed in the senior consular officer. Should I not have said something to her? Where were my balls? But then if I had, would I have my passport today? I need to travel very soon. Might she have delayed me a day, a week, a month? Or perhaps prevented me from renewing it at all? Would I have had to deal with others shushing me? Maybe someone might have agreed with me; or might they have all turned on me? And so I said nothing. I didn't stand up for a principle; I put my own needs first. I lacked courage.

I get my passport but I walk out of Nigeria House on Se-cond Avenue drenched in my own shame.

It isn't as if the consular officer's remarks are a rare thing from someone in a position of power. Sexual minorities in

Nigeria are such an easy target, even from those one wouldn't expect to resort to scapegoating.

Just a few months later, when the fifty-four year old and very well respected Emir of Kano, Lamido Sanusi Lamido, a former governor of the Nigerian Central bank and a noted public intellectual, anti-corruption crusader and all-around truth-teller, announced that he'd settled on a fourth wife, it set off a firestorm of criticism in the media. The criticism is not because he has decided to marry a northern princess, but because she is an eighteen-year-old who's just finished high school; some of his own children are older than her. Nigeria has had issues with men marrying child brides, and while this bride had reached the age of consent, it doesn't stop women and men from holding their noses publicly.

The royal father took to social media to respond, arguing that those who criticized his marriage had no understanding of his culture, and it was none of their business anyway. Royal families, he said, have a duty to select brides from other royal houses who have been brought up in a certain way.

That might have been an adequate rebuttal, but then he lambasted the West and took a swipe at gays, calling us foul and repulsive. "Is this something I expect a European- or Western-trained or feminist mind to appreciate or endorse?" he wrote in his public response. No. "But has any American been bothered about my views on men marrying men or women marrying women who frankly I find primitive and bestial? No, and my views do not matter. These are cultural issues."

No Nigerian gay person or group, or Western gay group, or any Westerner for that matter, had waded into the issue of his marriage; none had publicly criticized him, if they even cared. His fellow heterosexual Nigerians were the ones who had castigated him and made fun of his baby bride. But it is a cheap shot he can get away with, and he uses it to great effect: distract your critics by referencing the 'primitive and bestial' gays who few publicly support and the matter is over. After all he is marrying a woman, even if she's a teenage girl, and it is 'tradition'.

Gays and their supporters are often silent, or their voices are drowned out in these conversations. And in Nigeria it is easy to toss them over the bridge because the government sanctions it. You can change any subject by invoking how terrible you think being gay is. It worked for the Emir and, mind you, he ought to know better: he was a former chief executive officer of First Bank, a major national bank, and he currently sits on the board of Black Rhino, a fund created by Blackstone Group, one of the largest private equity and alternative investment banking companies in the world. He occupies the second highest traditional post in the north of Nigeria; he currently operates in the first world, appearing on CNN and traveling the world. Yet he knows the way to easily deflect any criticism of himself is by throwing homosexuals under the bus, even when they have nothing to do with the issue.

The following year he is on record advocating for a minimum age of eighteen for Muslim brides in Nigeria.

Over in Accra, even Dadzie, who was in general optimistic about the future of his beloved Ghana, had to take a break from radio journalism and head to Canada to take part in a doctoral program. "We're not going to get to the point of same sex marriages soon, but we'd get to a point where people will decide, 'He's gay so what'," he hopes. "Maybe when I'm dead and gone we can get to same sex marriages, but I'll be surprised if in my lifetime we talk about same sex marriages in this country."

"Your silence will not protect you." – Audre Lourde

NINE: GIVING IT ANOTHER SHOT!

"**C**hikaaayyyyy," squeals the tall, lithe lady with the clear complexion now strutting towards where I am sitting at the bar. Her smile is big and bright. Her jet-black braids are glossy and extend all the way down to the small of her back. She is a vision in a formfitting ensemble of traditional African prints sewn in the style of a Western skirt-suit that shows off her curves even though little skin is exposed.

Her heels clank loudly on the cement floor as she approaches. The jewelry about her neck is bold: a gigantic red semi-precious stone sits above her breast, attached to a thick gold string that competes with the bronze necklace and ropes of coral beneath it. Her earrings are large too, and her bangles, of bronze, coral and gemstones, make soft sounds as she moves. She is totes a large leather Louis Vuitton handbag. On her right forefinger is a gold ring adorned with an Ethiopian Coptic cross.

As I stand up to embrace her in greeting I can feel the eyes of all the men in the room on us, see the necks craning to get a look at her swinging hips from behind as she moves in to hug me tightly. She is stellar, and the male patrons of Monsoon, the bar-cum-eatery on Accra's Oxford Street where I've arranged to meet her, are mesmerized. She's a wet dream for many of them: the African-American babe in Accra. Later she tells me that one of the many hats she wears is that of jewelry connoisseur and seller. What she has on today are one-of-a-kind statement pieces: she is a walking advertisement for herself and her business.

Monsoon is a nice enough restaurant in downtown Osu with a sushi bar attached. Its upstairs outdoor seating area has a good view of the main shopping drag. On this June night in 2008 there is a funky vibe, with a nice mix of expatriate workers and locals. I've been retreating regularly to Monsoon for a glass of wine or a Bucks Fizz, the champagne-and-orange-juice cocktail. For Christa, who is my dear friend as well as the personification of a hot babe, her drink of choice is the Kir Royale – champagne, a dash of brandy and a dot of angostura bitters on a sugar cube. She might live in Accra, but she is a bougie American chick, and that's all there is to it.

Our relationship started as a professional one and soon turned into a close brotherly-sisterly one. When she first met me she immediately began using my Igbo name, Chike, and has never stopped. Few outside of my close friends do, but she did, and introduces me that way all the time. She also immediately tried to set me up with a lovely, dark-skinned woman who worked for her, Anthoinette. "He's a professor and he lives in New York," she whispered to her a little too loudly in my presence. Christa would soon learn that, as lovely as her colleague was, I wasn't on offer and never would be. I wasn't going back in the closet even when working in Africa, and I wasn't going to waste anyone's time. She loved that, as all the gay professional men she'd met in Accra seemed to end up getting married to women, and she found that extremely problematic, for both the women and the men.

"It's sad but that's just the way it is," she would sigh.

The following summer I invited her to my first 'guinea fowl and wine' birthday party in Accra, and some wonderful men and women I had become friends with in the meantime also came along. Christa met a young man that night who she would later marry, in a wonderful seaside ceremony in the Central African island nation of São Tomé & Principe, in the autumn of 2015.

Back when we first met I had just arrived in Accra to work for an extended period teaching young journalists who hoped to become foreign correspondents, and she was my first real and true friend there. I also got back in contact with another resident of the city, my Nigerian/Peruvian friend Timi Jose Zapata. A fashion designer who had grown up and worked in Lagos, when we first published the *AFRican* magazine back in the early 2000s, the stylists and fashion-savvy folks I worked with brought his work to my attention for us to feature: this designer was doing great things in Lagos, they told me. I met him when he came to New York on a business trip and we became fast friends, as if we'd known each other a long time.

By the time I went to Accra he had already moved there, and he showed me all the gay hangouts.

Chester's, which I mentioned earlier, was the first stop on our Saturday nights out. In Ghana gay establishments cannot exist as such, but some places would become known as welcoming to all, and Chester's was one of those. At the time the Coconut Grove Regency Hotel hosted a weekly Wednesday night salsa party around its large swimming pool, a popular hump day hangout that was also a welcoming and seemingly safe zone, and we often went on there. Those dancing appeared to me to be mainly gay men and straight women. The party has since moved to another venue, Afrikiko, and while it certainly pulls a crowd, it seems fewer gay people attend.

There was also dancing every week at posh venues like the South African eatery-cum-club Rhapsody's, in the gleaming new American-style Accra Mall. Rhapsody's is not a gay magnet, but there is always a corner the bourgeois gay men and women stake out where they can chat and dance without being bothered. And without bothering the hordes of straight people trying to pick each other up.

Beyond this there are of course the discreet house parties that gay men organize, which are fun-filled. My buddy Ian, who routinely hosts such shindigs, moved to Accra a few years ago, after years in New York and London. He also spends a fair amount of time in Salvador da Bahia, Brazil. He's a busy but fabulous Welsh gay man who loves African sugar, and I love spending time with him in Accra because he's so realistic in dealing with work situations. He's had many iterations of a career, veering between working for corporate entities and becoming a published author to getting involved in setting up small businesses. His advice to me on dealing with difficult colleagues and bosses has proved invaluable over the years. He doesn't waste time or opportunities sulking, but finds ways to get around the stumbling blocks.

This busy, successful businessman also parties harder than most people I know.

On my first visit to Chester's I strike up a conversation with Timi's roommate Ekow. He is short with lovely, dark and very smooth skin. He smiles big and can hold a conversation.

A few days later we are out on a date, and he takes me to the beach at Kokrobite. Kokrobite is twenty miles along the coast west of Accra. Like Prampram it's a predominantly middle-class refuge where many people go on weekends to escape the crowded city, play ball, eat fish, swim, surf and lie around on a clean, unspoiled beach. (The beaches within the Accra city limits are generally not the cleanest, and while people go to party there, no one really 'escapes' to those ones.)

Wow, I thought, as I spread the sheets and towels on the white sand and looked out at the waves of the Atlantic crashing down, what a lovely place. The waters aren't blue here, they're a dark concrete, but it's still breathtaking.

I soon notice a huge number of surely queer men milling around, their oiled black bodies glistening in the sun. Some I recognize from Chester's but others are picked up by my gaydar. They are enjoying the beach like all the heterosexual couples, taking Saturday off, sitting in twos or threes, gazing into each other's eyes, sprawling in the shade of the palm trees, or following each others' backsides as they dive playfully into the soothingly cool gray waters.

I'm plainly there with Ekow, but other men I've exchanged numbers with at Chester's saunter up to me, all of them suddenly wanting dates. It is disconcertingly aggressive. I am new in town so am probably fresh meat, but the forwardness is something I had not expected. Bizarre, I thought: all these men hitting on me and yet I'm in Accra, not New York. I was pleased that gay men here had created a safe bubble for those who are different, and it seemed they were left alone by the straight majority.

That is, if they even noticed: some heterosexual Ghanaians tell me they don't know any gays even when gay people they know are all around them. It is odd, but I truly believe they don't notice – hence this semi-invisible coexistence. Perhaps these daring men on the continent might be fun to date in a way that Africans abroad can't be? Maybe the hang-ups are gone and people have moved forward?

By the end of that year Timi has relocated to Cape Town, and I have had to move on from Ekow, who I dated for several months. At first I found him interesting, funny and Good On Paper. He has a job, drives a Volkswagen Jetta, and is generally fun. Or so it seems.

We haven't gotten to know each other very well before I start to get this nagging feeling that he isn't interested in me, but only in what he feels I can bring to the table. In addition to weekly tales of woe, explaining why he needs money for some emergency or other, he has, it transpires, many concurrent boyfriends, of which I am only the latest. In the end I felt he was fundamentally a juggler. He seems to relish coming to me with stories that don't add up but always involve getting cash out of me, from car accidents to his mother needing help with medical expenses. In the end I couldn't get past his alligator's arms and frequent requests to be bailed out of one situation or another.

I tried not to let my experience with Ekow color my view of all Ghanaian gay men. It wasn't easy.

The most vexing incident happens on a bright and sunny Sunday afternoon in the rainy season. He has been asking for weeks that we go to brunch at The Dynasty Chinese restaurant on Oxford Street in Osu. I finally agree. It is supposedly a fancy eatery, and since my only experience with Chinese food is no-frills take-out I haven't been keen to go. But I am leaving Ghana soon so I say yes. As I'm getting ready to be picked up, Ekow rings to inform me that his mother will be joining us. He's told me often that she wants to meet me and make us lunch, but every time our meeting was scheduled she had to cancel for a funeral or some emergency or other. The cancellation would usually come shortly after I had made my financial contribution to whatever emergency Ekow claimed she was having. Great, I thought, I finally get to meet her.

We get to the restaurant and are seated. It is packed, smart, has red walls, white tablecloths, and waiters in penguin suits, and seems like a 'look-at-me' crowd kind of place.

In the car on the ride over she'd said hello, but not much else. Once we are seated and have ordered I turn to inquire how she is doing, and about her wellbeing, since I've been given to understand she's had many medical emergencies. She doesn't respond to me but turns to her son and spends the next forty-five minutes having a conversation with him, and him alone, in their native Twi. Ekow knows I don't speak their tongue, and when they pause for drinks they don't care to respond when I try to engage them in conversation in a language we all speak. It is surreal.

Ekow says nothing to me but continues to chat with his mother all through brunch and dessert. They order everything they want, and fill their bellies. At this time Ekow is close to thirty-years-old, lives on his own (albeit with a roommate), works for an international courier company and seems on track for a bright future. He is one of the few brandishing the newly-released and very expensive iPhone in Accra before it becomes ubiquitous the world over. Yet when the bill comes, as usual he turns to me. His mama looks away. Their arms become like alligators' jaws.

I smile and pick up the tab. It is costly in Ghanaian cedis, but very moderate in dollars. His mother then complains about the tip I'm leaving for the waiters: she thinks it is too much. She makes a production of saying they didn't deserve anything.

Tipping isn't particularly common in Ghana. But later on, when I tell Ekow that in all my life I've never seen a family so lacking in basic manners, and so inhospitable, he tries to explain away his behavior and that of his mother as nervousness. I'm unconvinced: everyone I know is polite in front of strangers. The more so when nervous.

"You and your mother just wanted to eat at a nice restaurant and you needed me to pay for it, just own it," I fume. "This would be shameful for a mother in Nigeria but maybe it's the norm for you guys." Ekow couldn't seem to get it. Or pretended not to. He just repeated that he was "nervous", and was eager to move on from it. But not as eager as me: I checked out on the relationship there and then.

Even after I'd moved on, and he'd moved on, he would still contact me in New York with requests for financial assistance. There would always be a car accident, a housing emergency, something. And the stories got more elaborate with each telling. I always listened, knowing I would say no, thinking maybe this would be the conversation where he might think to begin with hello, just because, before going in on the hustle.

When I returned to Lagos for the Christmas holidays that year my Ghanaian friends kept calling, wanting me to come to Accra again, and telling me of Ekow's latest boyfriend dramas. In the next year or so I made several visits, all of which I enjoyed. I made great new friends and did some good work reporting on politics and government. I even waded into the dating pool again, this time with Kosi, an Ashanti man a few years younger than me. He was very dark-skinned, and stout. We met dancing salsa at the Coconut Grove Regency Hotel. He too was funny and seemed great on paper, and he was relentless. He was also very forward when we were out; whenever we came to a safely-screening tree or shaded area he'd pull me aside and lean in for a kiss. And then we would saunter back to the street. I didn't mind the interruptions to our progress.

He called a lot, always made himself available, and seemed to have a good head on his shoulders. He knew of my relationship with Ekow and, having heard the stories, didn't want to come off that way, so while a lot of his interest in me was feigned, he made sure to request nothing, at least at first. He did some daily work for a tourism board, and said he had some sort of agricultural engineering degree from the science and technology university in Kumasi. He also said he had a small farm outside Accra, to which he went on the weekends to supervise his two workers. He showed me pictures of the crops on his phone and promised that we would drive there. It was a small commercial venture and he had one client, his maternal uncle, who produced industrialized packaged pineapple juice, for whom he was one of the suppliers. Great, I thought; he's busy.

Kosi wasn't exactly out to his family – but then most people weren't – but he dated a lot and had recently broken up, he claimed, with the married son of a formerly very high-ranking government official.

It was fun for the first month or two, but then the soliloquies from the drain-the-foreign-boyfriend playbook started: "My car is problematic. I need this part. My house situation is horrible. I have rats, I need to move" blah, blah, blah.

Around this time my brother Vic, (on his way to being Big Vic), had been building up a beverage company, Cintron, on the continent, and South Africa was his base of operations. I'd been there a few times to visit him and support his promotional events, and found I really loved the Western Cape. Vic was spending so much time there that he decided to buy a home, first across the way from the diving enclave of Muizenberg, then later on up in the mountains overlooking Hout Bay, not far from Cape Town.

Hout Bay is a charming fishing community with a working harbor that is also a popular tourist destination. It has a long stretch of beach that is popular with dog walkers and is at the foot of the entrance to the famed Chapman's Peak drive, a twisty mountainside road with spectacular views of the ocean. A large sign at the entrance to the village reads 'Welcome to the Republic of Hout Bay'. Local lore has it that, once upon a time during the apartheid era, one resident made up a Hout Bay passport and used it to travel through Europe, successfully fooling customs officials at the various borders, who had no clue where or what Hout Bay was. I've no idea if the story is true, but whenever I arrive, as I pass the sign I am filled with calm. Hout Bay feels like an artists' enclave, and each weekend its village lawn is filled with artists selling their work outdoors at a local flea market, while down by the harbor artisans and clothiers peddle their wares inside a gargantuan, warehouse-like building. There is live music and craft beer for those tired of beachcombing, and who come in for the fish and chips the village is known for.

Families of color who own homes here are few, but over the years I've noticed an uptick, and many in my family return to 'the Republic' year after year. The mountain house looks down on its moneyed neighbors, and has a wraparound balcony with views of the Atlantic Ocean, and the Table Mountain range to the north. I often escape there to write, research, or simply to rejuvenate myself, and I feel like a local. I sit at the same desk when I use the library, I worship at the tiny S$^{t.}$ Anthony's Catholic parish nearby, I work out at the Velocity Sports Lab with its floor-to-ceiling windows that face the ocean; and when I'm in town I try to go to the Hout Bay Coffee Shop every afternoon at 3 p.m. The faces have all become familiar.

In those early days Big Vic would throw a poolside braai (barbecue) to celebrate my being in town. These days I may get a drink; dinner if he's in a good mood, but no parties in my honor. And that's fine: after all, I'm a local.

That year he was having an event at Camps Bay, another tony seaside suburb of Cape Town. I was supposed to be going to Accra for my buddy Peter Tawia's birthday, but decided at the last minute to head to South Africa instead. Rather than meeting up with Kosi in Accra, I arranged for him to join me in Cape Town. It was supposed to be a romantic treat for him and a relaxing few days for me but soon turned out to be anything but. The instant he gets off the plane it is clear he's never been outside the region. He is amazed by sidewalks, for example, despite having claimed to have been to London several times.

Years later, a good buddy, Allotey, who was educated in English boarding schools and universities, explained the concept to me of the 'locally acquired foreign accent'. Apparently there are Ghanaians who, through the power of the internet, television and film, have imbibed so much American and British culture, slang and music that they can even turn on the varying regional accents of those countries as if they had once been locals. Kosi was one of those. I had believed him when he said he'd been to the UK with his father, but when he finally arrived in South Africa I noticed he had a brand-new passport with zero stamps in it.

I didn't take him to the Republic of Hout Bay, but rather to a comfy, inexpensive bed and breakfast at the foot of Table Mountain in Cape Town, which is close to all the touristy sites and the gay village in De Waterkant. I'd hoped for a short but restful couple of days of sex and sightseeing. We took one evening to go to my brother's function in Camps Bay, which was being held at a once-exclusive and still elegant club called Saint Yves. Cintron Energy, my brother's beverage company, was the night's sponsor, and was supposedly now the official energy drink of Saint Yves.

But Kosi just didn't fit in, and his complexes began to spill out. I tried to get him to socialize with the others, including a very beautiful and friendly former Miss Namibia who happened to be seated next to us. All to no avail. Maybe her stunning looks, her intellect and ease of conversation with others contributed to his feeling intimidated. I'm not certain, but he had no intention of making friends or meeting people in my circle, or even trying to keep the conversation going by taking a polite interest and asking questions.

For the rest of the trip he just wanted to acquire stuff. Like a market trader stocking a stall he demanded things every time we went out, and soon even when we were alone in the guest-house together. This was a different side to him. Perhaps the real side. I had planned on a fun time for us that would certain-ly include some giving of souvenir gifts on my part, but not financing a whole bunch of things for him to sell once he returned to Ghana. But the real kicker was his desire to cut our days together short so he could spend time with another 'friend' in Johannesburg.

After a few days of this I was spent, and not even bothered by his endlessly gaping alligator arms (he never felt the need to buy even a bottle of water for himself). I needed a vacation from my vacation, and was pleased I never took him to Hout Bay: the demands would have been nonstop. And they contin-ued once he returned to Ghana. In his mind, I was to provide for him and his mother and her new sons. This was the 'dowry' I should pay for dating him. What a prize!

When I got home I decided to end this waste of time. Peter told me afterwards that Kosi had never even been on a plane before I brought him to South Africa.

Before I could engineer an amicable break, the playbook continued: "Mum's sick, I need help," he would say. I sympa-thized and empathized but offered only a shoulder to cry on. A few days later he informed me that he had come to a decision: for the good of our relationship he must come to America to pursue a graduate program. I was to make that happen. After all, he was going there for me. My response was to give him a good strategy for pursuing his admission. I then gave concrete steps for him to use to approach schools, and asked that his family set aside funds for tuition and a student visa. I was to be no part of it officially, but would help with the school applica-tions, and be happy to welcome him to New York and into my home if he made it there on his own merit. And with that it was over. Since I wasn't willing to finance his move to America, we were done.

I later learned that his job at the tourism board was a form of extended service internship and the farm wasn't his but his uncle's; he was obliged to go there and help out.

By 2009 I wasn't even remotely entertaining the idea of dating a Ghanaian, but I didn't let my experiences deter those of my friends who did. In fact I encouraged it, particularly if they were straight. But I did tell my heterosexual friends of my interactions with these men, and a version of the scenario of Kosi and his former well-connected boyfriend made it into my pal Nicole Amarteifio's critically-acclaimed hit soap opera, *An African City*, in 2016.

Nicole is my 'Uncle' Nat's actual niece, and when one of the writers wanted to include a slice of gay life in the Season Two series finale, I recounted to her the story of Kosi and the politician who was my predecessor in his dating life. The politico, you will recall, is married with children, and I howled with laughter as I watched the episode.

The screen version had the boyfriend being courageous enough to tell his lady that the relationship between them would be for show only, but that she should put up with it because as his political star rose, so would her societal and monetary status.

By contrast, among many of the gay guys I encountered it seemed poverty meant they would sleep with anyone who could drop a few notes on the table. They rationalized it by saying it wasn't money for sex but – for instance – "just a little help with transportation". I hooked up a couple of times but made no connections. It was fun and they didn't need much convincing to have safe sex. It was refreshing that I didn't have to always be the one to bring it up, and sometimes they came prepared. But I told my buddy Peter that dating two of his countrymen was enough. After Kosi Peter agreed with me, I think.

Peter is fifty-one. Love at first sight may be a fairytale, but friendship is not. From the moment we met we knew we were kindred spirits, and over the years our mutual admiration has deepened.

It was a Friday night back in 2008, and I was in the bar at Rhapsody's, the South African eatery in the Accra Mall that was all the rage then: all the hip Accra guys and dolls passed through there. After eleven p.m. the DJ would switch up from music to nod your head to while conversing, to the hits that got booties shaking on the dance floor.

In one corner, across from the DJ booth and overflowing onto the edge of the verandah, gays and lesbians clustered inconspicuously, dancing with the rest of the crowd, sometimes next to their partners, other times with their friends. At first glance one wouldn't guess there was a 'pink' corner, just happy revelers.

That night I was happy too. I wasn't on the prowl, I wasn't looking to pull anyone and I wasn't dressed to the nines, unlike the other patrons. I had a striped blue T-shirt on, along with my thick black-framed Gucci spectacles. I was sitting at the bar chatting with a friend about how my fashion-designer pal Timi Jose Zapata had left Ghana.

"Good! He can go to Nigeria or Brazil or wherever he came from," said the fellow in the seat next to mine. I looked round, surprised.

It turned out the slender, handsome guy next to me had dated Timi. I didn't mind the intrusion because of the unusual way it had happened. People in Accra are never normally so forward, and few men would ever openly say they had dated another man in mixed company – Rhapsody's had a cosmopolitan crowd, but it wasn't exactly a gay place, and at the bar anyone could overhear. And as I'd come to learn, Accra's denizens thrive on salacious gossip. Anyway, I turned to see who this dude was and turned on my inquisitive self: "You dated Timi? When? How?"

Despite having raised the subject, he's not keen to talk about it. But he tells us he is called Peter and proves to be a fun chap to booze with. Like me he has spent a fair amount of time abroad. He holds a European Union passport, and has navigated Accra's social shark tank quite well. He's just begun dating Kwabena Obeng, who he would go on to settle down with some years later. Before that he'd dated Timi, but had got pissed with Timi's dating antics. It seems Timi was too flaky for him.

Peter inhabits the high-end hospitality industry. He was trained, and had a decades-long career, in the United States and the United Kingdom. When we meet at Rhapsody's he's only living in Accra part-time, but is soon to become a full-time returnee. The rest of the time he's in the U.K., and back then every time I passed through London, which was several times a year, I'd make sure to look him up. Sometimes my layover would be just a few hours, and we'd hang out in a café near or at Heathrow airport, catching up until it was time for me to go to my gate. I found in him a kindred spirit: an intelligent gay African man who I could talk to without needing to explain much. He just instantly 'got' me.

The son of one of Ghana's early post-independence diplomats and member of the ambassadorial corps, Peter has always kept one foot firmly planted in Accra, and though he shuttles between London, Geneva and sometimes the U.S. he is Ghanaian through and through. Today he is settled in a tastefully decorated three-bedroom flat in the East Legon section of Accra, and his home is frequently an intellectual-cultural salon where good food and good conversation is guaranteed. Kwabena, his younger, hunky and brainy lover, is always close by, joining in with the talk, or just playing host and seeing that everyone's wine glass is full and plates are heaped. The food is always plentiful, with a fair share of imported goodies such as cheeses and hams, often from the high-end grocer Harrods, in London.

Peter's country retreat is in Cape Coast. The famed seaside town is seventy-seven miles from Accra and is best known for the enormous European-built slave castle there. Many African-Americans who visit Ghana stop at Cape Coast, and also make a pilgrimage to the nearby, older Elmina slave castle, following the footsteps of the millions who passed through the 'Doors of No Return' in chains, on their way to a new world from which they would never come back. Both castles date back to the 1600s and have been designated UNESCO World Heritage sites. President Barack Obama brought his family there in 2009.

Peter's home, which is just a stroll away from the castle, is where he escapes most weekends, leaving the bustle of Accra behind, and he and Kwabena entertain there as frequently as they do in the city. It's a modern, spacious single-story house with a tiny bit of land around it, and the walls are hung with loads of colorful paintings, including one of Peter and his brother. All the artwork is by local artists. His parents are deceased, but he is close to his younger brother, and has known for years that he'd end up returning for good to Ghana.

Today he is running an interior design concern with a higher end clientele, and is one of the rare gay men who are fairly open in Accra: most of his friends know, and invite him and his companion to events as a couple. He tells me he hasn't broached the topic with his brother. The brother lives abroad much of the year, but I find it difficult to believe that with Peter's no-nonsense style he has not figured it out.

When I first met Kwabena he was rather young and often accented his responses with the emphatic phrase, "Yes of course!" I took to calling him 'Young Kwabena' because of his age and Peter dubbed him 'yes of course'. Peter has met Kwabena's mother and grandmother but tells me they have no real clue about the nature of this now nearly decade-long relationship. "I think they see me as a big brother to him," Peter says. He told me he didn't mind the characterization; he is, after all, decades older than Kwabena. "We can't do 'husband and husband' in this country; we can just live together. To the outside we can be roommates."

They met at the (since-defunct) gay-friendly bar Henry's in Adabraka, and have been practically inseparable ever since. Back then Peter hadn't fully moved home from London, but once he did it was all Kwabena, all the time. In the intervening years I've watched as Kwabena has grown from a baby-faced young man fond of replying, "Yes of course" to a mature adult running his own transportation business.

Kwabena is also a gym bunny and has transformed himself physically. When we first met he was skinny. Today his arms bulge like gigantic yams, his chest is enormous, and his waist still hovers around thirty inches. When he wears a T-shirt he looks like those musclemen with six-pack abdominals who model underwear on the covers of *Men's Health* or *Men's Fitness* magazines. And his smile is bright, a little gap between his front teeth hardly diverting from the band of white that shines like the insides of a freshly hacked-open coconut. He's blossomed into an extremely desirable man for many, but he's with Peter.

And Peter, like many 'repats' – those Africans educated abroad, or who have had careers in the West and have returned home – has had to make concessions. The Peter I know wouldn't have contemplated dating a married man when he lived abroad, but he is very clear about where he is, and is sure that eventually Young Kwabena will get married. "[Or] if not get married at least have a child at some point, if they pressure him enough," Peter says. "He's younger and his mum is alive and his grandmother is alive and they will lay on the pressure. I'm a very adaptable person, so I just go with the flow."

He goes on to say he's done all the partying he needed to do abroad and rarely goes out now, and when he does it's to social functions with pals in his age and income bracket. He rarely posts things on social media but others do, and often in New York I see photos of him dancing at someone's fiftieth birthday or sixtieth wedding anniversary, or just at a party for partying's sake. Peter can be a 'dancing queen' when he feels up to it. Just not in the clubs. That's because he isn't about to march back into the closet. "When I go out to a gay place I like to be openly gay but most times you can't be, so if I'm going to go out and have to do that I might as well stay home."

Young Kwabena is strapping enough that he doesn't elicit stereotyped suspicions at first, second or even third glance. He blends in well with Accra's nightlife denizens: whether at the upscale Shisha Lounge in Osu, or the hip Republic chop bar, Kwabena is at home with all and sundry, chatting, dancing, drinking and being at the center of things. But Peter's in love, and even after eight years doesn't think there is anything out there for him – though "every now and then you need to be naughty."

He's extremely cautious about men purporting to be gay, however: "You have to be careful – they might be setting you up for getting bashed."

True, but every now and then, at places like Monsoon or Republic, though they are straight venues, one can spot a male couple happily sharing libations with each other.

"Love does not consist of gazing at each other, but in looking outward together in the same direction."
                                                    – Antoine de Saint-Exupéry

TEN: SCOTT (THE GOOD DOCTOR)

After spending much of the summer of 2011 working in Ghana, I return to New York, pick up my partner Scott, and we head to Scotland for a long weekend. It is now early September. The British Airways flight to London Heathrow is comfortable, and on arrival we have to clear U.K. customs and immigration before flying on to Edinburgh. We are going to attend the wedding of two of my very dear Nigerian friends. It is being held in a secret location: all we have to do, we are told, is get to Edinburgh, and from there we will be whisked off to our mysterious destination.

The immigration officer who looks over our documents is a handsome, bespectacled black British man. I smile at him and he smiles back. He asks me to fill out the address where we are going and I immediately say, "Oh, I don't know. We're going to a party," and I try to explain the wedding's secret location scenario. Well, that is the wrong answer, and he immediately begins to lecture me hectoringly. He says that no one could pass the U.S. border control in New York's JFK, where Scott and I flew from, with no address or idea of where they'll be staying, so why I did I think I could do that in London? Scott has never really spent any time in the United Kingdom and this is meant to be a lovely getaway for us both, so I apologize profusely and say that actually oh yes, I do have it after all.

He gives me a look. It is the weekend of the tenth anniversary of the September 11 terror attacks, security is heightened, and I worry I have opened a can of worms that will delay us. I fill out the forms with the address and telephone number of my aunt who lives in Willesden Green in North London. Thankfully they are committed to my memory, as I spent many summer months there with my brothers when a teenager, and it was where I lived when I worked at the bakery all those years ago.

He looks at the address, nods and sends us on our way. The U.K. border officials who have given me grief over the years have consistently been of color. When ethnically English customs officers encounter me at Heathrow the conversation is less aggressive, one might even say good, and their curiosity about me and my journey seems genuine.

Once through, we go straight to our domestic flight, which takes an hour. After the haul from the States we are sick of being stuck on a plane, and upon arrival the car that has been pre-booked to pick us up isn't there. It takes several phone calls to find the event organizer. When we do, she gives us the secret address: "It's near Haddington" – which of course means nothing to us – and off we go in a regular taxi. The ride is an hour-plus trip, and all the while the heavily-accented driver regales us with tales as to how awful the English generally are to the Scottish, and how it has been that way for generations. Scott and I look at each other. Neither of us can easily tell these Brits apart.

Scotland out the window is all green. At least it seems from this ride that rolling hills and sheep farms are all the rage here. By the time we arrive at Garleton Lodge, a charming, family-run inn in the style of a country farmhouse that is surrounded by miles of grass, and boasts a hot tub on the property, it is three o'clock in the afternoon. We check in and pass out in our room, exhausted.

I wake to the sound of Nigerian pop star D'banj's hit 'Booty Call' pumping from somewhere within the building, and Scott and I get up, wash up and go downstairs. During our doze loads more people have arrived, and Garleton Lodge is now full of Nigerians, all of whom are here for the party; and even before the official party begins Nigerian pop music is blaring all evening in the common areas. The owners of the Garleton Lodge, a husband and wife, seem genuinely thrilled to have us here, and have no issues with hosting a gay wedding group. I imagine they have not had so many Africans taking up every room here, ever. They politely shake to the music too and chat with us cheerily. *I love that booty, I love that booty, I love that booty, it's a booty call!*

They also fill our night with tales of Scotland, and good advice as to what whiskey to take home (Glenmorangie is best, they say), and suggest tartans with appropriate symbolism for the kilts some of us will be wearing before, during and after the party.

It was to be a three-day extravaganza in picturesque East Lothian, east of Edinburgh, to celebrate the joining in matrimony of two of my closest friends. Their families and friends have flown in from all over the world to celebrate and be treated to the best of British and Nigerian hospitality – British in the sense that we are going to be hamming it up all weekend in an ancient castle, refurbished and repurposed as a luxury hotel, amidst the trappings of the landed gentry. There are over a hundred of us. The first night we have a quiet dinner, all of us together in the local pub. The pub grub is good but the conversation is better.

Over dinner my partner Scott, who is Japanese-American, and who has met many of my family and other friends over the years, gets to meet both grooms for the first time, along with an old boarding school mate of mine, Yomi. Yomi and I have not seen each other in over twenty years, and he tells me he is dating one groom's sister (they will go on to get married some time later.) Only one mother-in-law has arrived so far, and she and her daughters seem genuinely taken with Scott – at one point during dinner they ask if he has a brother who could be introduced to one of the daughters for a love match. Nigerian mothers are often on the hunt for potential husbands for their daughters once they reach a certain age. Scott ponders for a moment and says, "Nooo. But I do have a sister," at which the ladies laugh boisterously. It is a good start to the weekend.

One of the grooms, Ralph, I have known for years, and is a dear, dear, friend. His now-husband Prescott I'd known of for years, and when I finally met him several years before this shindig I fell in love with him too. He is perfect for my buddy; a delightful, charming, intelligent and caring man. He's witty and always makes great conversation. A hunk who is also a thinker, over the years I've grown to love him as much as I love Ralph. Today I think of him not just as a friend, but also as a brother.

Oddly enough, it turned out he'd once been close to my first boyfriend Lamido back in Lagos. (Paulie says they dated, but Paulie is always full of salacious gist so I took it with a grain of salt and didn't ask Prescott about it.)

Together they make a dynamic and caring couple, and I wasn't surprised by how many people, both gay and straight, had flown in from Nigeria for their wedding.

The following afternoon is spent chatting and shooting clay pigeons on the lawn (the happy couple are too ethically-minded to engage in shooting live animals for sport). The weather is warm and the Pimm's, a traditional English summer beverage of gin, liquour, mint-leaves and chopped fruit, flows. And so does the bubbly.

After a display of falconry, and a reenactment of Scottish history by participants who seem to really take their feuding seriously, there is a traditional Nigerian feast to picnic on. I am thrilled to see the moi-moi – stuffed with shrimps or chopped boiled eggs, it was a staple of my youth in Ikoyi. I rarely get this delicacy in the Big Apple and I munch on it happily. It is a joyous time, and when evening comes we are treated to an excursion for a fancy dinner back in Edinburgh with some sightseeing sprinkled in – more castles, including the current Queen's residence of Holyrood House; and an afternoon at a spa.

The weekend culminates with a romantic and charming humanist wedding ceremony that sees the two men have their hands tied together while their mothers watch proudly – I am informed that hand-fastening is part of the humanist tradition. It is September 11, and Scott and I are happy to not be in New York, where we would have been surrounded by harrowing memories of the 2001 terror attacks. We still have our Big Apple pride though: I sport my orange-and-black New York Mets cap all weekend, until it is time to glam up. The giant orange 'NY' is the point, as is Scott's deep blue New York

Yankees hat.

That evening we look on as two beautiful and kind African men get hitched to each other, and afterwards we have yet another gourmet dinner, this time in the castle dungeon, which has been transformed into an elegant dining room, festooned for the occasion with blue and silver balloons. This is followed by dancing. All night. Everyone is elegant. Ladies wear shimmering evening dresses and have intricate fascinators perched atop their heads; the guys are in tuxedos and fancy bespoke suits. And the grooms and some of their mates don kilts in true Scottish fashion. It is a feast for the eyes.

I decline a kilt and opt for traditional Nigerian attire, a starched white embroidered caftan with a traditional purple cap, balanced just so. After I am dressed Scott sees me and changes out of his suit and tie, deciding to also wear a Nigerian outfit, a black caftan with shiny, diamond-looking sequins that he's grabbed out of my suitcase. The fancy suit he brought goes back into his suitcase, even though he'd had the inn owner's obliging wife adjust the pants so it would fit better. Scott relishes being in his Nigerian finery all night. It is not only comfortable to wear but it gets him admiring looks from our friends, and is a conversation-starter for the folks he doesn't know so well.

Back in the fall of 2009 my friend Kent, who I'd met years earlier at Kai's home in Fort Greene, was having a party for his husband Damon. Kent was then working for AmfAR, the American Foundation for AIDS Research. They had recently returned from living in South Africa and were now ensconced in Brooklyn. I'd just got back from the U.S. Open tennis championships in Flushing and was really too tired to go to a party. But it was Kent's, so I prised myself off my couch and headed there.

While I didn't stay long I'm glad I went, because Scott and his friends were laughing up a storm in the kitchen, and we started chatting and haven't stopped since. He's dressed in jeans and a black T-shirt with bold prints on it. His jet-black hair is slicked back, and even though he's in a cluster of other Asian doctors, (his colleagues, and one best buddy who is in finance) he breaks free, comes over to me, introduces himself, and we talk. He's sexy to me, and I expect him to be in his twenties because of his radiant baby face, but it turns out he's a good two years older than I am. After a while, much as I'm enjoying our conversation I'm so tired I have to leave. But as I drove home he rang me on my cellphone and we talked some more, and when I arrived at my flat we made a plan to meet later for breakfast. He remained at the party and went to a nearby nightclub afterwards.

Scott turned out to be not just a good talker but also a good listener, and gets along well with everyone he meets. My family, particularly my parents and siblings, have embraced him wholeheartedly. After we had been dating for a few years he spent a year in Myanmar with Doctors Without Borders; on his return we took the plunge and moved in together. Previously he had been a regular corporate worker, only deciding in his mid-thirties that he wanted to become a doctor – and so back to school he went, struggling for years, working day and night to make it happen. While not being an immigrant, he shares the same struggle that many of my people have, and I'm inspired by how he always finds a way to make things happen. For him medicine is a calling, particularly treating those who have little access to it.

His work took him to Myanmar (Burma) to care for an oppressed minority, the Rohynga, in Rakhine state, on the country's western coast. That year we could only see each other once a quarter or so. His patients had endured brutal clashes with the Buddhist-majority Burmese in the area, were often derided as Bengali (and therefore lower-caste), and were in effect rendered stateless as they could not even get passports to travel.

Scott's work has also taken him for long stints in Zambia and Uganda. Today he's the medical director of a program in New York that sends doctors and nurses to far-flung shelters throughout the New York area to provide medical care for homeless families. I love that we have a meeting of minds on social justice issues, though I never like to march and protest as he does, because I feel it could compromise my integrity as a journalist if I end up reporting on the issue. But I happily partake in economic boycotts. When one of our favorite grocery retailers donated heavily to antigay causes I stopped shopping there, and Scott joined me even though up until then he had been a loyal customer. We had to begin renting cars and driving forty-five minutes to get our weekly shopping done. It was worth it. It took months for them to do an about-face, and even more months before we went back there.

We still won't buy any Dolce & Gabanna products – not suits, not fragrances – after the duo behind the company repeatedly mocked unorthodox families. Both our families have been blessed with additions due to adoption and surrogacy, and we cannot imagine ever supporting D&G again. Scott is kind and generous, even forgiving, but has principles that don't fall away when inconvenient.

I love those qualities about him, but also love that in addition to being a good man he's hot and looks younger than me. His sunset-colored skin is always radiant, and his thick head of hair is jet black with barely a speck of gray. While I have to work out with a trainer three hours a week to keep myself somewhat presentable, he does a seven-minute workout most mornings and remains slender. I can barely swim, but he loves diving, and somehow we find ourselves cooling off by a pool anywhere we are. Our banter is always easy, and wherever I am in the world, he's with me.

When we've made our annual trips to his family home in California I too have been warmly welcomed – though it took a moment for one parent to warm up to me; I guessed it was because I am not an Asian woman. But warm up they did after a few visits, and nowadays I'm totally comfortable in their world, just as Scott is in mine.

And he blends in so well with my friends, chatting amiably and having fun. Dancing the night away at this wedding where he knew no one but me, Scott makes friends easily and is happy. This is where we meet Dike, a handsome Nigerian who lives in London and is here with his equally dashing partner Lekan, with whom we become fast friends. It is a wonderful weekend. Gay and straight Nigerians, boogieing till dawn. The best man is straight and gregarious. I look on and wonder: why can't we be like this at home?

"People are trapped in history and history is trapped in them."

– James Baldwin

Eleven: Shall We Return?

At the wedding dinner we are seated at a table with a Nigerian pop star who is a good friend of both grooms. Her breakthrough album, the one that catapulted her to the top of the pop charts, was released in 1988, and I remembered seeing her perform way back in 1989, when I was a student at the University of Port Harcourt. All weekend I'd noticed her and her handsome husband at the festivities, but we hadn't spoken beyond exchanging the regular pleasantries. The disc jockey is good, but the singer upstages him and surprises the guests when she stands up and serenades Ralph and Prescott with Shania Twain's 'Still The One' right after the couple are pronounced civilly partnered, her voice still as strong as it was all those years ago.

Of course, being a gay wedding, there is also an appearance by a drag queen – Scotland's best, I am told. She's very tall and her heels make her even taller. She's warm in manner, decked out in pearls, very blonde and very glamorous. She also puts everyone at ease with her high-wattage smile. She doesn't so much put on a performance per se, but is a jolly, comedic hostess.

At the end of the night, paper lanterns are lit and turned loose outside. The orange contraptions are better than fireworks, floating upwards and lighting the sky, but not fizzling out after an explosion of light. They are steady like my buddies.

Ralph and Prescott are very happy today. They are now officially partnered, as close to married as the law of 2011 allows, and their best friends and family, many of them heterosexual, are here to give them unqualified love and support.

This joyous celebration could not have been commemorated in Nigeria's capital Abuja, where they lived for many years. They are respectful of everyone, unfailingly considerate of the feelings of others, but won't sit at the back of the bus for anyone. They demand respect for their relationship, and if you can't give that, you don't deserve their friendship. There is no closet big enough for these two. But the reality is that their wedding, recognized in Europe, isn't in Nigeria; and subsequently they both decamp from Abuja, initially to East Africa.

Of course that transition wasn't without drama, and it saddened me because for years they tried to make it work, first in Lagos and then Abuja — being open and honest and living their lives with integrity while never bothering anyone. They were an example of what seemed possible however hostile the legal and wider social climate.

They lived a luxuriously decadent life in Abuja. I always loved the ostrich eggs and peacock feathers they had prominently displayed in their home, which was camp in a way that only queers would recognize; they even had a massage table.

Ralph had worked with multinationals and in international development, as had Prescott. Even though the climate for gays was getting worse in Nigeria, they approached investors and made long-term plans to build and run a one-of-a-kind boutique hotel there. There are many hotels in Nigeria, but in general they cater to a business crowd and are utilitarian. Having travelled the world with these two, I knew the unparalleled levels of hospitality they wanted to offer. The kind of before-you-ask-for-it-it's-done service that we'd received at top-tier hotels around the world, particularly in Asia; like the Banyan Tree hotel in Bangkok, Thailand, where we spent a week in celebration of Prescott's fortieth birthday, a gently perfumed and calming environment despite the grit blowing about just outside its doors. Sure, several hotels in Lagos and Abuja are wonderful, but there isn't anything like what Ralph and Prescott had in mind, which I knew was fueled by all the spa escapes and business trips they had taken over the years, in the course of which someone would always sigh, "Why don't we have something like this at home?"

Ralph is a perfectionist, and with Prescott's business acumen they could have made their investment work and provided a good many jobs in the process. And taken hospitality in Nigeria up several notches. But in the middle of all this, as the anti-gay rhetoric was ratcheting up there, Ralph got into a spat with a female neighbor in their housing estate over the parking spot next to his house. The following morning a police officer knocks on his door and his neighbor is standing next to the officer and begins screaming, "He's gay! He's gaaaay ooh!!" with all the arms-flailing drama that market women are sometimes known for.

She's come with the specific intent of inflicting a public humiliation, to get the police involved and, who knows, maybe make an arrest and bring charges under the sodomy laws. All over a parking spot she thinks should be hers.

Fortunately the policeman is more interested in resolving the parking dispute than getting into the gay matter. But the ugly confrontation changes everything. To hear Ralph tell it, as he later did to the UK's business newspaper, the *Financial Times*, it was an eye-opening nightmare. "I'd always known Nigeria wasn't gay-friendly, but I hadn't felt directly targeted. Now I realized I was at risk."

Just before this happens, Prescott – who is always in demand for international development gigs – is offered a good position in East Africa. Ralph isn't keen on moving again: they've already moved from London to Lagos and then to Abuja, have made a beautiful home there, and on my visits I enjoy the salon environment they have created for Abuja intellectuals and like-minded friends of all stripes. So even though the offer is good and Prescott wants to take it, Ralph is considering a commuter relationship. Plus, he has his own work.

On one visit, just before the kerfuffle with the neighbor, I advise Ralph to go along with his man: my feeling is that they belong together rather than apart. East Africa is too far to do the weekend thing or the once-a-month trip, I tell him. He resists, but when he is attacked by his bitch of a neighbor, it is too much. That makes him pull the plug on the whole hotel project, and they leave.

Both know they have made the right choice when Goodluck Jonathan agrees with the homophobes in the legislature, and in 2014 signs into law a bill that would have gays thrown in jail for fourteen years, just because.

"We're so glad now we didn't invest in Nigeria. In retrospect, that incident was a stroke of luck," Ralph tells me. This saddens me. The couple moved to southern Africa for a few years after the East African job ended, but today have ditched the continent entirely in favor of Asia – and of course their home in Scotland, not far from where they got married.

I wonder how many highly-skilled professionals my country has lost, and continues to lose, because of its government-sanctioned homophobia. Ralph and Prescott don't travel with Nigerian passports anymore: they are British, and have jobs representing British interests around the world. Nigeria has lost out on their talents for good. With their skills, first-class and first world education, my friends can work anywhere. Africa had them and took them for granted; now Asia has them, and Scotland too. It saddens me that they were compelled to leave Nigeria, a place that needs them more than they need her. How many more bright Africans who have the power to not just invest but to bring in good investors are turning to countries other than their own because of antigay hostility?

Over the Christmas holiday season in 2014 Ralph, Prescott and I meet up for dinner and cocktails in South Africa's mother city, Cape Town.

As far back as the eighteenth century, the indigenous people of the Western Cape, known as the Khoikhoi, had terms for male same-sex relationships. They used 'koetsire' as a term for men who were sexually receptive to other men, and described friendships that involved same-sex masturbation as 'soregus'. South Africa's post-apartheid constitution expressly protects sexual minorities, and gays and lesbians can legally marry here. This official protection doesn't mean South African gays are free from discrimination; however Cape Town, with its pride celebrations and queer village, attracts a fair number of those

African gays who can afford to vacation there along with all the other partygoers. And so we do dinner in the Cape Quarter, dining alfresco on a cool summer night next to a gigantic fountain. The restaurant is located near the hip De Waterkant village, with sufficient eye-candy for all of us.

Even all these years later, when Ralph thinks about how he left Abuja it still stings, though he waves the pain away: "My dear! The country's loss! We wanted to bring some real sparkle to the leisure industry but alas it won't happen with us," he says. He's looking forward to other opportunities, just not in Nigeria.

Despite such tensions the pull of home is strong for many African professionals who have been educated in the West and have had successful careers there. And it was at that time that I myself, since I'd been offered a good job with a Lagos media house, felt it was time to return to Nigeria full time. Perhaps it was also time for me to return to a newsroom full time. Scott had loved Lagos when we were there, and had talked unprompted about working in Nigeria. It had been wonderful meeting with friends, swimming, going to museums and galleries, getting to see hidden artistic treasures at the homes of collectors – even navigating the traffic had been exciting, though I suspected that thrill would pall soon enough.

When we were in Las Gidis (that's Lagos for the cognoscenti), there was a nationwide strike over increasing fuel prices that paralyzed the country. On the first day of the strike Scott and I went to watch the demonstrations for a while and he took pictures. Workers paraded down the streets with signs, chanting in pidgin that Goodluck Jonathan would get tired and give in before they did. The few cars on the roads had shrubs tied to their bumpers to signify solidarity with the workers: if you tied greenery to your car you were not seen as part of the problem.

All along the main thoroughfare in Ikoyi, across the Falomo Bridge and into Victoria Island, we saw folks marching and chanting. Those not marching who couldn't get to work stayed home or indoors, though I spotted young people playing soccer by the side of the bridge, uninvolved. There was an uneasy calm around town. Scott loved being in the thick of the marchers, and I briefly went into work mode and wrote a news story for the *New York Amsterdam News* and sent in several of Scott's photos to accompany the article. On the second day of the protests his social justice leanings kicked into higher gear and he wanted to return to the streets and spend all day with the protesters, but I nixed the idea. He's a foreigner on a visa, and who knows what could go wrong. I felt one day was enough. Besides, our friends Oskar and Wanda had invited us out sailing for the day.

Oskar is an industrialist whose family has been involved in various Nigerian businesses, from shipping to aviation, hospitality to journalism, since the early days of our nation's existence. His wife Wanda was educated in New York and we share friends there, along with a Big Apple sensibility through which we view the world. Both are more than close friends to me: they are my family, and they welcomed Scott to Nigeria with open arms. Knowing most businesses would be shut because of the strike, and that people were generally staying away from work, they decided to have a day out on the water, and we joined them. Wanda and Oskar brought a fantastic basket of yummy picnic goodies – cheese, cookies, sandwiches, pies and of course multiple bottles of bubbly – and as we chowed down and drank they showed me and Scott Lagos from the water.

It is an afternoon of blue skies with few clouds anywhere, and from this vantage point I can appreciate even more than usual how beautiful my city is. Once you boat a few hundred meters out past the lagoon into the Atlantic the waters are a breathtaking aquamarine, and I find myself wishing Lagos had more marine mass transit.

Soon after, Scott and I leave for South Africa, to hang out with Big Vic. But during his time in Lagos Scott talks to people about working there. Opportunities are available for him to treat patients in some good private hospitals but he wants to continue his work in public health. In New York he runs a project that treats the very poor and homeless, and is keen to do something similar in Nigeria should we move.

In the 2000s the media narrative of 'Africa Rising' as a continent is in part made true and plausible by returnees, many of whom are gay. They are often called repats, and are easily identifiable because they speak a little differently and have first world work-experience and, often, concomitant expectations in terms of efficiency, customer-oriented service, consistency and infrastructure. The narrative of Africa Rising may have been derided since, but at the time it rang true. Economies were getting bigger and Western returnees were coming home in droves. I was excited about the possibilities, and even today remain optimistic about the continent.

Lagos isn't the only place where this is obvious: while working in Accra I met Ghanaian gays who had lived in the West and had packed up and moved back there, not just to contribute to the homeland, but also to make a home they could be proud of. Some were looking to retire in and around Accra. Even with the tempest surrounding being gay there, there were those who had pushed that aside and were prepared to make adjustments. Or thought they were.

That was the case with a dreadlocked, fifty-year-old marketing expert I befriended, Tom Awotwe. Around town he is known as Ashanti-Dreddy because of the flowing locks that fall past his shoulders and hang down to the small of his back. Often mistaken for a practicing Rastafarian, in reality he is an atheist. I meet him at one of Ian's parties and immediately take a liking to him. He spent much of his formative years living in the United Kingdom, splitting his time between London and Kingston, Jamaica. He's been married and has two daughters but has lived a fairly open life. While not embracing the label 'gay' he's had relationships with men and been open about it; and by his own account isn't likely to have a lady companion in his life again.

Tom lives in a sprawling three-bedroom house in a gated community in Perakau, just outside Accra, having resettled there as a single man three years earlier. His children, now grown, elected to remain in Europe. His heritage is Ashanti and he's by most standards handsome, a DILF with locks. Business is good but his social life is so-so. His German shepherd Kofi keeps him company, along with a string of lovers who pass through, but there is no live-in companion. I wonder why, as he has ample sex appeal, a lovely home and his independence – all the checkmarks for good husband material. He's Good On Paper and good in reality.

I've visited him sometimes at his home and he makes a good dinner. But I prefer to remain close to Osu's main drag and my workplace, so we more often meet in town for drinks after work. He doesn't mind coming with me to one of my favorite haunts, the Republic Bar & Grill.

At first glance Republic seems no different from the myriad chop bars that dot Accra's streets. It is close to Duncan's, another favorite of mine that has been in Osu from time immemorial, and is as crowded as Container, another original chop bar that is a local favorite. But on closer inspection Republic is overflowing with expatriates, local professionals, photographers and artists of all stripes; Accra's hippest folk are to be found seated on the plastic chairs outdoors on the roadside, away from the red revolutionary-themed walls within, adorned with photos of the nation's founder, Kwame Nkrumah. A small stage is often host to live music and spoken word, and the spot has WiFi, a rarity for a roadside chop bar in this country. And nowadays there's even karaoke.

The menu too is different from the usual. Rather than vodka or gin, the cocktails are made with a local brew as the base liquor. So caipirinhas are made with akpeteshie, a traditional Ghanaian palm spirit much like the ogogoro we have in Lagos. It is often referred to as 'Kill Me Quick'.

Tom never liked joining me on group outings but would come out alone for a jug of iced kokokroto – the mild cocktail of akpeteshie and hibiscus juice that Republic had created, and that I could never get enough of. It relaxes me and loosens our tongues. "I get a lot of attention in Ghana because of my hair and this persona. I meet a lot of guys who want to hang out and smoke a spliff. In that sense it's easy to have same sex contact with men," he says.

Tom tells me about at least three men – two married – who he has slept with on numerous occasions. All purported to be heterosexual, and yet were available for no-strings sex with another man. "It's all well and good having sex with someone who is unsure of their sexuality," Tom says, "but at my age I want something more from a relationship with another human being than just a quick thing in the sack. What I found easier here is not the kind-of-identifying-as-gay men, but men who are married who may sleep with their drivers or houseboys, these kinds of relationship. It's much easier here."

However that – along with dating someone who had a

partner abroad to whom he remained committed – had left Tom feeling slightly used, and was a scenario he would not have entertained in London.

"I don't really have a gay life [here]. Being a fifty-year-old man there are certain expectations that I have in a relationship. I'm not particularly interested in twenty-four-year-old boys or young men, so that also puts a limit on what is possible for me. I'm much more interested in mature older men. Thirty-plus. I'm looking in this environment. If I were in England I'd be talking to you about men forty plus, about my age. But I'm here and what's available is young men of various degrees of immaturity."

But surely, there's got to be someone else in Accra available, I say.

"I haven't met any gay men in their fifties, full stop."

I would have introduced him to Peter, my other close friend who is also a returnee from the U.K., but by then he's been taken off the market by Kwabena.

Tom always says there is nothing to write home about, about being gay in Ghana; that it's not much different from elsewhere – though he's had to adjust to the fixation the gay men he's met both online and in person have with sexual positions. "People are preoccupied with the question 'top or bottom' first of all, and it would seem that most people are bottom and they want to be bottom," he says.

Another adjustment that had to be made was to do with marital status: the unavoidability of dating or going out with married men. His ideal partner has to have integrity, be honest and hopefully age appropriate, but doesn't need to be single. "If I don't want that to be an issue I have to take myself off somewhere else. Somewhere like South Africa, or back to Europe or America or wherever." I empathize. I know from being here that he's absolutely right.

For someone like Tom, who's lived an openly gay life in the West, that's easier said than done. And as a 'repat' the social cues back home in Africa aren't always easy to pick up on. "I can understand that you could be married with your wife or your kids and have a relationship with a male. Tons of people do this. I can understand – which is probably why I'm single – but whether I can live with it is another matter."

Every time we are out he insists on walking me to my flat, which is in the well-to-do Ringway Estate area of Osu, before flagging down one of the ubiquitous downtown taxis seeking passengers to take home. When I go to his for dinner in Parakau I have to sleep over as it would be too late after eating to look for a taxi. If he's so caring with a friend, I imagine he ought to be even more caring in a relationship. He is in the middle of constructing what he says will be a beautiful home up in the hills of Aburi, to the north of Accra.

Aburi is a mountainside enclave where many of Accra's middle-class residents have country homes, and to which some wealthy Nigerians also escape – particularly to the ultra-deluxe Lansdown Aburi, an eight-villa resort known mainly to the cognoscenti among Nigeria's upper crust. Hidden away up in the hills, it's difficult to find: there's no advertising, just a single sign and a long, narrow road going in, overhung with vegetation. This is intentional; either you know about it, or you don't.

Once one has driven up the unpaved – and in rainy season muddy – road into the mountains, and passed through a high gate that is all but concealed by a mass of untamed greenery, one arrives in a wonderland, an Eden. The view from each colonnaded, two-story villa is of rolling hills and yet more greenery, but it's the colors that hit you: scarlets, golds, magentas, royal purples, turquoises; every sort of flower seems in perpetual bloom.

The nerve-center of social activity in the resort is a large clubhouse. It overlooks an Olympic-sized swimming-pool, and houses a restaurant where the chef is capable of not just whipping up delectable local dishes in minutes, but surprises me with many of the offerings one could hope for abroad. The décor is African-inspired, the marble floor sparkles, and the ever-smiling staff, all in bright green tops and black trousers, are eager to please. Nearby is a tennis court.

In recent years power cuts – 'dumsor' in local parlance – have become routine in Ghana, and escaping to Lansdown, where one never hears the racket of generators, is enjoyable in itself. Lansdown's management keeps things operating at a high level despite the lack of infrastructure around them.

I've spent weekends in this oasis being pampered by Oskar and Wanda when they visit from Lagos, and it has always been a blessed escape from reality.

Aburi is one of Ghana's gems. The mountaintop is verdant and always temperate, and offers sweeping views of the metropolis below. Once Tom had hoped to retire there; now he isn't so sure, but is still keeping the option open. "I might find love but whether I can do anything with it is another matter. Pigs might fly." If he does find the right man he believes they could live in Aburi together, safely insulated, in the home that he is building. "He could be my son, my driver, or any number of scenarios that people would buy here." Or they would have to move abroad, which he says would be a shame.

And so Tom did the Accra thing, but shocked me in early 2016 with an abrupt announcement: he had decided to move back to London. He'd tried, but after six years in corporate marketing in Accra he'd given it all he could, and he wasn't happy. He found a new home for his German shepherd: another expat couple took Kofi in. The Aburi mansion was put on hold. And so Ghana and the continent lost another very talented and highly-skilled professional.

This returnee, like Prescott and Ralph, could work anywhere. He had chosen to come home to Ghana. But Ghana, with its open derision for gays, had not tried to hold on to him. Yes, the falling economy and leadership failures contributed to his decision to leave, but not being able to be in a relationship that was reasonably normal didn't help. I know that in London he won't consider dating married or even closeted men – an indignity he endured in Ghana, though when he was there he did his best not to see it that way.

He's ended up back in his well-appointed flat, not far from the tony Kings Road, in London's upmarket Chelsea neighborhood. When I drop by to visit, I am thrilled to see he has the same Bruce Weber photo of Naomi Campbell that holds court in my Brooklyn living room. He didn't display it in Accra, where it would have been considered too provocative to be acceptable, and it had been in storage all that time. In London no cares about the bare boobs staring back at you.

Since he now has no dog, he has invested in a plush, deep blue carpet that caresses one's feet. Masks he brought back from Ghana live on his red walls, and Ashanti stools are dotted about. Though his living quarters are smaller, he's managed to bring a chunk of Ghana with him back to London. Contemporary art from Nigeria and elsewhere in Africa adorns his walls.

It's always seemed to me quite scary to start over when older, but Tom is alright. Accra's loss is London's gain: within months of being in the U.K. a play he wrote decades earlier is about to be revived, and will go on to receive solid good reviews. Things are looking up professionally. And he's dating out gay men again.

"Being willing to sacrifice a false life is the only way to live a true one."

– Charles Blow

Twelve: Fatherhood & Family (purporting to be straight)

Over the years I've wondered about my gay friends who become fathers. It seems a magnificent experience to not just bring a life into the world but shape it and do one's part to raise a good human being. Scott and I have discussed parenthood. I'm not convinced yet that I should take the plunge, but I'm not against the idea. Our compromise and happy medium for now is that we could one day take in a child whose development is challenged, and whose family cannot handle the burden.

Participating in what the Americans call a foster care program would require much larger living quarters than we have now, but would be possible once we move to a bigger home. Years ago my brother-friend Marcus became a father to two sons, twins, and watching him and his partner Christopher parent them has warmed me to the idea of fatherhood. Watching my Congolese friend Etienne come to terms with being a gay parent over the years has been wonderful to see too; the happiness of his now-adult child, who is well-balanced and successful in life, a great advertisement for out gay parenting.

But in much of Africa it is extremely difficult to be a parent who is open about his sexuality. Take Lamido's pal, Jacques the gardener. His ex wife and son eventually left Nigeria and relocated to Scotland. As he would tell me when we reconnect-ed in 2015 he supports his son, but his mother, knowing of his sexuality, creates roadblocks to their keeping in contact.

However, it is fatherhood while purporting to be straight that I find supremely challenging, even though several gay men I know seem to be doing it with ease: Lamido, Chidi, and many others I've met are husbands and fathers. Those fathers are rarely able to share their true loves with their children, and to me that seems a deprivation on both sides. Some fall into the part willingly enough; others have no choice. Most of us are concerned with doing the right thing. Families often come first, and no one wants to bring disgrace or embarrassment to them. Ultimately, for many gay men in my society there is simply no choice: one must marry; then one must procreate. Almost all my gay friends who remained on the continent after we finished university, or who went back later, end up married to women, and it baffles me how they carry on year after year. Of course once the knot is tied an issue or several must be pro duced otherwise there is a whole new set of worries: is the wife infertile? If she is, why not marry another?

It can become a never-ending cycle of denial, and for men of a certain age the pressure is on. Younger gay professionals, almost always from Nigeria or Ghana, frequently write to me trying to find a way to get to work in a different country. Often they say they are at their wits' end because the marriage pressure is too much. If they were abroad, studying or working, they would be too far away to have to deal with it daily; if they remain at home they may feel compelled to succumb. And these younger men are urgently looking for ways to buck these forced relationships.

The pressure is even worse for women. For most it is mar-riage and then motherhood that is the crowning glory their families expect, regardless of any other professional or personal accomplishments.

In Ghana this scenario is playing out for my pal Peter's long-term boyfriend Kwabena, who is now in his thirties. 'Young' Kwabena is a lifelong Accra resident. His mother lives in Tesano, an upscale neighborhood in the city; he also has a grandmother who lives there, in Santa Maria. For Kwabena Accra has always been home, and he is now a successful entrepreneur, running a transport concern that moves goods and passengers between Accra and Cape Coast.

Kwabena is tall, charming and loquacious, bodybuilt and seemingly heterosexually virile. He has a huge smile, and throws his head back often to let out peals of laughter as the beard on his chin points in your direction. When he speaks he focuses on the face of the one he's talking to, and stares with an intensity that makes some avert their eyes. Or in my case look up at his bushy eyebrows. His business is doing well, and in all ways but the one that matters he'd be a catch for any woman seeking a husband.

He nominally lives with his family in Tesano, but in actuality is so constantly with his partner Peter that to most it seems they live together. Even though Peter feels – and says – that he might one day give in to the pressure to marry, or at least father a child, Kwabena repeats to me emphatically, in conversation after conversation, that that will never happen. Even though he's an only child, and the pressure to produce grandchildren will become intense, he says he'll just keep playing the broken record of not having found 'the right girl' yet with his family.

"I think they think I'm straight," he said to me. "I sit with straight people and we have a normal discussion about girls. I do give them one story or the other. 'I had sex with this girl' and 'this girl likes me'. They are all lies."

Not being in any way effeminate, he can get away with it. He's grown up living a double life, and slips in and out of the various social circles he inhabits with apparent ease. On any weekend night he can be seen out at one or another of Accra's hot spots, drinking and socializing, flirting with girls. At home with Peter he is filled with a different, more authentic joie de vivre, is a great host, and can be very gay-flirty.

Though he thinks his mother doesn't know of his sexuality, Kwabena tells me she once found a gay magazine in his room and said something to the effect that if her son was gay she'd kill him. And he recalls how she and her brother ostracized a cousin, a chef in one of the hotel resorts up in the Aburi mountains, who turned out to be gay. Despite this, Kwabena believes his mother is only bluffing when it comes to him: sometimes those who make the most vicious statements turn out to be the ones who come round most surprisingly. She continues to nag him about marriage, and though he is her only child he isn't ready to cave in. Over and over again, he insists to me it can never work.

"I've thought about insemination, of getting a child, but not marrying. I can't! It won't work, just for three days. If I were to get married for three days it won't work. I will pack, or the lady will pack!"

While many gay men can, when it comes to the crunch, perform sexually with a woman, Kwabena's never had any interest in women when it comes to intimate situations, and so the horrid specter looms of being forced into marriage and then being unable to even nominally satisfy his wife. His first sexual encounter was in high school, and by his count he's dated and slept with close to twenty-five men – though hasn't been in love until his current relationship. And while his small circle of friends (as well as Peter's friends) know he is gay, he's determined to keep the façade going. "I won't tell. I'll just keep it as it is. This is Africa. There is this mentality, if you are gay you are evil; if you are gay you are sick upstairs. Yes I wish we had something that said gays is accepted, or we had a law that says you can come out and tell people you are gay, you won't be killed, you won't be hunted down, you won't be gay-bashed. But then this is Africa so still I won't."

In Africa as in most places family comes first, but so long as you are a father and husband, and so are fulfilling social expectations, it doesn't mean you can't have fully-fledged love affairs with whoever your heart desires, even if they are of the same gender. This is the route many have taken and are continuing to take every day. And in this way gay men and lesbians are rendered invisible down the generations – a survival tactic that has the downside of making gay rights activism the more difficult.

It is the spring of 2013 and an acquaintance, a longtime and notorious Accra man-chaser, is getting married to a woman. He is close to forty and it is 'time'. His bride is barely out of university and is in her early twenties. They are to have a big reception. It is the talk of the town. Peter refuses to witness the charade; other people we know are heading over for the party and to see for themselves.

For some gay men, if they can manage to become fathers ahead of the actual ceremony, they can remain engaged to the child's mother and, so long as they offer the appropriate financial support, keep on putting off the marriage itself. This gives them some cover – they are engaged! I suppose it's integrity of a sort, to pay up while not misleading the woman you became involved with quite all the way. And so a fella sires a baby then jumps back into the scene, chasing young guys all over town.

This was certainly the case with my buddy Joshua Kofi Roeper. A certified chartered accountant and a tall, chubby, gentle giant of a guy who always has a big smile on his face, Kofi's almost forty and has one son. He dated – and allegedly broke the heart of – another friend of mine, Fred Mahama, a tall but skinny, light-skinned and charming man from a town called Bolgatanga in Ghana's northernmost region, close to the border with Burkina Faso.

Bolgatanga, like many of the northern areas close to the Sahara, is predominantly Muslim, with pockets of Catholics like Fred's family. It's generally a conservative area whichever side of the fence one falls on, and Fred bolted the first chance he got, headed south, and ended up in Accra, working as a security guard by night while attending the University of Ghana by day. Somehow he found time to meet and fall madly in love with Kofi, and seemed shocked and utterly mystified by the subsequent break up. But then Fred can sometimes be a tad dramatic, and favor convoluted explanations for matters of the heart.

Kofi tells me a different, much simpler, tale, saying that they broke up over sexual positions and dominance. Who would give and who would take? And how often? Apparently Fred wasn't willing to bottom much, if ever. Also, Fred's a player, with a legion of Accra dalliances ranging from powerful entrepreneurs to police officers to men in government.

Before he and Kofi got involved, Fred knew full well that among Accra's gay circles Kofi too was seen as a man-about-town. Knowing this, I laugh hysterically while consoling Fred over his 'unbearable' pain and histrionic heartbreak.

A few weeks later he is entirely over it.

Kofi lives in an Accra suburb with his elderly mother and

ten-year-old son. He's been engaged to the mother of his son, who lives in Kumasi, Ghana's second city, for some years now, but the next step, marriage, somehow hasn't happened.

"I don't think it's going to happen," he says, as if the decision has little or nothing to do with him. "At a point in time, yes, but now it doesn't seem so. There is a child between the two of us but that is what is keeping us going." I nod, and wonder if it matters for a son to never truly know his father. Surely it must. Yet who of us truly knows anyone else?

When I'm in town Kofi and I go swimming in Accra's nearby resorts, particularly at the upscale Royal Senchi Hotel, which is adjacent to the Akosombo dam on Lake Volta. Our poolside conversations often take in Ghana's political scene, and how he would like to make a difference if he could, perhaps by running for office. Invariably there is the question of what to do with this or that boyfriend.

Kofi had girlfriends well into his thirties, though all the while he was dating men on the side. One of these girlfriends became more serious. He didn't discourage it, though when she left Ghana for further studies in the United States he was relieved. However, while he was 'alone' his friends introduced him to another woman. Though he had been happy when his girlfriend left because it meant uncomplicated time with the man he was seeing while having the cover of a girlfriend living abroad, for reasons I don't really understand he became involved with this new woman. I suppose that, while predominantly preferring men, Kofi is really bisexual. Within months they got pregnant.

He and his family acknowledged the paternity, and then had to follow native law and custom and perform a ceremony of betrothal. This entailed his family going to the girl's family home with alcoholic drinks to ask for her hand. This ceremony is often referred to as a 'knocking on the door' or 'a knocking'. In other West African communities it's called a 'wine-carrying' or simply an 'introduction'.

Once she was properly betrothed to Kofi, their son could be born without societal stigma. However, Kofi never followed through on the marriage, they've never really lived together, and once he even tried to break off the engagement. "But the lady's family says 'No'. It's hanging, but I guess she's made up her mind to move on, but we do chat a lot; it revolves around the kid."

So his family believes that he is straight and simply not interested in marriage, a playboy who prefers the single life. And Kofi is a good father to his son, of whom he is, and always has been, the custodial parent. He is there at school activities, and spends his Saturdays watching or playing soccer with his boy. Most outings he makes are scheduled to get him home before his son goes to bed or wakes up. His devotion is total, so his family members, many of who are themselves married with children, see him as a good parent who will settle down once he finds the right woman.

"Once in a while there is pressure, but my family is a liberal family: they will accept who you are – though they will not accept who I am. I will say I'm bisexual because I have intentions, perhaps. If the pressure mounts and becomes insurmountable then I'll have no options but to settle down with a lady, which I can easily do. But the other side of me? No, I can't do away with."

Kofi once set a goal that by August 2015, his fortieth birthday, he would make a decision as to whether to try and somehow live with a man in Ghana – which for him would mean sending his son to live with one of his married brothers so there would be a mother figure in the house for the kid; right now his son has a grandmother at home all the time – or get married to a woman, which he maintains he can "easily do".

Birthdays have come and gone since then, but the decision is pending, and the 'easy' marriage is yet to take place.

Kofi did fall in love with a new man. That relationship brings him joy, but of late his mother has expressed displeasure at them being so close, and the man cooking for him, and this has caused tensions. The young man no longer visits, and Kofi is looking to relocate with his son away from the family home. It's not easy as housing is costly in Accra, but he's working on leaving.

In my chats with friends, and friends of friends, I end up having the same conversation repeatedly: I keep finding that a man loves another man and then marries someone of the opposite gender who he doesn't love.

The story of one couple from Tema particularly moves me. Tema is a port city on the Gulf of Guinea, sixteen miles east of Accra. It started out as a small fishing village but today is an industrial hub, and owing to its proximity to Accra, many people are in and out of both cities like they are one. It has a sizable number of lesbian and gay residents and is known for its house parties.

Neither half of this couple has university education; both are blue-collar workers, and neither has ever left Ghana. They are both happily married to women and have children. Atta Samuel Afiriyie is thirty-six when we first meet, and has been a Tema guy from infancy. His family is originally from Kumasi and he's a proud Ashanti. He's a tailor and runs his own business. He's very skinny, has a shy smile, and is always nattily dressed, favoring long-sleeved oxford shirts, well-pressed and neatly tucked into his trousers, which are sewn to look like skinny jeans.

Atta's been sewing since he finished junior high school. He went on to apprentice with a grand Tema tailor who turned out to be gay too, and through him Atta was introduced to other gay men in the area. From then on he never lacked for male companionship. He has been married ten years, and has two children with his wife.

At the time we first meet he's just lost his third child, and is still pained at the passing of the three-month-old, the pain sharpened by the cause of death being unknown at the time. He says he deeply loves his wife and can't imagine living without her, but for the past few years he's had a steady boyfriend who he also can't be without.

"I'm a gay man," he says. He's known so from his child-hood, and even though he's been with his wife for much longer than the decade they've been married. He's been with his current boyfriend peacefully and clandestinely for two years now, though his cover was blown several years before that by a jealous ex-boyfriend.

"He came and disgraced me in my house. He said I'm flirt-ing around. The boy demanded some money from my parents and my family."

When the family stood by their son, the heartbroken ex (who Atta had apparently left for his current boyfriend) went to

Atta's church to turn up the heat. "He told them, 'Hey this boy fucked me,' and he's not feeling fine so I should give money [for him] to go to the hospital."

The church declined assistance, and refused to pressure Atta to pay up, but stopped him from singing prominently in its choir, and made him sit in the back row of the congregation thereafter. He moved to another church, but the deed was out, and though he denied it to his family, and they pretended to accept his denial, they know. "I like my wife because my wife supports me. The first time she heard, she said I should not do that. The first time the boy comes to my place, my wife didn't know I was doing something. She said she would pray for me." Nothing more was said about the matter.

He's always been monogamous with his wife as far as heterosexual leanings go. "I like my wife but I don't like women, different girls or ladies." Sex with his wife is regular, he says. Atta loves his wife, but he loves his boyfriend Kwame more. "In Ghana if you don't marry they will say that you are a gay. You have to marry so they won't say that you're a gay."

And he really is gay, he says; not even bisexual. His wife is the only woman he's ever been attracted to. It's interesting to me that this does not change who he feels he fundamentally is; that there are things we do that feel like deviations from our truth rather than embodiments of it. In the last few years he's dated and had dalliances with at least twenty men, but then fell head over heels for Kwame. He tells me that once he met Kwame his behavior changed and he stopped participating in Tema's party scene.

His wife would be okay about it if she found out about Kwame, he believes, but his family not so: "They will kill me. They told me I've married so I should stop." He will never leave his wife, though, and admits that Kwame sometimes gets jealous, but he handles it: "I can't do that [leave his wife]; we have children. [but] I love Kwame, I love [Kwame] more than my wife."

Kwame is twenty-eight. He married young and has two children, one ten, the other five. He married his wife a few years after she gave birth to their first, a son. He lives in Tema but works in Tarkwa, a gold-mining town deep in the Ashanti region. Kwame isn't a miner but works in support services. He lives with the miners for twenty-one days of the month and spends the rest of the time at home. Atta makes the trip to Tarkwa several times during those twenty-one days, to see Kwame in his room in the hostel-like miners' accommodations. That works fine, but when they are in Tema, with both of them being married, seeing each other is a bit more complicated.

"For sex matter we go to a guesthouse. At times, sometimes I will tell my wife I'm going somewhere and I will not come back, and he'll tell his wife the same and we meet at a guest-house."

Mostly this works. However, once when Atta came to Kwame's home, someone saw him and then mentioned to Kwame's wife that they thought her husband's friend was gay. "My wife asked me and I denied it. I said he's not like that. Because I didn't know her mind." He thinks she believed him. He believes Atta's wife, though knowing her husband is attracted to men, "doesn't know what is going on between us. [She] considers me as a brother. I've always been asking, supposing she catches us one day?"

Atta, he says, brushes off his concern, preferring to deal with it when it happens, if it happens. Kwame says that while this current relationship is his first real one with a man he's always been interested in men. "I was in a relationship with someone for six months but nothing happened with him. It was not serious like the way it is with this one."

Atta even gave him a ring. "He is the first person I had sex with, but it was in my mind before I completed JSS [Junior Secondary School]. That was thirteen years ago. What made me wait was because I get married early, that's why I couldn't put myself too much into it."

Under no circumstances would Kwame consider giving up his marital home for a gay relationship, and yet he has no plans to give up his relationship with Atta either. He is, it seems, happy. "I like both of them. The other one has given me children, but he has given me happiness." This life, he says, is his secret. But he knows it can't stay secret forever.

I never ponder much about the wives, but perhaps I should. I do know that, as Uncle Nat reminds me, marriage in Africa is about many things, and love and sexual fidelity aren't always at the top of the list. Growing up in a region where polygamy is no more than mildly sneered at, and then only by some in the educated classes, I find it hard to believe that anyone in my part of the world today gets married expecting complete sexual fidelity. And maybe some can truly be happy in a relationship while knowing there will be others to fulfill other things. Monogamy is admirable in its way, but I now believe equating monogamy with happiness in relationships is purely a Western construct, and that these wonderful men can't and shouldn't conform to that, unless it has been agreed to by all parties. This – Western Africa – is a society where even men who aren't making loads of money have two wives and a girlfriend. Why should married men who have same gender love interests on the side be looked at any differently from their heterosexual friends?

At first glance it may seem to those in freer societies that some of my friends lack courage, that they are players who can't seem to openly pick the side they truly desire. Not so: living a double life is fraught with danger and anxiety. And I empathize, because what will 'courage' get you if you are openly gay and you lose your job after a lifetime of study and preparation? I can't imagine what courage will do for a person if they are ostracized from their family. Or as my buddy Peter, one of the few out and proud men I know in Accra, always warns: "In certain situations you have you be careful or you might end up gay-bashed."

I love the activism that is flaring up on my continent, and I am proud of those courageous enough to come out to family and friends, but I won't condemn my friends who have not made it there yet. Their struggle is real, and they are not just cads playing both sides of the field. I believe their time will come.

"Taboo is a very dangerous force." – Salman Rushdie

Thirteen: The Shea Prince

It's taken twelve hours on a 'luxury' bus to get here. My noise-cancelling headphones block out most of the relentless gospel music the driver favors. I rock to my heathen divas – Tina, Mariah, Beyoncé – and look out the window, watching the Ghanaian landscape slowly change from verdant to sparse.

My first impression of Tamale is that it's dry, dusty and low-rise, not like modern, overcrowded Accra. The Twi I hear there is replaced here by smatterings of Hausa and Dagbani. I haven't crossed a border but feel I am in a different country. I've journeyed up north in search of those dynamic women who, after trudging for miles at dawn, pick up shea nuts and process them into butter by hand.

This butter is used in confectionary products, but is better known for its hair- and skin-nourishing properties, and is now a key ingredient in the cosmetics trade. The women who pick the nuts have rarely had the chance to have an education themselves, but the income from shea enables their children to stay in school.

One of those 'shea babies', now an adult, is helping me navigate the terrain. His name is Will, and he's a heartthrob. I've come to write a journalistic piece on economic development, but my focus is derailed and Heartthrob Will is the culprit. To begin with we converse earnestly about shea but quickly veer off onto other things. I'm not sure how old Will is, and like many Gonja people he doesn't have a birth certificate, but he estimates he's thirty-seven. He was born in a hut near Navrongo and uses a national holiday here as a birthday, putting that date down on forms, and also celebrating himself on that day like other people do.

Will made sure his own children were born in hospital, where births are officially recorded. Today he's a clerk for a non-governmental organization, and has dreams of owning a coffeehouse. He's been married, divorced, and though he married again, he remains a babe magnet. The women hover, and it's easy to see why. Though he's skinny and very dark, his savvy fashion-sense makes him stand out from the other tall dark men of Tamale. He favors form-fitting tees, jeans and sneakers in a place where traditional dress is de rigueur for most. He has a full head of hair, and delights in sporting Mohawks with shaved-in lines. His goatee and a high wattage smile emphasize his deep dimples. He oozes vitality. In laid-back Tamale I've found a dandy.

Will comes from a long line of shea processors, and I am impressed by his deep knowledge of the craft. But it is his melodic way of stringing together common words in English, his particular form of elocution, that makes me smile even when he isn't saying anything profound. I take notes though I feel I will not use him in my story; instead I find myself inviting him to join me and my friends for dinner at Mike's Place, a pizzeria with alfresco seating that is popular with the expatriate crowd.

My pals, who have visited Tamale before, are foreign NGO types, and all have some project to make the lives of rural people in this region better. They are talking shop and I'm listening to their gripes and grumbles and small successes and soaking it all up. Will is listening too, I think, but looking only at me.

While we eat he says little but focuses on me intently, staring whenever I speak. I think we might be in flirtation territory: there is an undercurrent, a nice vibe that feels like 'we should be talking alone and not with your friends'. I get nervous in the way one does when things seem possible, and wonder why he isn't wearing a wedding ring. When he bids me farewell and says he'll be in touch, I'm not sure I'll hear from him. Maybe I should have invited him to eat with me alone.

However Will calls the next afternoon, while I'm on the bus back to Accra. He tells me – doesn't ask but tells me – that he'll be visiting me the following weekend.

"You're not going to ride the bus twelve hours just to see me, are you?" I ask, somewhat incredulous.

"Of course I am," he says.

He reminds me of Lamido, my first love; that Alhaji who gave me my first taste of the brutal reality of losing at love to culturally appropriate choices. Will – William – converted from Islam to Christianity. The name he has adopted is not what his family uses, and I take to calling him his northern name, Anass. Our banter is easy. He has this way of punctuating his sentences with emphatic exclamations – "Perfect!" and "Yes please!" – that is pleasing.

While speaking on the bus ride back, he asks if I am married. When I say no, and that I am gay, he moves on to other things. No surprise, no curiosity, no questions. As if I've just said I don't like socks. Often Ghanaians I encounter will say they've never met an openly gay man, or might mention a cousin they aren't close to; or will simply make a religious comment when such a subject comes up. But Anass just keeps talking. This seeming lack of upfront complicatedness is very attractive to me.

When he gets to Accra the next weekend – I meet him at the Shisha Lounge in Osu and we stroll to my apartment together – he wants me to tell him all about Nigeria. He seems to know plenty about my homeland already, and regales me with the plots of Nollywood movies he's seen. He often pronounces a variation of my Igbo name: "Chikenna!" On occasion he calls me Omalicha, or 'the beautiful one'. Anass has never left Ghana, but such is Nigeria's soft power that he knows and uses intimate Igbo phrases as if he was born to them.

We speak in hushed tones, with wide eyes, and I think to myself, are we toasting each other?

In the spacious flat I'm renting we spend a lot of time reclining on the king-size bed, and I listen as Anass uses pidgin English to describe his conquests.

"I chop am well well oh."

"I just dey fire dey go!"

When he has his clothes off, I can only stare: Anass' lean, muscular physique silences me. On his belly are a series of long Gonja tribal scarification marks. I begin to refer to them as 'the wall clock' as there is a large circular marking, and twelve long slim tribal marks radiate out from his navel, three 'hands' each, to north, south, east and west. The marks are elaborate and I find them beautiful, a work of art etched on the flat canvass of his stomach. I often trace them with my finger.

That first weekend he's with me we spend a lot of time indoors, in bed. Chatting. When he arrives he calls the Mrs. briefly, and says, after hanging up, "There are some things you must do as a husband." He adds that the reason why some men aren't married is because they don't want the responsibility of taking care of a woman, or having to check in with her like he is doing.

This way of reasoning is so old-school, but I can't bring myself to chastise him for being chauvinistic; nor do I when he says to me that he no longer cooks because he's no longer single. "Why should I go to the kitchen when I'm married?" That is the wife's domain, just as picking shea is women's work. Yet in my flat he joins me at work in the kitchen and cleans up afterwards.

Or there is the way he explains his penchant for chasing and fucking younger women: "I can't be with a girl my age or older. That's too old."

"Too old for what?" I ask.

"To have children."

I say surely that can't be the sole reason for marriage? He laughs. He always laughs. With me and at me. It's contagious. We laugh at our disagreements.

Like me he loves animals, and has several cats and birds.

I've grown up in the megacity that is Lagos, attended university in America, and work professionally in journalism. I'd call myself worldly; he calls me Western. He grew up in a rural area near Navrongo, where farming was his way of life until he completed high school. His worldliness comes from pop culture. He loves Nigerian music and introduces me to new artists I haven't yet heard of. Yemi Alade's hit 'Johnny' becomes our favorite song to dance to at home. The hilarious ditty is about a lover looking for her man, a lothario who is juggling many women.

Anass starts coming to visit most weekends, and I find myself more eager than usual for Fridays to come around. He's been to Accra before, during his school years, but when he visits me he's charmed by the city anew, or at least by the slice of it I inhabit. Every time we leave my flat he smiles and runs his long black fingers over the big, carved-wood butterflies that are affixed on doors and walls around the complex. There is a welcoming butterfly by the door of every flat. An old roommate of his drops by a few times, but mostly Anass ties himself to my apron-strings.

On Saturday nights we go to the Shisha Lounge. We don't always dance but we soak up the ambience. We have nightcaps at Republic Bar & Grill. I down several kokokrotos as I share my spicy roast chicken and fried yam chips with Anass, who is a teetotaler.

On Sunday morning we go to church with friends of mine. He engages lightly with these accomplished and moneyed professionals but keeps his attention on me. Later Anass will tell me how impressed he was by them, mentioning that he is particularly fond of Andres, an American foreign correspondent who is a brother to me.

When we go to one of Andres's Sunday Fun Day poolside gatherings, Anass chats briefly with folk in the expatriate circle, making a pleasant impression, and then swims with me. Every restaurant I take for granted is a revelation to him, from the Senegalese French bistro Au Grand Ecuyer to the Nigerian Thai sensation Zion Thai, off Oxford Street.

Weekends with him remind me of the first time I went to London. I was awestruck by everything from the pavements to the underground Tube trains. Now I'm awestruck by Anass being awestruck at our outings in his own capital city, even though he's seen it before.

"But not like this. With you everything is nicer," he says over milkshakes at Pinocchio, an Italian ice creamery in Osu. Up until now he has chosen the northern cuisine he knows, rarely desiring anything different: Tuo Zaafi, popularly known as 'TZ', and kontomire soup, a spinach delight, have been sufficient for him. Sometimes we chow down on another northern staple, guinea fowl roasted on an open fire. It is fun to go on these – to me – routine outings with someone who is close to my age but doesn't know how to drive, and is bowled over by Thai Ice Tea.

Strolling at dusk is our favorite pastime. We rarely venture far from Osu after our routine early dinners. In the rainy season we listen to the crickets in the night, and sometimes the toads croak as we make our way to the kebab-stand near Epos bar, passing the Ivorian ladies and the lines of people waiting for their achekes. He is happiest when we make our way home and turn in for the night. He doesn't mind going out with my friends but prefers being in the apartment with just me.

My pals find Anass charming and assume we are dating until he says something about his wife and kids. They are certain I wouldn't be dating a closeted man, and so they accept it when I smile and murmur, "He's not gay. We're just hanging out."

My friends are mostly heterosexual but Anass is new territory for me. None of them talk to me in soft whispers, or look me intensely in the eye, or send me text messages telling me how grateful they are for my existence. I never wonder if my friends are toasting me, and I have no desire for romantic moonlight walks with them. When I'm out of town none of them wait for me to call and say I've arrived safely. Anass does, and says, "I have to keep vigil until I know you are safe. Now I can go to sleep." With Anass I feel special. I feel loved.

My brother-friend Binyavanga says that one day I'll have to accept Anass' invitation to stay at his home in Tamale rather than my preferred hotel. He says I'll have to be prepared for the moment when his wife pulls me aside and explains that she is aware of our relationship and happy to have a co-wife. I burst out laughing as he continues, "She will tell you she has a lot of work to do with the children so you will have to be on duty all weekend handling his dick so she can rest."

These jokes make me more confident. The next time we meet up and are luxuriating in my bed I ask – does he not want us to sleep together? I want to. And I've wanted to from our very first handshake.

He seems nervous, and then he says, "You know I have children. For us that's a taboo."

I'm not sure who the 'us' is. His Christian community? Or

the Gonja people, perhaps? Or maybe he just means being Ghanaian in general. He says he knows it's not that way in America, where I spend a chunk of my year working, but he lives in Ghana, and while Chikenna is free to be who he is, Anass isn't.

I put myself in his shoes. Recently Ghana has been embroiled in a nasty national discussion about gay rights. Talk radio's favorite topic is which alleged gay to demonize next, and how to respond to governments like that of the United Kingdom 'imposing homosexuality' by tying development aid to LGBT rights. Evangelical groups are dispatching emissaries to rural chiefs to warn them about the 'ills' of gays. This is the charged climate I slip in and out of, but in which Anass lives all year. I try to empathize while also feeling superior, a citizen of the wider world. Looking at me as if to knock back the smug look I have on my face, he says, "Who told you I haven't been with a man before?"

Wait, what?

I let that statement hang in the air a while, then say perhaps it isn't a good idea for us to be so cuddly if we are simply friends. His mood darkens.

"But why, why, why do you want to break the relationship?"

Anass insists that we are special in our own way, and that when I get married he will be proud to be my best man. Everyone gets married in Ghana, he says, even the gay guys, just like in Nigeria. And when the children come, after ceremonies in Nigeria we will do an outdooring, a public 'sip and see' with the baby, here in Ghana. As he talks my mood lightens, and soon I'm howling with laughter.

Later I wonder about Anass to Peter and Kwabena. They say I'm being gullible. "Gay for pay!" they chorus. But Anass asks for nothing; in fact he often insists on sharing what he has with me. Perhaps the escape from humdrum Tamale is enough for him. Maybe it's the stories of the places I have traveled to he craves. When we are together he often asks to see pictures of anywhere I've recently been to – Lagos, New York, São Tomé, Johannesburg. Sure, I always pick up the tab at the bourgeois eateries we frequent, but that's because I chose them; and he constantly showers me with gifts, especially the traditional clothes and scarves I fancy.

One particularly expensive gift he gives me is a fugu, a woven top indigenous to Ghana's north. It is made of fine cotton, dyed and perfumed, and much nicer than any of the ones I've purchased myself.

I see the first flash of anger in Anass when he thinks – mistakenly – that I've re-gifted that present to another friend. He frowns, sulks and hisses. But it is brief. Some of my more urbane Accra friends advise me to drop him. He's settled, they argue: a wife, children – and now he has an emotional boyfriend (me). They say let him go get a real boyfriend if he has the gumption to.

But I don't.

I justify it by saying that openly gay men and straight married men can be close and I'm not going to overthink it. This is my lie. Anass isn't just a pal. There is a deep mutual attraction, one we both feel powerless to act on. Yet I love the unbridled joy that emanates from him when he sees me in public. The smile gets wider and he puts his arms around himself in a hug. Once indoors, Anass looks deep into my eyes and tells me how much he appreciates me. I enjoy hearing him reiterate how special he finds me. And, as he smiles, his quivering blood-red lips come so close to mine – and then stop just before we touch. Arousal and confusion follow: Anass never goes further.

As we lie in bed, he brags about his past pussy conquests and I trace my fingers over the wall clock on his belly, wondering what on earth I am doing.

When I return to America he WhatsApps me frequently. By then I'm dating Scott, and am happy in my relationship just as he is happily married. Everything seems tidy. But I get upset when I miss his messages. I make an effort not to reach out too often, but when he messages me I always respond.

After many months have passed I return to Ghana. I have in my mind moved on. I head to Tamale. It is the rainy season. The moment I see him, his big smile appears. The moment no one is within earshot, he remarks how cute I am. He shows me his new home, a house he is building that he says is ours. In the humid air the statement is oddly intoxicating. When he insists we return to his current house because his wife has prepared my dinner, I worry it will be weird. But any trepidation I feel disappears when the food is served, and, seated with his wife, children, and assorted relatives I eat the TZ. I feel at home.

I return to Accra and at weekends he visits. Again and again he remarks how great I look. We talk about making love. Now he is insisting that our relationship couldn't ever be taboo. "When I tell my wife everything you do for me she says 'he loves you'."

That night he tells me tales of divorced women who strut their stuff in Tamale, and of his friends who pursue them. The women are dubbed BZs – Bazan Wara, or women who are mothers but have left their husbands.

Somewhere between the story of the BZs and my nodding off he puts his arms around me and whispers, "You can never know how someone feels about you. I love you. Just because nothing has happened doesn't mean I don't love you. You don't know the future. Be patient." I turn to him and he looks me in the eye and declares, "Chike, me and you na forever oh."

He's whispering. But this time with an intensity to make sure I get it. Eyes wide open, eyebrows arched, unsmilingly he repeats, "Chike. Me and you na forever."

"Empty Barrels Make The Most Noise." – Proverbial

Fourteen: Eko Oni Baje O! (Lagos Must Prosper!)

I've loved Lagos for as long as I can remember.

I use every excuse I can to return – for weeks, months, a few days, a weekend, whatever. Sometimes I sneak in; other times I announce to my pals that I'll be around. I can't afford to have a place of my own there so I just show up at my brother Don's home and camp out in his spare bedroom. Don's an attorney and runs a law firm in South-West Ikoyi. He also lets me take over a desk in one of the rooms in his chambers so I can get my own work done.

It's the summer of 2015, and I'm excited about a literary evening in Accra hosted by the Ghana Writers Project. I'm to share some short stories I've been working on, and while I'm excited I'm nervous because they're still very much works in progress. I go on first. It seems to go well, and before I'm allowed to leave the stage to make room for the main event, I get lobbed a few insightful questions and compliments. Afterwards we all listen enthralled as the Kenyan author Binyavanga Wainaina reads from his seminal memoir, *One Day I Will Write About This Place*. The audience, a mix of cultured Accra denizens, hangs on his every word.

After the readings are done, the organizers and some of their guests, including businessmen and diplomats that I've invited, go out for libations and more conversation at a nearby hotel in Asylum Down. The barman this evening is my buddy Roderick Opobo, and he takes great care of our party, which numbers about fifteen. I get talking to a European industrialist who runs several factories making building materials. He spends a lot of time in Ghana, and has made Accra his part-time home. He's tall, a silver fox with a chubby build, and was invited by Ian, who came to see me read, to join us after the event.

The fellow compliments me, and we discuss the progress I am making trying to tell stories that have been overlooked by the conventional media. I say with a laugh that my hope is the next generation of journalists will do a much better job of it. It turns out we know a few people in common, and he mentions that he has a Nigerian partner who like me grew up in Lagos. I ask him if he's ever lived in Lagos, my wonderful city, and he says no, but he has visited. He met his Lagosian partner in Accra. The fellow is getting a drink at the bar, he says, and hadn't been able to make the reading because he was at work.

When we make our way over to refill our cocktails he touches a tall, strapping and shaven-headed man on the shoulder. The man turns and I am confronted by a somehow very familiar face, dark and lovely; but I'm unsure until the hunk opens his mouth and I see the gap-toothed smile. As the businessman tries to make introductions, Jacques – for it is indeed him – just keeps babbling, "Chike, Chike, Chike, Chike?"

"Wow."

"Is this you, Frankie?"

"You know each other?" his partner asks, seeming sur-prised.

"We have history but it has been years," I respond, amazed that all this time Jacques has been right here in Ghana.

It turns out that, after ditching the hotel manager in Asaba, he left Nigeria for Ghana to work with my friend Timi, and after a period of shuttling between Lagos and Accra, is now firmly ensconced in Kumasi, Ghana's second city. Many in Ghana believe his boyfriend is a diplomat, but he is actually an honorary consul, which is an unsalaried position – meanwhile running a lucrative construction business using Ghanaian workers.

After catching up with Jacques I promise to keep in touch properly, especially since I am in Accra fairly often. He looks older but still has a great physique. Shaving his head conceals a receding hairline. He doesn't work in horticulture anymore and now has a job dealing in office supplies. His son and former wife still live in Scotland. He's never been there. He seems content. It has been years, and standing here at a hotel bar in Accra I realize I've missed him.

And I did look for him. I looked for him because, despite our sexual shenanigans, he was a fundamentally nice person. As recently as a few summers ago, while in Nigeria I'd kept an eye out for him as I ventured out to nightspots frequented by queer Lagosians. But none of them had a clue where my friend Jacques the gardener was.

Lamido isn't in Lagos anymore either – he moved first to Abuja, then on to Kano – but several of my mates from boarding school now live or work there, as well as a generation of lovely cousins, so it's always hectic when I'm there.

Connecting with the family in Lagos is tough, though, because the ubiquitous traffic jams wreak havoc on any plans that involve darting from one side of town to another. I often have Paulie, my childhood friend and cousin, come meet me for drinks or dinner so we can reminisce about the good old days. Paulie's grown up to be a property developer, and is, so he says, happily married. Sometimes he'll drag me to some hip bohemian spot in Ikoyi like Bogobiri House, a boutique hotel that is also a meeting point for local artists, and is on a quiet street just off Awolowo Road. Other times we end up in some roadside drinking spot and gist like we have since we were young.

Once we are imbibing, Paulie regales me with stories of his latest 'TB' boy (TB – tops and bottoms – which I learn apparently has a counterpart for lesbians : 'Lola'), and whoever is his current partner, he introduces me to. Often he brings young men who make good conversation and are trying to get a foothold on the corporate ladder; other times they are neighborhood toughs who sometimes seem like unemployed 'area boys', and talk is rather stilted.

As close as we are, I've never been introduced to Paulie's wife. "Her whole family is homophobic. They wouldn't know what to make of you," he says. I don't push it.

Paulie is often good for an after-work pub-crawl, as is our other buddy, Muyiwa Alakija. One summer night I ask them to meet me at Freedom Park, which is in the heart of Lagos, and is one of my favorite haunts. Freedom Park is a walled oasis on the very busy Broad Street. During the colonial era it was Her Majesty's Broad Street Prison, and following independence it lay dormant for many years – until some geniuses turned it from an emblem of oppression into a creative hub. Movies and documentaries are screened there on a regular basis in the outdoor amphitheater, and there is often excellent live music. But there are also gardens with fountains, spaces for reflection. Plays are staged there, and cultural festivals, but I go more for the good food, conversation and music.

One of my favorite nights at Freedom Park is Afropolitan Vibes. It falls on every third Friday, and features a live concert, with the audience rocking to Afropunk, Afro-Hip-Hop and AfroBeat. Guest artists show up to perform with Ade Bantu and his twelve-piece band, whose set anchors the night. On this visit I ask Paulie to join me there as I'm also going to meet up with my friend Jacob Basboll, a Danish journalist who is stopping over in Lagos.

Jacob's part of my New York City posse, and is taking time out from doing journalism in Europe to study for a post-graduate degree at New York University. He has a longtime girlfriend back in Denmark. As part of his graduate work in Africana Studies he's been assisting me, training undergraduates in how to carry out research in Africa and do journalism on the continent. We've travelled four times to various parts of West Africa together.

Now Jacob is doing a project on the militant separatist group Boko Haram. He's due to fly to northern Nigeria the next day, and this is my chance to show him a good time before he dives headfirst into what will prove a grim subject in a difficult area. As we sit listening to the musicians jam we are joined by Jahman Anikulapo, a newspaper editor and cultural connoisseur. I make introductions and we chat a little. I also strike up a conversation with a handsome man sitting nearby, who introduces himself as Razaq. He joins our table before Paulie and Muyiwa show up, and we have several large Star beers and multiple suya sticks together. Razaq is a travel agent and, though he says he has a girlfriend, I think he is gay.

We chat and laugh. Later in the evening Jacob whispers to me that Razaq seems really into me. I think so too but say he says he's not gay. At this time my partner Scott is working in Myanmar for a year, and Jacob, while not wanting me to be lonely, also doesn't want me to succumb to temptation.

Razaq is macho and handsome, and there is a vibe between us that is palpable. Then Paulie decides it is time for us to leave. Razaq and I make plans to meet up alone the next night, the band finishes, he leaves, and at Paulie's suggestion Paulie, Muyiwa, Jacob and I head over to a club in a private home in a walled compound on Victoria Island. Entrée is by invitation. It soon fills with TB boys and Lola girls and some who are in between, and the energy is off the charts. The bar is stocked with top-shelf liquor and the decor is all red. There is plush carpeting throughout and everyone is dressed to the nines.

Jacob and I are surprised. We had both assumed that, like in Accra, there would be no explicitly gay venues, and that if there were any, they wouldn't be so crowded – the more so since the passing of the anti-gay law the year before. This place is jammed, wall-to-wall guys and girls, all (or at least most) of them clearly into folks of their own gender. Here too I look out for Jacques. It is a nice evening, but not being much of a drinker I decide to turn in fairly quickly, leaving Jacob in Paulie and Muyiwa's hands. On the ride home I think to myself, there may not be any gay bars in Lagos, but there are probably loads of places like that where the elite, at least, can chill. OK then.

I hear later that Paulie and Muyiwa took Jacob to yet another club that evening, finally dropping him off at the South African diplomat's place on the Lekki Peninsula where he'd been couch-surfing barely in time to pack his bags before heading to the airport.

Paulie and Muyiwa have been friends for a long time and I always enjoy Muyiwa's company, but they are very different from each other. Muyiwa is tall, skinny and effeminate. He's not married, doesn't plan to get married, and is as openly gay as one can be in Lagos. A chain-smoker and very well-read, Muyiwa is at ease with himself and everyone around him: he can converse with the area toughs or the butter children. He's an original Lagos boy, born and bred.

"I gave up women in my early twenties and focused totally on men," he tells me one afternoon when he drops by my brother's Ikoyi office to see me. "I'm openly gay. My whole family knows: my brothers; my sisters; my stepmum; my dad before he died."

Muyiwa has five brothers and three sisters. He had worked in customer service for several companies, but the worsening unemployment situation in Lagos means he's not held a steady job in a few years. He's had some short-term contracts here and there, but no real, open-ended employment.

Family acceptance came slowly.

First from his eldest brother, who lives up north in Kaduna, about four hundred miles away. Muyiwa said his brother knew instinctively and brought it up himself. "We were out one day and he said, 'I don't care about your sexual orientation; just be discreet. Think about the family you have.' That I have his blessings, I can do whatever I like, but be discreet. What he meant was that I shouldn't do anything that would bring odium to my name and by extension my family."

That scenario – of not embarrassing the family – is one I've heard over and over again from gay men and women across Africa, and I press him to tell me what it would mean in his case. He says an example would be if he slept with someone and then they came and made a scene at his home or in public. This reminds me of my Ghanaian pal, Atta the Tema tailor.

"We are too hypocritical in Nigeria," Muyiwa says. "Even people who are gay will come out publicly against you. The people who are the dominant ones, there have been instances of – the people sleep together… he wasn't raped: he took off his clothes and he did it. But he goes back thinking, 'What have I done?' and he goes to plan with other people to embarrass you."

Muyiwa never dates people from the Suru-Lere neighborhood, where lives with his family, as a result of a particularly hurtful incident involving his late father. A local man he'd had sex with wrote a letter to his father afterwards, warning him his son is gay.

"He showed me the letter and said what do I have to say about it? And I told him that the person must be mad." That was close to twenty years ago, and Muyiwa's not bothered with anyone local since.

In the strange way that things can sometimes go, Muyiwa and the letter-writer eventually became friends, and the man now has a girlfriend who knows nothing of their dalliance or the subsequent drama.

The two men first met at a local drinking spot. "We happened to be sitting beside each other and I was drinking. He was sitting next to me and I kissed him. Yeah. We were both high, he kissed me back and I think he went home – you see in Nigeria, you have this problem of sometimes you'd meet people who will kiss you and play around with you and then he goes off and thinks, 'Does that mean I'm gay? Oh you caused this, I hate you. You brought it out in me,' forgetting he's an adult and he knew what he was doing."

This scenario of shame after sex, or even just fondling, followed by instant denial, has played out many times in Muyiwa's life, and continues to do so, so he's become more careful. "There is this place in my area where a lot of boys hang out. They sell Indian hemp, beer, cigarettes. Usually a lot of guys are there and sometimes they play football on the side, so I gravitate towards such places because sooner or later someone will make a pass at me."

I've seen this sort of thing many times: "I don't step to people," Muyiwa continues. "I just be myself, my effeminate self, and one person out of ten will make a pass. So I don't mind waiting."

When he is out he crosses his legs like a lady and always has a cigarette dangling from his long fingernails. As the gays say, he 'gives good face'. Sooner or later someone says hello. Interestingly this all happens in public, with the apparently heterosexual men who witness it ignoring what is going on. And so his life carries on in exactly the sort of area and situation one would expect to generate an instant lynch mob.

While I know he has his pick of men, in all the time I know Muyiwa he never seems to have a boyfriend. At sixteen he was kissing boys and girls, but by the time he graduated from Catholic high school in Lagos, he knew where his attractions really lay. Then a supposed friend pimped him off to a politician, a man in his forties, someone he'd seen in the newspapers, and that was his first sexual experience. Now forty-something himself, he's never looked back, and is at peace with his sexuality, even though things are difficult in Lagos. A good friend of his who ran a drinking spot for years on Lagos's Bar Beach on tony Victoria Island was so brutally beaten he eventually died from his injuries. That chop bar was always a gay-friendly place. In its heyday it attracted foreigners with cash and biddable area boys, along with a sprinkling of the butter children, and Muyiwa thinks that's why his friend was attacked. The beach itself was and is often filled with a surreal mix of local toughs and white-garment-clad church people, and at night it can be unsafe, with shady characters lurking at the shoreline. Following the attack the gays migrated to other spots, such as the secure club he and Paulie took Jacob and me to. Or to the chop bar in Costain, though Muyiwa says his visits there are infrequent. "I don't want to be a known face there. I'm sure trouble is going to bust there one day so I don't want to be part of it. And when I do go I don't sit in the cluster. I tend to sit a bit away. Not that I'm ashamed of being gay, but I'm not going to put myself in a position where someone would attack me for my orientation. Especially people I don't know, and maybe in the general melee I get hurt."

Muyiwa may be cautious but that doesn't mean he doesn't delve. He's dated foreigners too, Brits working in Nigeria. One, Harold, was a consular attaché who helped him study while he was at the University of Ibadan, and used to visit Muyiwa on campus every weekend. After three years Harold left Nigeria and they've not seen each other since. It was over just like that, but Muyiwa still believes Harold is his great love.

"I've never met anybody as loving as white men," he insists.

"Really?" I ask. "How much experience have you had?"

"I've dated three for at least a year," Muyiwa says. "They never cheated on me. White people are very faithful. They always gave me a nice time. Because they were working we didn't have to see each other every day, which suited me fine." Nigerian men he believes can be a bit clingy. Having lived in America, I think he is conflating race and economic status – all these men are comparatively well off, so helping out financially costs them little; and as short-stay residents in a country where being gay is severely penalized in law, it suits them to have a reliable casual boyfriend handily on tap: convenience, then, rather than fidelity.

Muyiwa has also had to sleep with a married man he didn't particularly care for because he needed cash. When his younger brother was getting married he, Muyiwa, was unemployed. Having to contribute his share for the festivities, he finally acquiesced to a longtime admirer who "had been chasing me for five years, and I was always playing him. I didn't like him. But I quickly decided that it is what it is. So I called him up in Ilorin and he said I should come. He gave me fifty thousand naira." The attraction wasn't there, but the wedding guests needed to be fed and that money was the equivalent of over three hundred dollars. Muyiwa didn't think about the man's wife or children, just about the money. "He's fat and I don't sleep with fat people. I grinned and bore it. I faked it. He got what he wanted and I got what I wanted."

Every time I'm in Lagos, I see Muyiwa's patterns remain the same. He's fun to hang around with, but as he's unable to gain steady employment, like thousands in Lagos he makes compromises. Now he seems jaded with love and the promise of it and he rarely dates. And when he does venture to open himself to someone, they are generally sort of unavailable. He last dated a twenty-six-year-old guy with a girlfriend. He'd cook and get hemp for both of them to smoke and they'd have sex. Then the man started bringing his girlfriend over too, and Muyiwa began to feel used. He cooked; they ate. He procured marijuana, they smoked it. And then the two of them had sex in his bed and Muyiwa couldn't take it. He could watch, they said, but not join in. And so he ended it. But with all his issues, at least his family doesn't pressure him to marry: they accept him.

By contrast, Paulie is married, as are many of his other gay friends. Even for those who are only wanting a leg up in their professional career, being married projects a useful impression of maturity. The pressure is far greater for women, and in their case it begins much earlier because the clock is also ticking for them to become mothers. I suspect some women knowingly marry men who are gay, turning a blind eye to their husband's extracurricular activities because it's better than being single and middle-aged in this society.

Nowadays Muyiwa is at peace. "I'm comfortable with myself but it took a while. In the beginning I was hush-hush, but now I just look at it like 'fuck all you all'. I can't be running for the rest of my life." But he rattles off the names of friends who couldn't take the pressure, the ones who left Nigeria because they were able to. They haven't returned.

My friend Timi is one of those who left. He's so Lagos in his demeanor, and when he moved to Accra and then Cape Town it was primarily because of his sexuality. It pushed him to embrace his South American side, and these days when he meets people he doesn't say he's Nigerian. At first this surprises me, but I understand it. He doesn't return to Lagos unless he has work there, and his last visit was to bury his mother. Originally South American, she had made Nigeria her home after marrying Timi's father.

Just like me, Timi grew up in Lagos, went to a Nigerian boarding school, and followed that up with a stint at the University of Ife, one of the country's premier tertiary institutions. And like me, all that time he knew he was different, 'peculiar'. Partway through studying for his degree he found work apprenticing for a fashion designer and decided not to return to university. He made friends at work with an effeminate drag queen type who "claimed to high heavens" that he was heterosexual.

"I could never understand that in my head. At that point in time you are just longing for someone to say the words to you that I'm just like you and we're okay. People were still ashamed to say they were gay."

Soon he was sewing, designing and styling for a television soap opera, and he found a gay support group. He went to one of their parties and saw the hairdresser there. But "I felt out of place, based on my background." He was one of the butter children, and eventually found a like-minded Ikoyi crowd. The soundtrack of their days was En Vogue's 'My Lovin' (You're Never Gonna Get It)'. Soon his crowd zapped, however; and after rumors began swirling, he too left for Accra.

Rumors, not violence. In retrospect those were the good old days. "There wasn't that much of an uproar, which is funny – unlike now, where even without that happening there has been a law enacted and they are witch-hunting everybody."

While it is true that many gay men and women who have the opportunity to do so have bolted from Nigeria, Lagos is also home to loads of people like my friend Chidi, who returned and has made a life here. Chidi is now married with children, and is happy in business and with his also-married boyfriend. Both men are successful and both seem happy in their closets.

Lagos is also home to a sizable number of repats such as my friend Cheikh, who returned there when he was in his mid-forties. Cheikh is tall, handsome, bespectacled and skinny. He's a swimmer and speaks with a gentle mien. He looks great in a suit and sometimes he throws on a traditional northern hat. At times a spurt of gray sprouts from his chin. He oozes a charisma that has been honed over the years by the luxurious lifestyle of the accomplished African.

A consultant with a doctoral degree in public health, he's built his career working on global healthcare initiatives on behalf of the United Nations. He assesses programs for many countries, particularly those focusing on sexual and reproductive health, as well as health and HIV/AIDS. His roots are Nigerian but he's also descended from a line of Mauritanians. During his years in New York he was always supportive of fellow African gays, especially those in the growing asylum network.

As high profile as he is, Cheikh has always been out. His activism abroad came to the attention of his family when they read online news reports about him. He confirmed his sexuality to his siblings. Though they accepted him, I was surprised when he decided to give Lagos another go. His mother and sisters are there, and he's close to them, but he has a longtime partner, and that man lives in London. I had assumed that if he ever decided to leave the Big Apple he would rather return to London, where he has had a home and a partner, than Nigeria.

I am wrong.

Lagos beckons in an intangible way that many middle-aged men find irresistible, especially if they've spent years working abroad. Cheikh is as satisfied as one can be, with a life in Lagos and a partner in London. The thing he enjoys most, he says, is "living in a city with incredibly beautiful men, and not facing prejudice about being an older man despite the younger age of my gay friends and acquaintances."

Today his life in Lagos is full. On some days he goes to the Ikoyi Club to swim with his mother before tackling his day's work. He's always trying to make a difference and bring about change. He would love to see more positive visibility for gay and transgender people in the Nigerian media, and has spent his years there working towards that end. He's attractive, and men flock to him for casual affairs. He makes no secret of the fact he's partnered. Still, he's wary:

"I am perceived by many as wealthy and upper class in a country with widespread poverty. I am always aware that I could be involved in a scandal or trapped by blackmailers from within the LGBT community."

"Culture does not make people. People make culture. If it is true that the full humanity of women is not our culture, then we can and must make it our culture."

– Chimamanda Ngozi Adichie

Fifteen: Best Kept Secrets (Lola Girls Rock!)

For as long as anyone can remember marriage has been central to our culture. This is true of every civilization there has ever been, but is, perhaps, particularly the case if you are African. And for women of a certain age, if they haven't tied the knot, it becomes an overwhelming issue. When is it going to happen, they hear all the time; if not right now, why not? When are the children coming?

The pressure on men can be heavy, but women are expected to marry earlier, to put aside any thoughts of a career more easily. However academically able or professionally driven they may be, matrimony is assumed to be their ultimate goal.

Two decades after it was released, Bobby Benson's seminal 1950s highlife hit 'Taxi Driver (I don't care)', a musical outpouring of defiance over a lost love, a disappointing love, was still a part of the soundtrack of my pre-teen years:

Sisi Seju, You no dey shame. Plenty husband is too much. Plenty drivers without labor, if you must go nobody cares. If you marry taxi driver, I don't care

If you marry lorry driver, I don't care
If you marry railway driver, I don't care
If you marry motor driver, I don't care
Sisi Seju, You no dey shame. Plenty husband is too much.
If she must go, don't you worry
Please let her go, nobody cares
If she marry taxi driver, I don't care
If she marry lorry driver, I don't care
If she marry railway driver, I don't care
If she marry motor driver, I don't care

Benson crooned these lyrics over an intoxicating trumpet-and-horn rhythm section that pulled listeners to their feet.

If you must go nobody cares. If you marry taxi driver I
don't care

It was not a question of 'if', of course, but 'who', and it was a given that you'd end up getting married, even if it wasn't to someone who loved you.

In 1986 Mandy Brown Ojugbana debuted like a shooting star on the Nigerian music scene with an album titled *Break-through*. One of her biggest hits was a reworking of that song, and she called her version 'Taxi Driver... Answer To'. Hers spoke to men, Lagos guys, the dawdling 'Brother Eko' who had not gotten around to getting hitched yet, and she opened with a traditional talking drum, before singing that if the brother married a hairdresser or a lady doctor or a market woman it didn't matter. As long as he got married.

In 2016 one of Bobby's descendants, Coco Benson, released her own version of 'Taxi Driver', making the case for choice in love and marriage as long as one was happy in one's choice. Even so, the assumption remains: that one will end up married.

Perhaps it was my years abroad that at one time skewed my thinking towards the notion that marriages were primarily love-affairs, even though as an African I've always known they are a lot more than that. I had forgotten that for us they are above all unions of families.

They can be tools of change too. I've been reminded by historians that Africans had our own version of slavery, and that that was why it wasn't seen as such a terrible thing to sell your enemies and captives to the European slave-traders, though no Africans knew those sold would end up being so brutalized. The key difference was, the African tribes that had slaves never viewed their captives as indentured for life. In some circumstances children of slaves could even be born royal, if the enslaved parent married a member of the royal household. Slaves could be married to people of higher status. They could own property and even buy their way out of captivity by dint of hard work. Or by marrying up. So marriage has been an engine of social transformation.

And so, when I was lamenting to Uncle Nat how sad it must be for some of my friends who have married because society expects them to, he looked at me incredulously and laughed. "Don't kid yourself," he warned. "Relationships are sad whether you are gay or not." People have strong criteria for marriage that have nothing to do with affection – does the proposed spouse have a good family name? Are they known for anything? What kind of bridal price can paid? Will there be any upward mobility? And of course, are they able to reproduce? These practical concerns are often the determining factors in who is chosen as a spouse. "This love for marriage thing is a really recent phenomenon here," Uncle Nat went on. Marriage "is families coming together and you darn well get along because if you don't we will keep the dowry. That's how it works."

For me, I recognized as a teenager that the path for women was shorter, and that marriage was the destination. When I returned to Federal Government College, Port Harcourt in 1986, a few months after graduating, to collect my school certificate results, it was a happy time for most of us. I had passed my exams and needed only to prepare for my university matriculation ones. There I bumped into one of my former classmates, Eugenia Okereke, a pretty, fun, light-skinned girl from the eastern part of the country, with whom I had been friendly throughout our time at F.G.C. With her hair straightened – perms had been forbidden while we were students – she looked great, and she had kitten heels on. She radiated happiness and seemed giddy with excitement, so I congratulated her on her results. But when she showed them to me I was stunned. She'd barely passed any of the subjects, and would not get any credits – truly passing meant getting at least five credits out of the seven or eight courses one had to take. If she wanted to get into any kind of higher education institution, she would have to take the exams all over again, in hopes of getting a General Certificate of Education – as opposed to the West African School Certificate one gets upon completion of high school. Yet here she was, brimming with joy.

Faced with her poor results I was reluctant to talk of future plans, but then she informed me excitedly that she was getting married: the bride price and dowry had already been negotiated, and her fiancé was simply waiting for her to be done with F.G.C. Eugenia was acting like she'd won the jackpot. It was the last time I saw her and she seemed truly happy. Who needs an education if you've got a husband lined up? Even thirty years later I wonder what became of her. When a WhatsApp group was created for our class she wasn't on it and no one seemed to know where she was. Even in the era of Facebook, she has proved impossible to find. I hope it worked out for her.

So what's a woman to do when she realizes she has no attraction to men or desire for a husband, but rather yearns for the companionship of other women?

In Lagos you can do a variety of things, as one Lagosian lady, Kainene, tells me. Like me she is a close pal of Muyiwa, we've shared drinks at the raucous and joyous Afropolitan Vibes dance party, and we hang out whenever I'm home. She favors long braids that extend to the small of her back and has a shy smile, with bright white teeth that contrast pleasingly with her very dark skin. She's a riverine area girl, and her hometown is in the Delta. I wouldn't peg her as a lesbian but she is one – a box she's checked only recently, but happily.

Her career as a theater and television director took her to Brazil for a few years and so she's fluent in Portuguese. She also worked in Australia, Germany and Ethiopia before returning to Nigeria. As a child she went to the International School in Ibadan and grew up very middle class. She's worldly and a thinker.

At fifteen years old, Kainene fell in love with a Lagos girl. Her paramour was eighteen, and they carried on for years until her lover broke it off because she wanted a chance at being 'normal'. This reminded me of my own first love, Lamido. Her friend got married and went on to have three children: she lives the 'normal' life today. Kainene was devastated. She thought she would die, she said. But she didn't: she picked herself up and went on and ended up with a successful career abroad. And all those years she too did what she thought was the 'normal' thing – though at some point began labeling herself as bisexual, because of her uncontrollable desire for women despite all the "nice guys" she was dating.

She soon realized this was a false identity, and that marriage was never going to work for her with any man. Her relationships with men never quite clicked the way they did with women; there wasn't that burning excitement, those stomach gyrations. No palpitations, no unexpected bouts of jealousy, no inexplicable longing.

At forty she had clarity. She wanted the woman next door. Her boyfriend, who up until then she'd been planning to settle down with, had to go.

"What made it glaring was that this was a really nice man. If he had been a bastard... but he is a good man. It was horrible for both of us. After we broke up I was single for a while. I didn't want to wake up and jump into the pussy pool and drown myself. There are a lot of women in Lagos who are conducting same sex relationships and they are married and they have children and whatever but I really couldn't see myself doing that."

Kainene and other women I know have told me that lesbians abound in Lagos, Port Harcourt and Abuja, but that many are married with children, and their partners are passed off as their friends. We've been out dancing at the hottest Lagos nightspots and Kainene will point out women dancing together and everyone is oblivious to the fact they are a couple: ladies dancing with each other is simply 'fun', and men get excited by it, so no problem.

So while lesbians aren't generally out front being activists, or having a publicly politicized sense of their own identities, there are hordes of them in Nigeria, and once they have fulfilled their obligations by marrying and procreating they are good to go. But some today are bucking the trend: Kainene, who hasn't had children herself, eventually moved in with a woman she fell head over heels for, and they have a large flat they share with her partner's eight-year-old son.

"I've had conversations with people where they say, 'Eh but so so and so has been having a relationship with that girl but she has a husband and some children. You can do that. What's wrong with you? Get a husband and have some children.' So at the end of the day it's do what you like but make sure nobody knows about it and don't be too vocal and gay about it. If you are not going to get married, have some children and give us grandchildren quickly."

Kainene's mother is dead. Her father lives in Abuja, Nigeria's capital. He is an intellectual who didn't freak out about his daughter being a lesbian, but did warn her to be careful and not to flaunt anything. In Nigeria even cooks, drivers and other working-class men sometimes have two wives, so unmarried women stand out. Right now, though she and her partner live together, they let neighbors assume they are cousins. Their friends know they are a couple and that's how to play it in modern-day Nigeria. They are as out as one could possibly be there without putting oneself in harm's way.

"Gay or straight, we are still products of our socialization and our conditioning where you have a certain generation of women who have been socialized that you must marry, and you have value, and your validation is whether you have a husband or not. But for a lot of younger women, their socialization is different: the world is their oyster. They don't have the issues that we have so it's a lot easier for them to say, 'I am a lesbian.' They are not going to rock the boat too much and carry placards in front of the national assembly, but they are just going to get on with it. And I find it strange here, where it's sort of an open secret. People will know that this person or that person is gay. They know. But as long as this big statement: 'be it, don't say it'."

It is as if the whole country believes that being gay is something that people do rather than who they are; an identity. For women, their sexuality is reduced to just being a conduit for the right penis to fertilize their wombs. "Not so long ago you were ostracized for having kids out of wedlock, or not being a virgin when you got married," Kainene says. "Now those whispers have gone away."

Kainene tells me on every trip I make to Lagos that the

'pussy pool' keeps getting bigger and that, though she can't partake, these days she's spotting lesbians everywhere. Many are married, of course, and the moneyed ones have multiple mistresses the same way married straight men do. "There are girls who are being kept. The same way they go to parties for older men, they go to parties for older women and you get a 'thanks for coming' and maybe a little bit more: 'thanks for staying'. A lot of women in government have access to that kind of cash; it's pretty much the same as the men. Governor's wives, ministers, commissioner this, that and the other. They have the means. They have fulfilled all righteousness and their husbands are off with little girls, so they too are off with their own little girls – or little boys as the case may be."

Perhaps, like many, I have only seen what I wanted to see and not looked deeply into my society. Out of the hundreds of millions I've missed the lesbians hiding in plain sight simply because I wasn't paying attention. Every hot new venue I go to, Kainene knows of it already, and she and her lesbian friends hang out there and blend in undetected. From Caliente Club to the Buka Hut in Lekki to the Hard Rock Café Lagos, "We are just everywhere. In general Nigerians are not expressive in public whether you are straight or gay. We don't snog or hold hands in public. But it's alright for women to be affectionate with each other."

Accra is not much different from Lagos when it comes to women and their sexuality. Lesbians seem to be an open secret there, and one community among the Ga people of Accra has been known to voice complaints.

As an outsider, it's always been easy for me to spot the numerous gay men around Accra, even if it seems difficult for my heterosexual Ghanaian friends to do so. "Really?" they ask, surprised and curious as to what I've noticed that they have not. "You think he is?"

My buddy Sammy, an investment banker fond of saying I was the only gay man he knew, recognized he had blinders on after his brother-in-law introduced his male partner to him, shaking his head and saying, "I just always thought they were friends!"

However I couldn't spot gay women easily. And with all the

talk in Ghana a few years ago about how gays were awful and shouldn't be condoned, there was very little dialogue on women. A few headlines, yes, but they lacked the vitriol that accompanied talk about gay men. Perhaps it is because women's sexuality and the forms of its expression are considered less important than men's. People told me of the sizable number of gay women there but I couldn't see it. I had blinders on, as others did when it came to gay men in Ghana.

"If you asked me I think there are more lesbians in this country than there are gay men," says the journalist and broadcaster Ato Kwamena Dadzie. "People tolerate lesbians more than they tolerate gays. I think people feel it's okay to see two women lying together than it is to see two men lying together. They express more disgust at male relationships than female relationships, but it's one of our worst-kept secrets that in almost every female school girls are sleeping with girls."

I wonder what happens when these girls leave high school: do they remain lesbian or become wives to men? Were they just experimenting? Are they bisexual and happy enough to go either way? Who knew? But as Ato said, they are there, have always been there, and everyone knows it. "In every all-girls school there is a term for it – 'supi' – and it is interesting that there isn't an equivalent term for gay people in all-boys schools. I went to an all-boys school, and I don't remember a single incident of people saying this boy was sleeping with this boy. You go to any girls' school and they can tell you which girl is sleeping with which one," Ato adds.

My boarding school was co-ed and I didn't notice much, but my favorite historian, Uncle Nat, concurs: "Oh sure, this has always been there. Occasionally you'd hear complaints from husbands whose wives prefer to spend more time with their girlfriends than them. And then they take to the airwaves to talk about this 'bizarre fashion' among their womenfolk."

He tells me that one place where this was particularly common was an area in the heart of old Accra called Ga-Mashie, which has the historic Jamestown neighborhood at its center, with its old red lighthouse, which has always fascinated me. Ga-Mashie includes what is called British Accra, and next to it is the Bokum boxing village. All the Ghanaian boxers who made a name for themselves in the international realm, from the late, great Roy 'the Black Flash' Ankrah, who was a Commonwealth featherweight champion in the early 1950s, to Azumah Nelson, who is considered the greatest African boxer of all time, trace their success to their early training in Bokum.

I've always enjoyed going there and meeting the indigenous Ga people. They are fisher-folk, not very tall but often solidly built. Their culture gives pride of place to physical strength and prowess – especially in unarmed combat, where the emphasis is on fisticuffs, rather than using spears or other weapons. In the old times they didn't have quays deep enough for ships to dock at, so many Ga became stevedores, manning the canoes and surfboats that went out to the ships anchored along the coast. Many still row, and their upper bodies, torsos and arms are usually well-developed.

I'd learned from my earlier forays there that the name Ga comes from the word *gaga*, a ferocious ant, and so their totem is a termite. They are an itinerant people who were among the earliest to go deep-sea fishing on these coasts, and even today these areas are filled with fisher-folk. The population is very dense and, despite its rich history, it is now one of the poorer parts of greater Accra.

"This is an area that has suffered a terrible amount of social distortions in the last fifty to sixty years," Uncle Nat informs me. "The men used to be mostly fisherman whose trade has been vitiated by outboard motors. And also by the port of Tema, which has taken away their livelihood." In fact the decline of their stevedoring industry began with the building of the first big harbor in 1928 in Takoradi, one hundred and sixteen miles from Accra. Then the Tema harbor was built just eighteen miles away, in 1962. Today the fishermen struggle.

"They are not highly educated. Their traditional way of living was going out fishing, bringing the fish home and giving it to their wives, who marketed the fish and controlled the family's purse strings. The men are no longer the obvious breadwinners and I don't know whether it's the consequence of this, but it's one area where these intense female friendships manifest itself." But this community is not unique. "I want to emphasize that it's not the only area where these female relationships occur blatantly and obviously, but it's the one area where they complain a lot. Among the upper classes women have latitude to do what they want. They don't have to do it in front of their husbands; they can always travel somewhere, take a trip."

Those wealthier women, he said, live in grand houses with many rooms, and so when their girlfriends come over it's easy to do things behind closed doors and away from prying eyes. "It happens."

It interested me that these macho men in Ga-Mashie were aware of these lesbian relationships among their women – after all, they complained about them – but also grudgingly accepted them.

In the midst of this dense, relatively low-income part of Jamestown there is a chop bar where local gay men congregate, and everyone seems to accept them too. Ian often hangs out with his Jamestown buddies there – fishermen, mostly, and tailors. They drink and have fun and in some cases have sexual encounters. No labels are used but the relationships are known of. Over the years some have gone on to get married and have children, and many have learned to read and write through Ian's generosity – he's paid for adult education classes for them. Yet in the country at large, even in the more affluent areas, these kinds of relationships are not tolerated, and family members are shunned if they dare to 'experiment'.

When I show Uncle Nat a newspaper article asserting that gay men could be tried in court, but that current Ghanaian laws were silent on lesbians, he laughs. Then adds more seriously, "We inherited a British legal system that condemned sodomy which is still on the books. These laws were written fifty years ago when they didn't dare think their women had sexual drives for men much less for women."

For younger people staying in the closet is proving more and more difficult to do.

Gemma Salifu was just twenty years old when Salase, a reporter friend, introduced us in 2014. Salase and I were friendly even before he came to New York to study at Columbia University. Now he has returned to Accra, and he makes time to meet up with me whenever I come to town. He knew I would find Gemma fascinating.

Like my friend Fred Mahama, she is originally from Bolgatanga. Though the area has both a large Muslim population and a small but centuries-old Catholic community, Gemma is a Jehovah's Witness. When we talked she had just been admitted to study art and sculpture at the Kwame Nkrumah University of Science & Technology in Kumasi, and was looking forward to beginning the fall semester there. She's always known she is a lesbian.

"When I was in first grade, my sister used to have all these friends come around. I liked them a lot and we used to play like we were getting married." By the time she was enrolled in Tema Secondary School she was very comfortable with her identity as a lesbian. She knew all about 'supi' in high school but says she never dated anyone there; she met her girlfriends outside the school environment.

Gemma is a pretty, slender girl with braids and dark chocolate-colored skin. Each time we met she wore colorful tops and jeans with boots. I wouldn't easily peg her as a lesbian, but I'm not good at spotting those who aren't overtly butch. The idea of sleeping with men freaks her out. "It just does. I like fem."

Meeting women in Accra she says is no problem. "My friend has a Facebook page where everyone on there is a lesbian: studs, fems, and stems." My newfound lesbian friend explains to me that studs are the women who take on the role of provider and protector in relationships, and tend to look more masculine or butch, while fems are the feminine ones, high heels, make-up and all. "Stem is a mix between a stud and a fem. The stems are stems because of how their family is." I take this to mean they would be studs if they could get away with it. As with feminine gay men, "Some of my friends say their parents burn their stuff. It is tough."

In Gemma's case, all her family now know she's a lesbian. When she was fourteen she confided in an elder sister who kept silent about it, but two years later the entire family found out inadvertently. "One time I was walking around with my girlfriend and we stopped to make out. It was not too far from my house." She says initially she was nervous about doing such a thing on the street, but "after our lips touched I didn't care. My brother was driving around. He just looked at me and just passed by and when I got home my mum was like what were we doing? It was pretty much awkward."

That brother had lived in Florida, so outside of telling the family he didn't make much of a fuss, but another elder brother insisted on trying to set her up with a man.

But "I told my mum I'm not getting married. Sometimes when I dress up she says, 'When I see you I get sad. You have a nice figure; why don't you just wear a dress?'" Gemma prefers button up shirts. "I just feel weird wearing dresses and wearing heels. It's just not me!" While her family hasn't tried to kick her out, she says other women get married out of that fear. "It's not everyone who has something to fall on, so once they say, 'If you don't stick by my rules, leave,' it kind of makes you think about stuff."

She's not dating now but was in love with her last girlfriend. It was often difficult to tell people that her 'best friend' was in fact her partner. They only felt free at clubs, she says, where they could mingle with other women and dance together, hiding in plain sight.

One club she mentions is Firefly in Osu, a favorite of mine and just steps away from the flat I rent. Firefly is a lounge bar with tall bar-stools and faux-brick walls. It has a wide range of premium liquors on offer, and is considered one of the places to go by Accra's sophisticates as well as its young expatriate crew. It's also an unofficial hub for some in Accra's Lebanese community. It is posh, then, and one's first impression is of a very heteronormative space that on the weekends is packed with elegant ladies and gentlemen dressed to the nines. How, I wonder now, could I not have spotted the lesbians there? But like the bars in Lagos, there's often a crew of gorgeous ladies dancing with each other.

Still, Gemma says, in clubs, "You kind of have to be wary when you see somebody who knows your family. Jehovah's Witnesses are everywhere. Some of them, they seem all spiritual in church and then you see them in the club. They go to Tantra [another upscale nightclub] and Firefly. When they have a few drinks then they start talking."

Like many young, middle-class gay men and women in Ghana, Gemma believes her future is abroad – most likely in America, where her sister has already gained admission to Columbia University in New York as a graduate student. She says it is hard to pretend to be straight, and harder still to put up with the crude Ghanaian men who offer themselves up to 'change' her. She always responds the same way: "'Why would I want to sleep with you? If I met your girlfriend she won't want to go back to you!' Sometimes they get really upset, they want to fight. I don't fight. I'm a lover not a fighter."

She won't be like the married lesbians in Accra, she says. "I know someone who is married to a guy, she has two kids and she has a girlfriend and her husband knows. He's okay with it." That life isn't for her, she insists, but her resistance is rare. These married women shower younger lesbians with gifts and cash, to seduce them into being their side chicks. Gemma had one woman offer her a couple of hundred dollars "just to hang out". In Ghana, that translates to over a whopping five hundred cedis. Gemma declined.

Gemma's pal Sabine Maier, who created the Facebook social page where gay women could share their thoughts freely, told me that in Ghana married women lavishing gifts and cash on younger girls is very common, confirming what Uncle Nat told me. "I've got a couple of [married upper middle-class Accra ladies] who offered me money but I didn't accept," Sabine, who was twenty years old at the time, revealed. She too didn't want to be a side chick.

"There's this married woman who wanted to have a thing with me. She's married with kids and she was offering me one thousand dollars." It was tempting. But Sabine doesn't do affairs. "Obviously they are not going to push their husband away because that's where the money is coming from. No woman in Ghana wants to do that." One even offered her a car. It's the way things are done with women, she insists. "A lot of straight women are broke. Most [side chicks] are 'gay for pay'," and transactional hook-ups are not uncommon.

Sabine is biracial. Her mother is Nigerian, her father is German, and she was born in Nigeria. She's lived in Accra since she was ten years old and to her it is home. She is cool and beautiful, light-skinned with strong features. Her hair is short but relaxed into curls. She favors T-shirts with bold, bright prints, jeans, and sneakers or boots. She is, she says, a stud.

"Studs are, they act more like the guy and try to be more responsible, to be the father. They are to be that one that is always going to be there for the woman and the kids." And indeed her desire is to settle down with one woman and have some kids. She won't be a mother though. "I will still be a parent but act more like a father. With me I think being masculine helps in so many ways, gives you some kind of courage. You look like a guy, and you have to take a lot of responsibilities from the guy's point of view." Sabine told me that one of the worst things about being so open in Accra was the way society judged her and other studs. "They look at you like you are going to burn in hell. Sometimes they look at you like the devil is here."

As in so many societies, everything in Ghana is okay behind closed doors but problematic once out in the open. Starting groups on Facebook to create a space for women where they can talk freely was Sabine's response to this. "Some people can't talk to anyone because they are just scared of what people might say, or what people would say about you, or where your name would be going. I just want them to be safe."

She's a tough stud. Even the hurtful 'devil' comments she says don't faze her; nor when market women don't want to sell to her. She just moves on. "I don't really mind what people say. People do talk. My mindset in life is, you do good, you do bad, you do this, you do that, they are still going to talk. They will never shut up."

Though young, she is remarkably self-sufficient, something that is especially difficult in a place like Accra. She works as a personal assistant, and has a small fast food concern and a tiny barbershop that she runs on the side. She has no plans to go to college in Ghana, and aims to relocate to Canada in the next few years.

Sabine's European father took her sexuality better than her mother, just expressing a desire to have grandchildren. (Her parents are divorced and her father is now married to a Ghanaian woman.) Her mother was another matter. "I told her when I was eighteen. She was about to slap me until I moved backward. She wasn't really pleasant with it." She remembers her mother trying to talk to her about it being "a bad thing, blah, blah, blah. Then I really knew I was [gay] so there was no turning back. Right now she's just trying to accept me."

Her mother now lives in Lagos with Sabine's younger sibling. The relationship is still strained.

Even as a little girl Sabine knew she was different. This was when she was growing up in Lagos, before they moved to Accra. She was sure by age nine, though she had no words for it, just, "When I see ladies I get really shy and try to be on my best behavior." She's currently dating a twenty-five-year-old, very fem girl. She prefers older women and so far it's smooth sailing. A few people know of the relationship but not her girlfriend's mother yet.

Like Gemma, and despite her studly appearance, Sabine gets her share of crass guys offering to turn her straight. "There was this guy that was bragging about sex, that he would turn me into a fem, and I said, 'OK, alright': I said, 'Can I have your girlfriend for one night?' He said, 'What are you going to do?' I said, 'Let me have your girlfriend for one night and I promise you she's not going to come back to you.' He gave me his girlfriend's number and I called her and hooked up with her and I had sex with her, and a week later this girl broke up with the guy and she was like she wants to go out with me. I said, 'Look I have a girlfriend, what we had is just a fling.'"

So for Sabine one of the best things about being a lesbian in Accra is that, every once in a while, "You get to tell a guy that he can't fuck better than a girl can."

Even as I feared for her safety in an environment so full of potential male sexual violence, I loved her laddish braggadocio.

She doesn't think she will ever marry a man.

"People who shut their eyes to reality simply invite their own destruction, and anyone who insists on remaining in a state of innocence long after that innocence is dead turns himself into a monster."

– James Baldwin

Sixteen: Holding On While Seeking Asylum

Accra, June 24 2016.

It is a Friday evening and I'm beat. I've been having trouble with the erratic behavior of an undergraduate student, one of my charges on an international reporting program I'm running out of Ghana. When I had him as a journalism student in New York he was a bit of an oddball but seemed okay overall; most young people have a weirdness adjustment phase, particularly in America, so to me this was no big deal. But since he landed in Accra a month ago he's become both combative and antisocial. A tall, lanky Asian national who keeps finding fault with his teammates and his surroundings, he is generally a pain in the ass, and I'm becoming worried he will hurt himself or others.

He has recently become addicted to extremely lengthy late-night phone conversations with me. Of course I tell my students they can call me anytime they want to, and they all have my mobile phone number, but most have some sense of boundaries. The situation is getting ridiculous, as these late-night calls are invariably about nothing in particular. Knowing

I view my position as the faculty member who brought them to Ghana as a permanently on-call one, and that I will always answer the phone to him, he'll call. And call and call, just to talk. And talk. And be argumentative. This means I have to pay attention, and it can become stressful.

One student was so unnerved by him when he began discussing terrorist extremists in ways that could be considered sympathetic, that he complained about it to me. This and the endless phone-calls have combined with his new thing of not eating to heighten my stress-levels across the last four weeks.

To relieve the tension I work out more often, at the modern Pippas gym around the corner from the flat I rent in the Maxwell Court complex. My entire Ghana support system is missing in action. Two weeks earlier my sounding board and brother Andres, the West Africa bureau chief for Bloomberg News, left to take up a new position in South America. After five years of being the West Africa bureau chief for *The Wall Street Journal* our mutual dear friend Drew, another sounding board, has also packed up his family and returned to America, en route to a new job in Europe. And even my pal Christa has decamped to Cape Town with her husband for the month; while my buddy Nii Obodai Provencal, the acclaimed photographer, has left first for Brazil, and then Europe.

And so I am left to stress out about this student with his jihadi mutterings by pumping iron at the gym, or pounding up and down the lanes of the new swimming pool the owners of Maxwell Court have installed, attempting to console myself with the thought that at least I am getting fitter.

This particular Friday night I am looking forward to relaxing with a couple of Buck's Fizzes and maybe some white wine later on at Monsoon: I could deal with the phone calls I knew were sure to come from there.

As is my habit I check my email before heading out, and I happen to see a note from one of the most respected gay Nigerians in Chicago, a man everyone fondly refers to as 'Uncle John'. The subject line reads: *Urgent! Urgent! Urgent!*

"Now what?" I mutter out loud as I click on it.

The body of the email, which includes his phone-number, asks that I call him immediately, or that I ring Mark, another activist I'm acquainted with who has been helpful to the community. As it was sent some hours ago I don't rush to make the call, but instead click on the next email, which turns out to be from Mark. The subject line reads 'Nigerian Traveler at O'Hare', and Uncle John is copied into it. I read on.

Hello Frankie – I hope you remember me. I am Kent Klindera's friend Mark. You helped me several years ago with my travels to Accra, and I met you in person last October at Kent's place when he celebrated his fiftieth birthday. I work with a group here in Chicago called CLASP (Chicago LGBT Asylum Support Partners). I have copied to our founder John. We are all friends of Kent and of Oliver also, in NY.

This morning I received a call from an ICE [Immigration and Customs Enforcement] *officer at O'Hare airport. He told me that they had a traveler who arrived on a flight from Nigeria. The traveler only had one local phone number in his contacts, mine, but the contact was listed as 'Eddie's Friend (SP?)'. The only Eddie from Nigeria who I can think of is you, from your last name. Do you know if someone from Nigeria is traveling to Chicago? Thanks for any help you can offer.*

Oh boy, I thought. Not again. Another gay man, probably after going through some trauma, has escaped, landed in the United States, and is seeking asylum.

After some mailing back and forth with the two of them I determined that I didn't know this person, and there seemed nothing I could do, but asked that they keep me in the loop.

Uncle John provides asylum support for LGBT Africans in Chicago; so do Housing Works in New York, and there are other similar groups around America.

In recent years the African LGBT asylee network has been growing exponentially, and the number of friends I know who are in this boat keeps swelling. Many of the cases begin with being ostracized, and then degenerate into violent victimization. That's how it was with Azziz, a dapper twenty-nine year old model I met several years ago, here in Accra.

Azziz was also dabbling in acting, and traded clothes from his living room while pursuing his creative work. He'd been in a few commercials, he said, though I'd never seen them. But then I rarely watched television when in Ghana. He was always one for bold colors, and he favored the woody fragrance fronted by Antonio Banderas, the heartthrob Spanish actor and filmmaker, the scent always announcing him before he appeared.

Azziz is an Accra guy. He was born and bred in Nima, a densely-populated neighborhood that is chock-full of Muslims like himself, and when I met him he still lived there, just off the Kanda Highway. His family originally came from Mali and are ethnically Hausa. As well as being extremely crowded, Nima is one of the poorest districts in Ghana's capital city, and is populated with families from the predominantly Muslim north, as well as from Nigeria, Côte d'Ivoire, Burkina Faso, Senegal and all around West Africa. No matter where they come from, though, almost everyone there speaks Hausa. It is as blue collar as it gets, and family bonds there are strong. Though poverty-levels are high, there is a sense of tight-knit community; and some here, despite being wealthy, still mingle with the push-carts and livestock – goats, cows, chickens – that stalk the narrow streets.

Azziz has never lived anywhere else and knows no other community. He has lived, as he puts it, "crowded" with other Muslims forever. "I am a Muslim. Pure Muslim. I pray five times [daily]; I go to mosque; I recite Koran." But he also told me, when I first got to know him back in 2014, that admitting his gay identity to his family, which he did in 2008, unleashed such a backlash in the area that he is still in shock. Even these many years later the feelings are so raw that the memory triggers a torrent of tears from the otherwise always jovial Azziz. He says he was just twenty-two, and dating a man in Nima, when a friend of his cousin happened to see him in the man's home wearing nothing but his boxers. The man was rumored to be gay, the friend told the cousin, and the legendary Ghanaian rumor mill began to churn. After having people in the community spy on him for a while, Azziz's mother, sisters, aunts and uncles summoned him.

"They called me and asked me, 'Are you gay?' Actually my heart jumped. I got scared. I'm from a big family. Very well-known family. In Hausa they say Dan Daudu. 'Do you sleep with men?'"

The accusations, made by a large group of relatives – folks he'd always been close to – unnerved him, but his torture was just beginning. The term Dan Daudu (or in some places 'Yan Daudu') can be loosely translated as not just gay but femininely gay, and is often highly pejorative. Azziz was cornered. But he didn't deny it. He looked them in the eye and owned up. He owned his identity.

"I said, 'Yes. I do.'"

His defiance was courageous. But it wasn't a freeing moment. The family began verbally attacking him and it all went downhill from there. "Trust me, it was very difficult. It was bad. I didn't know what was going on." They confronted him with the names of men he had visited in the area, four of whom he'd slept with. "They know much about it, so when they asked me I didn't deny... I was shocked and surprised and... it was very embarrassing to me. I was twenty-two, very young and beautiful. They were so mad at me, hating me. They called me names: 'Banza!' It's like outcast." But his humiliation didn't end there. Admitting was one thing, but refusing to change his ways was a whole other drama. "They asked me to stop and I shouldn't be gay. I said, 'I can't change my sexuality. I can't be straight. I can't be 'normal'. It is who I am.'"

Since the shaming wasn't enough, they then told his father, who hadn't initially been present, and then all hell really broke loose. His father fetched his dagger and tried to cut Azziz. Azziz ran from the room to avoid being stabbed, and that was the end of him living in the home he'd grown up in. His father chased him out. As if that was not enough, his father then "burned all my stuff, my clothes, my documents, my high school papers [certificates], everything." Azziz was taken in by a maternal aunt who lived nearby – in Nima quarters are tight, and he knew nowhere else to go further afield. More cripplingly he was left with no proof of education or even identity. He had to start over.

Father and son have not spoken in over six years. "He's nearby but he doesn't want to see me. He despises me," Azziz says, in that matter-of-fact way that says either he's come to terms with the rejection or is pushing down deep pain. "He hates me." During this time his mother passed away.

Azziz is certain that he's not the only gay one in the family, just the one who had the misfortune to be exposed. "I have cousins who I know are gay. It's very difficult."

His maternal aunt, the one he went and lived with, continually asks him to pray to change, and also to try and make overtures to his father – as do his two sisters, who live in Germany. These women are the few family members he's on reasonably good terms with. His skin has grown thicker in the passing years. He's no less gay, and is defiant with extended family members, and with strangers. His focus is on success in his chosen careers, modeling and acting.

"Everybody in my family knows and it's not everybody I talk to. You can't confront me and ask me because [now] I'm very rude and harsh. Yes I am. I wouldn't tolerate it. I don't take nonsense."

He speaks to some of his brothers but they don't accept him. His work in commercials is seen as a gateway to homosexuality and is not lauded as a worthy career choice.

While he's let go of the fear, the hurt lingers, and anger has crept in to stay. He has no plans to make up with his father because he is still furious with him. Most recently he'd been in a relationship with a man who was supposedly heterosexual and had girlfriends. Azziz claimed he loved the sex, and pretended to be the man's buddy to keep it going. I think he craved the intimacy far more than the sex, and would take it in any form he could get it. The relationship cracked when the boyfriend – despite being 'straight' – began getting jealous, and accused Azziz of cheating on him with other men.

After that he refocused on his career, every now and then paying a certain 'man prostitute' he was fond of for intimacy. He fielded many offers too, and – ironically enough – sometimes charged for his company, particularly in dry revenue moments when the commercials weren't coming in.

"I have people who want to be in a relationship with me. And I have some friends that, when I financially need them, I call them. Sometimes I give them sex. Then they pay me. I've been with so many married men. Like, twelve. Some are Muslims, a few in Nima. I need what they have, their money."

Back in 2014 Azziz had no plans to leave Nima, but said if he got a chance to escape Ghana entirely, he would love to. "I want to run from Ghana, so I could have my life, my gay life and wear the colors of gay. I want to be gay, fully gay entirely."

I remember an urgent email I got from him the following summer, in 2015, similar to the one I just received from Uncle John, saying that he'd found his way to California, and had begun his long, hard slog to claim asylum and live freely. We emailed back and forth about lawyers and resettling, and he began the process, but his American dream was slow to materialize. While he waited for approval to work, living hand-to-mouth, his struggle continued.

Azziz was ultimately granted asylum in 2016 and settled in the Bronx, trying to begin all over again. Working not at modeling or acting, but just to put a roof over his head, he found another pal of mine, Agaba, an Idoma man from north-east Nigeria who had also been through the asylum process, and he stays with him sometimes, using his address as a base.

Agaba is a quiet, slender and very handsome chap who I've always enjoyed being around. We aren't the closest, but I admire the dignified way he carries himself when we are out at bourbon nights or at parties in the Big Apple. Agaba was one of the first Nigerians I knew who'd successfully applied for asylum in the U.S. based on sexual orientation and fear of persecution for being gay. He'd been an aspiring singer in Abuja, while earning a living by working as a sexual health peer educator in neighboring Nassarawa state. His role was to educate men in underground networks about safe sex, with the goal of reducing rates of sexually-transmitted infections, particularly HIV. A sheltered 'born again' Christian for most of his life, when he finally had intimate relations with men in Abuja, Agaba knew little about sex. And then he got infected with HIV. So he worked hard at his job.

In 2010 he worked on a project financed by the Global Fund to Fight AIDS, Tuberculosis & Malaria. He went deep into Hausa communities, working with interpreters by day, and in the evening throwing parties with friends who brought friends along to have fun and talk about sexual health. As Nassarawa was, and is, a majority Muslim community these were all-male affairs; he had zero access to women. "In the Hausa community in Nassarawa the women don't have power like the men. Some of those men – even though they were young, some of them were married, and they have families and they have male lovers. Many of my clients were married. A lot."

Some months after their arrival, Agaba and his team were summoned to the traditional ruler's palace and were questioned. He began to have problems once the emir spoke to him. He recalls it was a genial conversation, but, "One of the things he told me was, 'We heard white men are giving you money to recruit homosexuals.' I said we are teaching men to take charge of their life. We know this is a Muslim community so it's the man that has power."

Agaba contacted his bosses, saying that to continue the project might be dangerous for him, but they insisted that the work must continue. He started getting threatening messages on his phone, with the senders describing his movements, what he was wearing that day, and warning him that his cup was full. Then a mob harassed him, scaring him more than the messages because he believed it was instigated by the emir's police, and he could have been killed with impunity.

At this time Nigeria's parliament was hotly debating the bill banning same sex marriage and, more generally, further criminalizing LGBT people. Agaba and many other activists had joined with other civil society groups to testify against it. That effort had yielded nothing, and he was left feeling uneasy and exposed. His music career was going nowhere and his activism work was going to get him hurt. So when he was notified that his sponsorship application to attend the International AIDS Conference in Washington D.C. had been accepted, he was ecstatic. Not only would he go to America to present on his work, but he would also get to sing at the conference.

He hadn't gone with any plan to seek asylum, but as the conference in Washington came to a close, the rhetoric in Nigeria was ratcheting up, and Agaba and two other attendees broke down; they knew they could not return to that climate of hate and violence. Another conference attendee took them under his wing and brought them to New York, where the AIDS advocacy organization Housing Works took them in. Agaba spent the next year and a half trying to get asylum. Eventually it was granted, and he was among the first wave of those who came from West Africa seeking help because who they were put them in mortal danger.

"After the conference there were people who flooded Immigration Equality," he says. "Other Nigerians that we that did not know. Because of the bill many didn't want to go home. They never had gay men from West Africa coming to America to seek asylum because of their sexuality [before]. Our face was known as the face of [the gay opposition at home]. We knew we were going to be in danger."

Agaba today, at the age of forty-one, has clawed his way up from the bottom of American society and lives a quiet, normal existence in the Bronx. He's gotten a university degree in entertainment business, and hopes to restart his singing career sometime. He hasn't been able to go home, and probably will not be able to until he becomes an American citizen, a process that takes years.

His stepmother, who is the woman who raised him, died recently, and he was able to participate in her burial preparations only via telephone. His family never talks about his sexuality, but in a subtle way they let him know they understand. "My brother said, 'What are you coming to Nigeria for? Haven't you suffered enough?'" And even before he left, his beloved sister used to say to him, "You don't belong here. Just go."

Now he works long hours as a healthcare advocate for Housing Works. His apartment, though it has only one bedroom, is open to newcomers, and somehow, through the gay African word-of-mouth network, Azziz found him when he landed in New York; they had never met prior to that.

Of course it's not unusual for immigrants in America to start over, clambering up from the lowest rung of the socioeconomic ladder, whatever the reasons for their arrival. Another dear friend of mine, Norbert Edet, like me grew up in Lagos. Ten years my junior, he's a college-educated accountant who had a career there as a retail banker. A chain smoker, he is soft spoken with an infectious smile. He's very Lagos, born in Mushin, a crowded lower-income neighborhood, and bred in Lagos and also Abuja, where his mother worked for a while as a civil servant. He isn't particularly religious, but his speech is always inflected with phrases like 'By His Grace' and 'Jesus' and 'Amen oh!'

By his early thirties he had all the trappings of a prosperous middle-class existence in Lagos. He lived in a nice three-bedroom flat and had a good car to go with it, a Rover from Britain, and was earning a stable and competitive salary. A dark and lovely fellow, a charmer and an Oceanic Big Boy, obviously he had the obligatory girlfriend to show off in public, as well as a string of secret boyfriends.

"I lived a straight life but I had a lover and some partners. I've always wanted to be with a guy. Since I was about six years old. I didn't know what to do or where to touch but I just had this feeling I should be with a guy," he recalls one day in my office in New York. He often drops by in the afternoons, sometimes to join me for lunch, other times just to gist a little between errands.

He'd never had full sexual intercourse with a man until he was thirty, and even masturbation sent him to confession. He had attempts, he said, at the university where he was studying accounting, but never went all the way. His gay life began in 2007, when he was befriended by a colleague and they began a clandestine relationship. The colleague showed him how to touch, how to kiss, and they masturbated together. Norbert dumped his girlfriend of more than a year. Then, "I told him I needed to experience the gay life in full. I'm new in this thing. I don't know if I'm going to be top or bottom but I needed... either you're going to fuck me or I fuck you. He told me he doesn't do anal sex. I could fuck his lap but no anal sex. So after we continued for about a year plus, he still was not going to give it to me, I told him, if he cannot give it to me then we can't continue because I really, really have waited so many years to have this experience, till now. I'm an adult. Here you are, not giving me what I want."

Norbert tells me he knew his guy had other men because his phone was always buzzing, and that because he was girly he got men making passes at him – something Norbert did not. Norbert had cultivated a macho manner that sprang out of his humiliation at being called a 'woman wrapper' as a teenager because of his then-girly ways. So no one made a pass at him, and he didn't know where to go to meet other men.

After they broke up, a friend with whom Norbert had had sex a few times, but had no interest in dating, introduced him to other gay men and showed him websites, and so he found a gay community.

The friend took him to the bars near the beach and to the theater, gave his number to others, and steeped him in the protective measures Lagos gay men have to take: always meet in public – like at fast food restaurants such as Tantalizers or Mr. Biggs – to scope a potential partner out first; never bring anyone home right away in case they turn out to be fraudsters and begin harassing you, etcetera.

"I always went for younger guys. I'd been having sex with ladies but I knew there was more. Being gay always gave me the satisfaction I desired. I was pleased and I was happy. It's just that you cannot express yourself fully; you are not allowed to hold hands or be with who you want to be, where and when. You have to hide, and fear to be caught."

He found himself a boyfriend with whom he fell in love, but continued to have wild sex with a lot of the other men he was now coming into contact with. All this while he'd been moving up the retail banking ladder at the popular Oceanic bank (later subsumed into the bigger Ecobank).

It all began to unravel in late 2013, when he used a gay website to chat with a man who was wooing him. Gay chat sites like Manjam and Planet Romeo are very popular in Lagos and Accra. He recalls the fella was a white guy who said he was European. Norbert loved the international connection, and the dude at some point said he was an architect and was coming to Nigeria soon on business. They exchanged photos, and Norbert promised to pick him up when he got to Lagos and show him around town. They chatted frequently about their jobs, and the man asked about the branch of the bank where Norbert worked, and if he could help him with money transfers. Norbert was open and shared information honestly.

They spoke every day for almost a month. When a request was made for racy pictures Norbert made a couple of short raunchy videos of himself naked, winding his waist and talking dirty. He dispatched one of these over his BlackBerry to 'the white guy in Europe'. It was on a Sunday afternoon, about four p.m.

At six p.m. Norbert got a menacing call from an unfamiliar Nigerian number, with a guy telling him he knew he fucked men and warning him to 'cooperate'. The blackmail had begun. In reality his European friend turned out to be Nigerian fraudsters. They let him know they had pictures of his car, and reminded him they knew of his ability to gain access to cash through his banking job.

Norbert panicked. The video showed his face and was full-frontal. Every day he got angry calls and texts. He deleted the number but the blackmailers were persistent. One day he became aware some guys were following him down the street. Coincidence? Fear gripped him. Nothing happened that time, but paranoia set in. Life was fast becoming unlivable, and so he called a policeman friend of his brother's and arranged to meet him in a bar. There he confessed all.

"It was really hard for me, but it had become a life and death situation and I needed help. I knew he wouldn't out me because he was my brother's friend. He told me not to pay any money because if I give they would keep coming back."

Norbert took the advice but the threats escalated, with the blackmailers saying they knew where he lived and worked, and that they would call his head office and get him fired. They also rained down abuses on him, calling him 'faggot' and 'idiot', and saying that he would be punished by God for his sexuality. He continued working, however, and the calls got fewer and fewer as he wasn't ponying up anything. It seemed he might weather this storm.

A month into the blackmail calls, Norbert's father died. This was in early September, 2014. In December he took some weeks off to go bury his dad in the village the family hails from. When he returned to work on January 7, 2015, he found a letter waiting for him on his desk, terminating his employment. No reason was given. He'd been working with the bank since 2007; his standing was high; he had never had any issues with his employers and was considered a rising star. He believes – I'm sure correctly – that, though the letter of termination made no reference to it, the video was sent to his head office. At thirty-four, and for the first time in his life, he was suddenly out of a job. He says that it hurt that after seven years with an unblemished record he was let go without explanation.

Months passed. He was living in fear: he had refused to pay up, and had a friend who was violently assaulted by someone who had blackmailed him. And so Norbert went underground. He had no job. He'd lost his career over a blackmail situation he could barely tell anyone about – after all he was gay – and nobody could do anything about getting his job back. Certainly his bank wouldn't want to deal with the scandal, and he was placed in the difficult situation of doubting he could go to them for a reference for other employers.

For six months he tried to find work, making ends meet in the meantime by selling his big ticket items, and making the pastry snacks called 'chin-chin' and selling them to individual buyers and to hawkers near his home. Norbert is a born and bred Lagosian, and the ability to hustle is ingrained. The profit was marginal but at least he had some sort of an income.

And then it came: the approval for a U.S. visa, which he had applied for while working at the bank. It was a short-stay visa to attend a business event. By then he'd managed to get a job as a teller in another town outside the state, but his mind was uneasy: that video was still out there; not only might the blackmail start up again, but he was also afraid of his family finding out, particularly his nieces and nephews, who saw him as a role model.

And so Norbert ended up on a plane to New York, and at thirty-four he was homeless, jobless, and having to begin his life all over again. He brought all his savings with him, a few thousand dollars in cash. All his certificates were from Nigeria so he couldn't just walk into a place and get a white-collar job, and in any case he had no work permits.

After hooking up with the trove of other Nigerians who had used programs for asylum seekers run by nonprofits like Immigration Equality and Housing Works, he decided to try for help himself. At some point while they were working on getting a proper legal application filed for him, he ended up at a homeless shelter on Staten Island. While he was there I would try to see him each weekend and take him places and keep his spirits up.

He looked forward, rarely talking about the things he had left behind, and adapted to the dusk-to-dawn curfews and other constraints of life in a shelter. A series of odd jobs followed – washing dishes in restaurants; delivering food. He always cooked, so I put him in touch with a rather unique restaurant near my office.

While to most patrons Colors is simply a spiffy Manhattan

eatery that serves gluten-free food, for those in the know it is also a training program for restaurant workers, particularly those on hard times who can't afford to go to culinary schools. Norbert did the program and learned commercial cooking, waitering, and how to do several other jobs in a restaurant.

That was the springboard for his finding a job as a short order cook. He worked in a restaurant by day, and went to classes to become a nurse's aide by night. No more banking for Norbert: he is on the verge of a new career in caregiving. He's also moved into a small flat on Staten Island while waiting to be granted asylum. His family has no idea of his shelter stay or his new life.

"It will hurt them to realize who I really am. I hope that someday I may have the courage to come out. Having the mindset, the culture back home of husband and wife, man and woman, and then them finding out that their uncle is something different, it's em... I'm embarrassed. I will lose my family and their parents will take them away from me. Apart from confusing them, I will not have access to my family. They will allow me to make my decision but they would fear that I would corrupt their kids."

Could he be wrong, I ask. Maybe once they know all he's gone through they might be supportive? But Norbert shakes his head and says it would be the end if they found out.

"I will become alienated, away from everybody. I feel nobody will want me. Being the kind of culture we come from, family is everything. I cannot imagine myself without a family. Who is going to share my joys or my sorrows with me? They are not that liberal when it comes to issues like that."

In the spring on 2017 Norbert was finally granted asylum. My buddy Kent and I had penned passionate letters in support of his application, and we were relieved. His siblings and mother came to visit but Norbert tells me he's kept the details of his odyssey from them. How mysterious they must find his life and choices!

Since 2012, Housing Works, an AIDS advocacy organization that fights for the marginalized, and the group that initially helped Norbert, has been working on an asylum program to help other LGBT Africans. This work was begun by happenstance, as a consequence of helping Agaba, along with two other Nigerians and a Liberian who were also in America for the World AIDS Conference, and couldn't return home after their sexuality was revealed.

That happened because a *Washington Post* reporter had thoughtlessly blogged about some African conference participants going to a gay bar in town and dancing freely. The thrust of his innocently-intended piece was that these men were enjoying a freedom to be themselves in a way they couldn't back home. But the article made its way to the Nigerian media, and those named were castigated on the airwaves.

Michael Ighodaro was one of the unlucky men but returned home anyway, only to find a firestorm awaiting him. "He didn't tell me he was doing an interview," Michael told Sahara-TV some years later. "I didn't even know he was from *Wash Post*. He took my picture and my name and published it online. I got back to Nigeria after the conference only to find my picture was there as a gay Nigerian talking about gay rights in America. I received threat messages, my house was attacked. I was forced to leave."

Agaba too remembers the reporter being friendly, and says that he, like everyone else, had no idea a story was planned, and that it was shocking to see their names and faces online. It was a grotesque and angering irony that a journalist reporting on gay men enjoying freedom abroad could be so thoughtless as to place those same gay men in jeopardy in their home countries. Perhaps he thought Africa doesn't have the Internet.

Agaba was also frustrated that the focus of the reporting became activists partying in D.C., and that their good work at the conference was ignored – they had done strong presentations on ways of improving HIV care, and access to that care, even with limited resources.

By the end of 2015 the Housing Works asylum project had assisted LGBT Jamaicans, Ugandans and Mexicans as well as Nigerians. As of this writing, at least two dozen people have been supported with housing while they await their initial asylum hearing, a process which can take up to a year. During this time Housing Works places them in volunteer positions, as a way to train them for job opportunities if they are eventually granted asylum, providing a modest hundred or two hundred dollar a week stipend. They also house them in rented apartments in Brooklyn until they get on their feet.

Norbert wasn't housed by them, nor did he volunteer with them, but he did speak with their legal assistance advocates, who helped craft his application. When he first arrived in New York he was optimistic, but as the process wore on, and it proved difficult to find meaningful work, the spark in his eyes dimmed. He worked day and night for meager wages, and to see him for lunch became a challenge. It was rare for him to have a free day, and when he did, he simply wanted to sleep.

Often when my buddy Kent had house parties I'd insist that Norbert come along, to get out of the house in a non-work-related way, see others in the same boat as himself, and meet some of those who'd been through it and survived. He's attractive and gets a lot of attention, but even the thrill of being wanted soon seemed to wane; the troubles of an asylee are heavy. While no reliable statistics exist for LGBT Africans seeking asylum in the U.S., to me it seems the numbers are going up. Uncle John's CLASP, the Chicago LGBT Asylum Support Program, was formed in early 2014 to help the many LBGT Africans who find themselves in this boat.

Others are helping those unmoored by the rising morass of anti-gay hate on my continent. A few years ago, through Kent, I met Bert Kay. He was a Ugandan activist whose 'husband' was killed by what he suspected were anti-gay men. His story, along with those of other LGBT advocates, was depicted in the documentaries *God Loves Uganda* and *Call Me Kuchu*.

When Ugandan president Yoweri Museveni allowed the infamous 'Kill the Gays' bill to unleash terror on gay Ugandans in 2014 many were brutalized, and many fled to neighboring countries. Nairobi, Kenya's capital, while not exactly a beacon of gay acceptance, was a destination for many. According to the United Nations High Commission for Refugees (UNHCR), in August 2015 there were some five hundred registered LGBTI asylum-seekers in Kenya.

A few, like Bert, ended up in New York. He was part of the group SMUG (Sexual Minorities Uganda) that sought to take the Massachusetts pastor Scott Lively to court for stoking the flames of hate in Uganda – a campaign that bore toxic fruit in the viciously extreme Anti-Homosexuality Act. Lively co-wrote

The Pink Swastika, a book in which he and co-author Kevin Abrams claimed that gays were the true inventors of Nazism. Essentially a nonentity in America, he's taken the culture wars abroad, seeing Africa as fertile ground for sowing his extremist antigay agenda under the cover of wholesome evangelical Christianity and 'protecting children'. He was being sued in the U.S. by SMUG for violating international laws and trying to deny Ugandans their basic human rights, and it was this legal action, which Bert became a part of, that led to his being in America.

At the invitation of evangelicals there, Lively went to Uganda in 2009 to deliver a seminar titled 'Exposing the Homosexual's Agenda'. As he would later boast, it had the effect of "a nuclear bomb". Lively's work is detailed in *God Loves Uganda*. He claimed that gays were coming to 'recruit' Ugandan children and tear their society apart. "They have taken over the United States, the United States government, and the European Union," he declared. "Nobody has been able to stop them so far. I'm hoping Uganda can." Soon after the seminar parliamentarians like David Bahati, who had heard Lively speak, went to work and drafted the insidious Anti-Homosexuality Act, also known as the 'Kill the Gays' bill.

While the preacher was happy – keen, even – to go meddling in the governance of a foreign country, it never occurred to him that the citizens of that country could return the favor, using his own nation's laws to call him to account. But that is exactly what happened. Lively's lawyers sought to have the case thrown out because the Ugandans were foreign. A federal judge disagreed. Judge Michael Ponsor, in his dismissal of that initial appeal, wrote, "The fact that a group continues to be vulnerable to widespread, systematic persecution in some parts of the world simply cannot shield one who commits a crime against humanity from liability." The case of *Sexual Minorities Uganda v. Scott Lively* could go ahead, he ruled, based on the centuries-old Alien Tort Statute.

The Alien Tort Statute is one of America's earliest, passed in 1789 by the first Congress, and it provides non-U.S. citizens with the right to apply to U.S. courts to seek relief for violations of international law. Human rights abuses were not part of legal discourse two hundred years ago, but in the twenty-first century they are. Activists in Uganda cannot sue their own parliamentarians or the Ugandan president, but in America, in Massachusetts, Lively's home state, they can, and they hoped for their day in court.

Lively's failure to get the case thrown out in 2013 was an encouraging start, but in June 2017 the judge ruled that it couldn't go forward because of a narrower reading of the revised tort statute that had been issued after it was filed. The case was dismissed on jurisdictional grounds because Lively's actions were primarily carried out abroad.

"The question before the court is not whether Defendant's actions in aiding and abetting efforts to demonize, intimidate, and injure LGBTI people in Uganda constitute violations of international law. They do," Judge Ponsor said. Ponsor ruled that even though there was evidence to support the Ugandans' assertion that Lively aided and abetted the repression of gays, the limitations of the statute made it impossible to continue the case. "The much narrower and more technical question posed by Defendant's motion is whether the limited actions taken by Defendant on American soil in pursuit of his odious campaign are sufficient to give this court jurisdiction over Plaintiff's claims," Judge Ponsor continued. "Since they are not sufficient, summary judgment is appropriate for this, and only this, reason."

The court ruling stated:

• "Defendant Scott Lively is an American citizen who has aided and abetted a vicious and frightening campaign of repression against LGBTI persons in Uganda."

• "[Lively's] crackpot bigotry could be brushed aside as pathetic, except for the terrible harm it can cause. The record in this case demonstrates that Defendant has worked with elements in Uganda who share some of his views to try to repress freedom of expression by LGBTI people in Uganda, deprive them of the protection of the law, and render their very existence illegal."

• The evidence "confirmed the nature of Defendant's, on the one hand, vicious and, on the other hand, ludicrously extreme animus against LGBTI people and his determination to assist in persecuting them wherever they are, including

Uganda. The evidence of record demonstrates that Defendant aided and abetted efforts (1) to restrict freedom of expression by members of the LBGTI community in Uganda, (2) to suppress their civil rights, and (3) to make the very existence of LGBTI people in Uganda a crime."

Even though SMUG lost, it was also in some ways a win for them, Frank Mugisha, the executive director, explained. "The court's ruling recognized the dangers resulting from the hatred that Scott Lively and other extremist Christians from the U.S. have exported to my country. By having a court recognize that persecution of LGBTI people amounts to a crime against humanity, we have already been able to hold Lively to account and reduce his dangerous influence in Uganda."

At least in America gay men like Bert don't have to fear death for asserting their legal rights. This is not the case in Uganda. Bert's compatriot David Kato was co-founder of SMUG and is considered the father of the queer rights movement in Uganda. After the notorious tabloid *Rolling Stone* splashed his name and photograph – along with those of some hundred others they deemed the most notorious 'homos' of Uganda – on their front page under the headline 'Hang Them', he and others sued. He won his right to privacy case but was murdered soon afterwards, in January 2011.

Authorities denied the two things were related; it was a burglary gone wrong, they claimed.

The Anti-Homosexuality Act was passed in February 2014, with life imprisonment as the penalty, rather than the death sentence earlier versions had called for. Despite this 'accommodation' there was an international outcry and some donors pulled their funding from the country. By August the Ugandan constitutional court had invalidated the act on the grounds that the parliament had failed to have a quorum when the bill was voted on. Every so often there are rumbles from lawmakers about reviving the bill.

Another tabloid, *Red Pepper*, continues to push antigay and inflammatory stories. In 2016 they published an interview with the country's minister for ethics and integrity, Simon Lokodo, a former priest whose raison d'être seems to be witch-hunting LGBT folks and breaking up get-togethers and pride parades. *Red Pepper* claims gays have threatened to rape Lokodo.

In the interview Lokodo, as well as regurgitating false arguments and conspiracy theories about gays recruiting children, announced that the government was investing in a gay detection machine. "We are going to attack and attack. I have fresh tactics. One of them is a censor gadget or machine. We are going to procure this machine and it will detect homos and porn actors, especially those misusing applications like WhatsApp with sex acts. The South Koreans are programming it. And very soon we will ship it into the country and all the evil will be busted." Lokodo claimed the government was willing to spend the money to get this device.

As of this writing, it has yet to put in an appearance.

Just like Victor Mukassa, the transgender man whose bank account was frozen because he was employed by the International Gay & Lesbian Human Rights Commission, Bert cannot return to Kampala, because LGBT organizations are illegal in Uganda.

And so the numbers of asylum seekers keep growing, and they come from many different countries. I thought about the young man stuck at O'Hare airport with just a phone number and a name he seemed to barely know himself, and wondered how long it would take for us to have safe spaces in our own countries, on our continent.

It doesn't seem likely to happen soon, as even heterosexuals who dare to speak up can be caught in the crossfire. Take the nephew of the Gambian strongman and now finally ex-president, Yahya Jammeh. A few weeks earlier I'd found out that Alagie Jammeh had been granted asylum in California. The reason he had claimed it? Because as a Gambian-sponsored student at the University of California he'd befriended a gay man and posted on Facebook that, "No one should be denied their fundamental basic human rights because of their sexuality."

This was despite his uncle having said he wanted to personally slit the throats of gays; and the government, well-known for having passed draconian anti-gay laws, rescinded his scholarship. Alagie Jammeh told the Washington-based *Blade* newspaper that the Gambian government demanded he return to his homeland and publicly apologize for his Facebook post. He refused, saying, "I can't go to the Gambia. I will be arrested – not only arrested, but killed. I'm never going to apologize for supporting gay people." Sometimes being an ally comes with a big price-tag.

Eventually I left the flat and did have a couple of Bucks Fizzes that evening, and I thought about the luck that some of us have. With Jammeh the strongman losing the election to Adama Barrow, and Gambian citizens finally saying enough is enough after twenty-two years, and other West African leaders forcing him to leave in 2017, his nephew might one day be able to return home.

Asylum in America is in no way guaranteed, however, and many just show up, blindly optimistic that it will somehow work out. Several months later, when I next return Stateside, and over breakfast with Scott Davis, the social worker who devised and managed the asylum project for Housing Works after the organization found themselves taking responsibility for Agaba and other gay activists, I ask him about numbers.

"I imagine in New York City alone there were hundreds. Hundreds. Because I alone had to turn away a few people a month, and we were by no means the only agency that people knew about that could be helpful," he tells me over coffee and croissants at Harlem's Lenox Sapphire restaurant – specialty Senegalese/Soul Food fusion. "I would say there were hundreds of asylum applications pending."

A spry sixty-something with a penchant for red sneakers, Mr. Davis and I first met at one of Kent's bourbon night meet-ups a year earlier, where he told me of his work helping folk like Agaba, Norbert and Michael. He's a white man, divorced and a father of two, who came out later in life. A former investment banker who worked for JP Morgan and Credit Suisse, his life unraveled after he came out: his marriage ended, and he became estranged from his children and many who were in his circle of friends. He renounced banking and became a case manager for Housing Works, applying himself to the job meticulously as he adjusted to his new reality as an openly gay man in Manhattan.

We meet periodically, to eat and stroll around a rapidly gentrifying and whitening Harlem. He's good company and I admire what he's doing. He's now comfortable in his own skin, and is proud to have helped resettle so many. While Housing Works is focused on supporting people with HIV, he estimates that about thirty percent of those he worked with didn't have the virus. These he would help anyway, and then refer on to another organization for final processing.

What all the Africans who landed in his office did have were severe psychological issues. "I got two mental health professionals to see them pro bono once a week to help them adjust. All had some sort of trauma. It was a high point in my career: I can make a difference. Although culturally many of them are not ready for that, but I still would refer a number of them."

Mr. Davis ultimately parted company with Housing Works; it became tougher and tougher to raise funds for the program, and by 2016 it was shuttered. At his last count some forty people had been helped.

When I inquire about the young man at O'Hare airport I find out that U.S. Immigration & Customs Enforcement turned him over to an activist who was now helping to process him. Another son of our continent – and my country in particular – lost to a raging firestorm of homophobia that needs to be extinguished.

How many more will flee, I wonder? In New York alone I've come across Ade, the creative director outed and chased away, now rebuilding his life in Manhattan; there's Mike, who came for a conference and was outed by a major international newspaper, and then had all sorts of threats sent his way at home; there is Chike from Port Harcourt; there is Deola in Coney Island; Edafe in New Jersey; Aziz; Agaba and, and, and...

"Out of the huts of history's shame I rise. Up from a past that's rooted in pain I rise. I'm a black ocean, leaping and wide, welling and swelling I bear in the tide."

– Maya Angelou, *And Still I Rise*

SEVENTEEN: SEE ME, SEE TROUBLE OH!

March 30 2016

It has been a busy week and now it's time to relax. Scott and I are parked on our futon in front of the flat-screen television in our living room. It is rare that we have time for television, so recording shows and bingeing on them when we can is the norm for us. Tonight though, we are excited. One of our favorite new shows, *Empire*, about an African-American musical family dynasty and their battles, is back after a midseason hiatus. We've fed the cats (Weber having acquired two siblings, Mos Def and Oskar), we've set out our wine and snacks, and are about to give ourselves over to FOX television, to be entertained by Cookie, Lucius, Jamal & Co.

In this episode, 'Death Will Have Its Day', amidst the usual intrigues one storyline involves Jamal, the gay son, being confronted by an openly gay music executive about his flirtation with a female singer and his apparent flip-flopping. Jamal insists that sexuality is fluid, and that even though he's gay he can be with this woman, and he doesn't see what the big deal is. The executive warns that it will be badly received by the LGBT community, which has supported Jamal as an 'out' musician, if it gets out that he is now dating women. Then the executive rattles off a list of ten countries where being gay could get one executed. To my dismay, Nigeria is at the top of that list: "Nigeria, Sudan, Mauritania, Somalia..."

Scott and I stare at each other. I am stunned for a moment and then Scott laughs – with me and at me. This wasn't news to me, of course. But it was still very sad to see that when Nigeria is mentioned in Western pop culture, it is for the fact that our Islamic laws mandate a death sentence for gay people. Death by stoning is the prescribed punishment, even though no sharia court in our federation has followed through, or been allowed to follow through, on that sentence.

Our civil laws are only slightly better.

In the days that followed, the Nigerian Twitterati took to the web to lambast Fox and *Empire* for not doing their research. A typical post would proclaim that we don't execute gays, we 'just' give them fourteen years. And I wondered, in 2016 is there anything to be proud of in saying we jail our gays for fourteen years rather than kill them? I'm often proud of Nigeria and Nigerians, but at the same time it has become imperative for me to hold up the mirror and look clear-eyed at what is staring back at me. And for us Nigerians, it's not always a pretty sight.

It would be easy to dismiss this as propaganda, as the West once again trying to make Africans look savage, and say that in fact no one is being stoned in Lagos or even Kano. But sharia judges are sentencing men perceived to be gay to public lashings and jail time, the kind of humiliation and social death that can lead to suicide.

Shortly after the episode aired, a lengthy – unrelated – report from the news website *The Daily Beast*, authored by a Nigerian writer, Philip Obaji Jr., landed in my inbox. It detailed 'the dirty war Nigeria is waging against its LGBT people and anyone associated with them', focusing specifically on the hunt for gays by the police in and around northern Nigeria.

A few weeks before, in February, police in Abuja were gloating over a 'gay marriage' raid they had executed at a hotel in town. A spokesperson, Anjuguri Manzah, told reporters that the officers acted "based on the provisions of the Same Sex

Marriage (Prohibition) Act signed into law in 2014.We received an intelligence report and acted fast by moving to the venue of the event to stop it. We arrested the intending couple, Ibrahim Lawal and Umar Tahir, as well as the sponsors of the wedding and the owner of the hotel where the event was billed to hold."

Obaji's report included accounts of other parties raided in Abuja, Bauchi and Kano, at which guests were arrested, then jailed and tortured to reveal the names of their friends. The police would then go arrest these friends, under the guise of following the law, but in reality to extort money from citizens who might – or might not – be gay. How can you prove you do not have gay desires? There was profit to be made from bail too. Nigerian human rights workers who followed the cases said the so-called wedding in Abuja was not a wedding at all. One said it was actually a traditional fund-raising ceremony – known in the local Hausa language as Ajo – where some participants, as he rather dryly put it, "socially cross-dress for the purpose of entertainment."

Not coincidentally, two weeks earlier my country's law-makers had failed miserably to pass a gender and equal opportunities bill. While lashing out at gays was now an acceptable national pastime worthy of any amount of govern-mental attention, Nigerian women, who make up roughly half the population, could not in 2016 get themselves taken serious-ly enough by our lawmakers to see a law passed that would start to close the yawning gap in our society between the genders.

Had it been passed, this proposal would have addressed gender discrimination in politics, education and the workplace. It would have prohibited domestic and sexual violence, and set a minimum age for marriage of eighteen. Scholarships and bursaries would have to be given equally to girls, ensuring more participation in formal education at higher levels. Advertisements for jobs with gender-neutral roles often explicitly state a preference for men, and this would have been banned.

The reason the lawmakers cited for killing this bill? It ran afoul of their religions' practices, Christianity and Islam. Nigerian women in 2016 remain less than their husbands, brothers, fathers and even their sons; and lawmakers are happy to maintain a status quo where women remain subservient to men. Widows continue to have less of a stake in their husband's estates than their children or their husband's siblings, and some will endure humiliation at the hands of their husbands' families with no legal recourse.

One senator who seemed sympathetic to the bill gave a mind-numbing reason for his colleagues defeating it. Eyinnaya Abaribe, a senator for Abia State in the eastern part of the country, said, "Some lawmakers started expressing deep worries about some parts of the bill that they think could give women too much freedom and lead them to prostitution, lesbianism and other social vices."

Of our one hundred and nine senators only seven are female. And while many women voice support for quelling any sort of gender nonconformity, they would do well to consider how the same societal and cultural norms that put gay people down put down heterosexual women too. Equality for one should mean equality for all, or else it isn't equality.

One female senator, Oluremi Tinubu, who represents Lagos and was a vocal supporter and sponsor of the draconian anti-gay law, soon found herself being pissed on because of her gender. In the upper house of our legislature one of her male colleagues threatened to rape and then impregnate her. When he faced pushback for his remarks, Senator Dino Melaye did not backtrack, saying only that Tinubu had reached menopause and couldn't get pregnant anyway.

I wanted to feel sorry for her, but these women who pooh-pooh LGBT rights shouldn't be surprised when their hetero-patriarchal allies disrespect their status as women.

That spring one of my very dear cousins, Jennifer, gets married to my buddy Kofi in Cape Town. It is a wonderful weekend, and a chance to connect with far-flung members of my family – cousins, uncles, and aunts from all over the world.

As the happy couple are having their personal wedding photographs taken against the backdrop of magnificent Table Mountain, on the quay of the elegant One & Only hotel, I am downing Prosecco and canapés with friends and relatives. I'm happy.

Somehow the talk turns to politics and the ongoing American presidential election campaign. With two New Yorkers in the running, I hold forth about the pros and cons of each of them. While many in the cluster I'm in are excited about the possibility of a woman in the Oval Office and the real potential of a Hillary Clinton presidency, one is not. She is an elegant senior lady with grandchildren, a successful businesswoman, and to me appears to be a sophisticated thinker. She is adamant that the Republican candidate, Donald Trump, will win, and will be the best thing for America, and the world. Many around us point out his negative position on immigrants, and his denigration of America's first black president, Barack Obama. But she is adamant. And then she flashes a bit of anger. "Trump will win and reverse gay marriage," she bellows.

I am stunned.

That is it?

This is her singular issue?

Indeed it was.

In reality, since the U.S. Supreme Court had ruled on the matter in 2015, no presidential action would be able to roll back marriage equality, but such details didn't matter to her; nor that Trump had not made reversing marriage equality a focus of his campaign, (even though upon assuming office he did at once start to chip away at gay rights using administrative actions). It didn't even occur to her that, there in South Africa where she was making this argument, marriage equality is the law of the land – indeed written into the constitution, having been achieved way back in 2006, long before it happened in America. And South Africa hadn't fallen off the map, been consumed by brimstone or turned into salt.

No one said anything. I didn't know the senior madam well enough to engage further, and besides, everyone was having a wonderful time, and it wasn't for me to ruin it. I just gulped more Prosecco and wondered, if a sophisticated, wealthy businesswoman, wife, mother, and grandmother – women of her ilk run Lagos – someone who I presume has traveled the world, is still shackled by such so-called cultural norms, and is so vehemently keen to keep others shackled, how can change come? If the vocal elite are firmly in opposition, will LGBT citizens on our continent continue to be on the losing side?

Could change come from the grassroots, then?

Back in February a Nigerian man, Akinnifesi Olumide Olubunmi, had been brutally beaten in a semi-rural part of Ondo state. The irate mob that set upon him believed he was dating, and had had sex with, a male councilor in the local government.

Akinnifesi would die the day after the attack, due to internal bleeding and other complications; the councilor would go on the run. But as horrible as what befell Akinnifesi was, nothing prepared me for the vile spectacle of his so-called friends gloating on his Facebook page. They shared bloody pictures of the deceased and celebrated his demise. One Facebook 'friend', using the name Ogbeni Ade Omo Ade, wrote on Akinnifesi's wall:

End of a gay! This will serve as a lesson to all the people that loves engaging in bisexual, homosexual, lesbianism and gay Akinnifesi was a guy that everybody in the community thought was a responsible person not until his secret was revealed when he was caught hands down with honourable Dotun who was a serving supervisory councillor in Ondo west local government in Ondo state he was beating mercilessly by Ondo youths that saw everything bad in a man dating a man he was rushed to the hospital but he later died of internal bleeding[...]

Another 'friend', with the moniker Adewale Victor Adeoye, wrote,

Akinnifesi Olumide Olubunmi When I heard this news of your attacked in Ondo on Facebook I was so disturbed. I said it to myself, that can this be possible that you involved in gay practices? Or it was a set up until I investigate the whole story. You disappointed many people including your family and friends[...] What police should do is to get the run away politician involved arrested so gay will not be spread in the community and it will serve as a lesson to others.

Another supposed friend, Mark John, wrote that he should, 'Rest in peace if you like.'

The posts were shared over and over again on social media,

gleefully, as if killing a suspected gay man is something to be proud of, something to spark jubilation. This attitude was now the norm in the country. A consequence of the antigay law, it was ugly, and to date no one has been convicted of the killing of Akinnifesi.

I witnessed this kind of ugliness on a smaller scale, in a WhatsApp group I was part of, that I had erred in thinking would be a safe space for all its members. Years ago a bunch of us American-based alumni of the Federal Government College, Port Harcourt class of 1986 began a tradition of meeting annually for a weekend of revelry and reconnecting. Each year we chose a different city. No real agenda was on the table, but there were always discussions about what we as alumni could contribute to the well-being of the current students back in Port Harcourt, as the school is no longer the premium institution it had been when we were students.

We'd met up in Chicago, Washington D.C. and Houston, and our thirtieth anniversary was sneaking up on us. Because of this, the group was extended to include our brethren in Nigeria, and a WhatsApp group was created to which members of our class were added daily. This online forum was a way for former students to reconnect with each other and plan for the 2016 reunion.

Friends pulled friends in, and before long over two hundred and fifty members of the class were on there. It was good to see how many of us had soared both professionally and personally – though the flipside was, it was also apparent that others had seen much less growth in the three decades since we studied together. However the conversations, though rowdy, were also exuberant, with everyone looking forward to meeting on the date that was eventually settled on.

The forum soon became a microcosm of all that we loathe and love about our nation today. A great deal of bluster was followed by inaction from the biggest talkers – the empty barrels, as is usual, making the most noise. Many were slow to pay the pledges they had made ostentatiously and without coercion. Those who donated least, the 'zero percenters', squawked the most, usually about some nonsense or other. It was all very juvenile at times. Misogyny reigned.

For me the excitement started to chip away very quickly.

While discussing what might be an appropriate tribute, a cabal of my former classmates decided on a mini-stadium. A stadium!

Currently the school is dilapidated. It wasn't in great shape when we lived and studied there in the 1980s, but photos someone circulated during our group chats revealed the current horror show: walls spattered with algae, run-down buildings that hadn't seen a lick of paint in decades; glass louver windows and even doors replaced with wooden boards. Rusted bunk beds with no mattresses, and actual potholes in the floors of the rooms where students sleep, are the norm. In our day it was primarily a boarding school with just a smattering of day students. Today, due to the state of the facilities, the reverse is the case. Mates who visited said some of the awful student dormitories had been taken over by the teachers as their residential quarters. It was hard for me to imagine grown men and women teachers living right next to boys and girls aged eleven to sixteen.

The eyesore the school had become was so terrible that some of the pictures ended up in a highly-read post curated by Nigeria's most notorious blogger, Linda Ikeji. She didn't even need to write an article; she just posted the photos under the caption, 'Sorry State of Federal Government College Port Harcourt'. Federal government colleges have declined generally, but the decline in Port Harcourt was so steep that those of my classmates who are parents wouldn't dream of sending their own children there.

Yet despite all this, here were a bunch of folk, some of whom lived in Port Harcourt, advocating strenuously for the construction of a vanity stadium so we could all put our names on it somewhere prominent.

Disconcertingly, Smiley, my first lover, was one of the stadium enthusiasts. In the years that had passed he'd become a husband and a pastor of the overblown variety. The firebrand public displays of worship by many Nigerians today – wanting to breathe fire before a bus begins a journey, or cast and bind demons before any meeting – have always baffled me. Growing up Catholic, Mass was never a big showy display, so I've never bought into the Pentecostal hysterics. And in today's Nigeria it seems every third person is some sort of pastor, or styles themselves as such. And now Smiley was one of these.

Eventually the group, which initially took on the name of our great principal M.C. Ebo, settled on the rather more useful and achievable task of refurbishing the kitchen, including a total overhaul of the facilities for student dining. Stoves would be upgraded from firewood to electricity or gas. This is how far the school had regressed. The food wasn't great in the 1980s, but it wasn't cooked with firewood! A few months in, there were allegations of improper handling of funds, and bid-rigging for the contract, for which we had raised about eight million naira (about forty thousand U.S. dollars). But the overriding mission – a successful reunion, and a respectable 'give back' that proved our members were doing well in their current lives – always brought us back to the table.

Outside of the jostling for the contract, the messages that flew fast and furious within the forum often centered on religion. Some took it upon themselves to preach and proselyt-ize each day without regard for the fact that this was a secular group for a secular school. Thirty years later there was a wearying assumption that everyone needed to be saved for Jesus, even when there were Muslims among us, and other types of Christians, and possibly atheists. One person would bombard the forum daily with long passages of Scripture. The devil was always on a rampage, it seemed, and God was always faithful. Actually putting money towards the project was not a thing she considered.

It was all so juvenile, so relentless, that I found myself una-ble to keep quiet. This group belonged to all of us, and yet a vocal minority of evangelical fanatics were taking it over. If I wanted to head to a T.B. Joshua revivalist gathering I now knew where to go, but the often interminable and sometimes hourly postings were now totally out of control. I got in a verbal tussle with one of the instigators of the pious postings on the merits of such religiosity. We didn't go to revival school, I said. All religions and denominations were to be respected, and here we were being endlessly bombarded with fire and brimstone. It was not the place for it, I felt. Of course the argument had to become personal on his side, with insults and mockery. I tried to remain gracious but steadfast. It was a low moment, with some friends reporting back to me about offline comments made by this same person and others about my supposedly heathen behavior and my sexuality, from which my disapproval was presumed to arise. I said nothing on that matter since the instigator hadn't made the comments public, but I pushed back against the incessant praying, and said if this was a born again convention I wanted no part of it.

As the insults flew I noticed that most of the North American friends of the school were silent, including all those I'd spent summer weekends with at the mini-reunions in America. Some took to calling me offline or sending text messages but refused to take a public stand on the forum. Interesting, I thought, thankful that I had other Nigerian friends, and that this group from F.G.C. was not the only one I could hold up as an example of how contemporary Nigerians think and behave.

One dear friend who lives in Lagos and also went to school with us called them pacifists, folks who didn't want to rock the boat. It's easier for them to say nothing, he said, and just wait it out until the moment passes.

Entreaties were made to me to remain in the group, and after much thought I chose to stay, but the madness of religiosity remained, a procession of hectoring daily sermons delivered without regard for the beliefs or feelings of anyone else.

In July 2016, a couple of months before the planned confab, and after the refurbishment work had begun, the instigator of the evangelical diatribes took it upon himself to compile a list of television programs featuring LGBT characters – whether major or minor – and content; and posted it on the forum, along with a warning to everyone to monitor what their children were watching, and asking them to circulate it to their pastors and friends, and do all they can to "shield our children from being shown LGBT characters."

This time others did speak out in a way they had not before, calling it inappropriate for our forum. Expecting uniform support, Instigator didn't seem to know what had hit him, and for a time left the forum in a huff. Some based in Nigeria dragged out the by then former president Goodluck Jonathan's anti-gay law, said the forum should be considered Nigerian, and that Instigator was right to drum up anti-gay sentiment. Others refused to fall into the old argument that it was only those of us who lived in the West who cared about these matters and opposed this.

Smiley's reaction was priceless. Here was a closeted gay man who had many male lovers in F.G.C., and who still flirts with me on the phone all these years later. Yet as a pastor he couldn't leave well alone, and launched into a spirited defense of the instigator, urging those of us in foreign lands to help 'protect the children' here in Nigeria as we had been protected in F.G.C. – this coming from someone who, as an eighteen-year-old, had routinely had sex with an inexperienced sixteen-year-old or two. How rich!

One of the forum administrators, a North American member, told Smiley he wasn't looking for tutorials on how to raise his children (Smiley has no children of his own) and to please stop with the lecturing. The discussion took on all kinds of dimensions, with members in the Diaspora finally speaking up for tolerance, privacy and human rights. Smiley was belligerent, claiming his 'pastorhood' meant his beliefs were the will of God and therefore overrode secular laws and institutions.

Tempted though I was, I chose to not blow up in the public forum, but said privately to him that his stance was disappointing; and that while he claimed to care so much for all these children he didn't have, he ought to remember that some LGBT people actually have children. What message would he send to those children – that their parents are less than heterosexuals? And frankly I just thought it was ridiculous for a guy who fucks guys on the sly, or at least did so for years, to be publicly defending homophobia when he could be outed at any minute.

He responded that 'these issues' are abnormal, that those of us who live abroad have forgotten our culture, and that he's a pastor. He said he had no 'adventures' with gay people. I wasn't sure if it was meant to be a joke, but I wished him well and haven't returned his messages since. I am willing to forgive his hypocrisy, but not when it extends to actual self-delusion; nor when it harms others.

Would my life have taken a different turn if all those years ago I hadn't asked him to share his bucket of water with me? If my first sexual experience hadn't been with him but with some girl, would I have ended up heterosexual? It seems unlikely. I would still have met Lamido back in Lagos, and he would have certainly been my first great love. I thought about how far Smiley had gone in his charade when he could have simply said nothing. Why? Here is what our society has come to – gay men married to women and deluding themselves that this makes them heterosexual, even though on every trip I make home he calls me up, eager to rekindle our affair. And here he is, agitating against gays online. It is really a betrayal of the rest of us. And of himself. I shook my head and deleted his number.

Of the ten countries mentioned in that *Empire* episode as having the death penalty for homosexuality, four were sub-Saharan African ones. The others were majority-Muslim Middle Eastern and Far Asian countries such as Saudi Arabia and Afghanistan. It is no consolation that Nigerians and Ghanaians are not alone in this kind of theocratic, undemocratic fuckery. And who gains? Our continent too often drives away its most precious resources – its own citizens – to the West, where, in an irony of history, their talent further benefits our former colonial overlords at the expense of those back home.

In the summer of 2016, Tanzania, which already sentences LGBT people to life imprisonment for homosexual acts, decided to ban intimate lubricants from the country, in a bid to limit sex between gay people. This brought snickers from many, and left the international community scratching their heads. There was a new government in place, and it decided to flex its conservative muscles by attacking a group who no one would defend. Prior to this, the anti-gay law had rarely been enforced.

The water-based lubricants in question had been donated to quell HIV infections in commercial sex workers of all sexes, and gay men in general – or rather, men who have sex with other men, as in those parts few would label, or perhaps even understand themselves as gay. The intervention to stamp out HIV had been agreed to by the previous government back in 2013, and safer sex packages containing condoms, lubes, gels, and educational information had been made available to these groups, paid for by the American taxpayer under the auspices of PEPFAR, President Obama's Emergency Plan for AIDS Relief.

Despite the fact that lubricants are also used by women, the new health minister, Ummy Mwalimu, decided that the money spent on them could be better deployed elsewhere. She would like to see the money spent on more beds in the maternity wards, she said – a peculiar equivalency, but good copy. Except she never told the Tanzanian public that the money was America's, not theirs. Following a series of coordinated raids on NGOs, orchestrated by the new Tanzanian government in order to show it was being tough on gays, the U.S. government took back the lubricants. One official told me tartly that the United States Agency for International Development balked at spending American tax dollars on Tanzania's maternity wards when Mwalimu's government could afford to do that themselves.

The HIV infection rates among gay men in Tanzania are estimated to be around 23 percent, compared to about 5 percent in the general population. The vulnerable population of sex-workers and gay men would continue to receive condoms through donor-funded groups, but not lube, and the government continued its crackdown.

Bashing gays has now become Tanzania's number one priority. President John Magufuli slammed NGOs that are providing services to the vulnerable. "Those who teach such things do not like us, brothers. They brought us drugs and homosexual practices that even cows disapprove of," he said in a speech in June 2017. His government had gotten into the fine details of the sex had in the bedrooms of its citizens, conducting raids and anal examinations, and didn't seem to want to get out of it. They now threaten NGO workers with deportation should they continue to assist gay Tanzanians in protecting themselves from HIV.

"One thing alone I charge you. As you live, believe in Life! Always human beings will live and progress to greater, broader and fuller life. The only possible death is to lose belief in this truth simply because the great end comes slowly, because time is long."

– W.E.B. Du Bois's last statement to the world

Eighteen: We Won't Be Tarred and Feathered! (where do we go to from here?)

Growing up in Lagos, I don't remember our leaders ever conceding that perhaps they just might have gotten something wrong. Understandably enough, they prefer to focus on what they feel are their positive contributions to what is probably Africa's largest economy. So when in June 2016 Goodluck Jonathan, the former Nigerian president, showed up for a Bloomberg News roundtable at the company's European headquarters in London to defend his governance record to the international community, I expected a spirited, likely overblown defense of his stewardship of the country. And of course defensive bluster from his surrogates, since upon taking the reins of government, his successor, Muhammadu Buhari, had accused Jonathan and his team of leaving an empty treasury behind.

As I watched him go on about how that was not possible I wasn't expecting anything different. So I was caught off-guard when Jonathan, in the middle of defending his government from what one has to call the standard allegations of corruption and bilking the Nigerian coffers, said this:

"When it comes to equality, we must all have the same rights as Nigerian citizens. In the light of deepening debates for all Nigerians and other citizens of the world to be treated equally and without discrimination, and with the clear knowledge that the issue of sexual orientation is still evolving, the nation may at the appropriate time revisit the law."

Okay, that only took him thirty months. But still.

Just days after his pronouncement came the grisly massacre of forty-nine gay people by a deranged gunman at the Pulse nightclub in Orlando, Florida. Jonathan, who as president ignored his gay constituents until the moment he threw us under the bus in an ultimately failed bid for the popular vote, sent out a message of condolence to the grieving families via Twitter. That small gesture sparked controversy among the Nigerian Twitterati, understandably confused by this man who had passed an extremely anti-gay law for which there had been small public clamor.

Being out of office, Jonathan cannot undo the damage caused by the Same Sex Marriage Prohibition Act, but he is not the only African former president who has expressed support for LGBT people once he has left office. After Jonathan signed the bill into law, former Mozambican president Jaoquim Chissano came out forcefully against it, and implored African leaders to make a swift turnaround and embrace all their people, particularly the gay ones. The former president of Botswana, Fetus Mogae, publicly chided Robert Mugabe and others who would deny LBGT citizens equality. And though this is frustrating since these leaders are out of office, I have hope. Hope for change. A change in attitude is underway, and while it may seem small, I'm confident that it will happen sooner than people expect.

Outside of Goodluck's change of heart, in 2016, a few months after my classmates said nothing in the face of anti-gay slurs and a whispering campaign, others finally stood up and put a stop to the gay scapegoating. More and more straight people are speaking up and expressing opinions that don't jibe with the sentiment of 'throw all the gay brothers and sisters overboard', or allow them to be the butt of every joke.

This new-found boldness reminded me of something I'd heard the late African-American poet Maya Angelou say many times about courage. In her life she often referenced her time in Ghana, where she lived for some years at the same time as the great African-American scholar and activist W.E.B. Du Bois. She said courage is built up a little at a time, but that it was imperative to have some, and to start from someplace.

I once saw her, already at an advanced age, being interviewed on television by the American talk-show host Oprah Winfrey. Oprah recalled being at Dr. Angelou's home some years earlier for a party. As the guests were talking, someone made a racist, homophobic joke. Even across the hubbub in the room the hostess heard the joke and stalked over to the offending party. Angelou immediately recalled the incident:

"I said, 'Is this your coat?

'Did you come with anyone?

'Both of you come this way.'"

And without further comment she walked them out of her home. To Oprah she said, "It's vulgarity and it's poison."

Today I see more and more Africans finding the courage to assert that what is wrong is wrong in small spaces and in big ones, in private and in public.

Privately, I hope those folks who find themselves in the space Anass and I did will one day have the freedom to be able to just love without barriers, unhobbled by excessive pondering about what our attraction to each other might mean in terms of who we really are, as long as no one gets hurt. To not waste time like I did, searching for ways to erase the relationship because it seemed the right thing to do when I fell for Scott and decided that my life would be spent with him.

Some years later, and after I'd put a ton of distance between us, Anass visited me in Accra, to celebrate my birthday at my annual guinea fowl and wine shindig. When the rest of the revelers had gone, and it was just us sipping Malta Guinnesses, he told me that, try as I might to forget, he and I are family. Our intimacy, he said, defies categorization, and couldn't be a threat to my relationship or his. We decide what we are, what we do, and what we call ourselves. And then he very calmly read me:

"You cannot delete me from your life. So stop trying. No forget sey me and you na forever. No leave, no transfer."

Unlike Lamido, who I barely hear from anymore, Anass and I remain in each other's lives and cheer each other on; and our support for one another is unwavering. Love, Anass said, equals making room in the heart. We had both done that for each other and continue to do so, whether we talk on the phone frequently or barely. So breaking off contact was futile. Whatever happened, whatever will happen, I'm in his corner and he's very comfortably in mine.

It is gratifying when some who are in the public sphere take a 'live and let live' stand. Like the Afrobeat singer Seun Kuti, son of the legendary Fela, who has called the attempt to deliberately hurt gay people in Nigeria what it is: "A cheap shot by an under-achieving government to discriminate against people because they are different"; and he predicted that as a consequence there would be a wave of asylum-seekers fleeing the continent to the West. He has been proved right.

In January 2017, data from the United Kingdom's Home Office showed a 400% rise in gay asylum-seekers since 2009. By 2014 the 200 people who were fleeing to Britain annually, seeking refuge from persecution for their sexual orientation, had ballooned to 1,115, with Nigeria and Ghana among the countries they were most commonly fleeing.

The novelist Chimamanda Ngozi Adichie has written forcefully about Africans like us – people now understood as LGBT – going back generations; African people born and bred here, who have never left the continent. This pushes back against the prevailing narrative of us as being in some obscure way un-African because of who we love. I'm hopeful when musicians like Uganda's Bobi Wine go from being virulently homophobic, and performing songs that incite violence against LGBT people, to having a 360° turnaround, and begin calling for tolerance. Okay, that may have had to do with a loss of income on the international music circuit owing to show cancelations and visa denials in the West, but however he comes to tolerance I see it as a good thing. We can begin by performing virtue, whether sincerely or otherwise.

I know that a lot of work needs to be done to build understanding and tolerance in our world, but the fact that Burkina Faso, Cape Verde, Djibouti, Guinea Bissau, Côte d'Ivoire, Niger, Mali, Lesotho, Mozambique, São Tomé, the Seychelles, Rwanda, the two Congos, the Central African Republic and South Africa don't criminalize their gay citizens leaves me hopeful. It doesn't mean they are all gay-friendly, but at least the state isn't using the law to hunt gay men down. I'm hopeful when I hear of legal challenges to the status quo in Kenya and Uganda. Change doesn't always come quickly, but I'm convinced it will come for our continent – especially when, even in the face of repeated arrests and disruption, pride celebrations go on defiantly in Uganda. Year after year, arrest after arrest, pride goes on, and each time it does, it leaves us with a little more hope. (Even though the celebrations were halted in August 2017 due to threats of arrest and violence from the government I know it will be back.)

The summer of 2016 gave me even more hope. When the odious hate-preacher Steven Anderson, a pastor at the Faithful Word Baptist Church in Tempe, Arizona, attempted to take his 'gays should be killed' message to Africa, it backfired spectacularly.

Anderson, following in the footsteps of preachers like Scott Lively, is known for jubilating on the heels of the June 2016 massacre at the Pulse nightclub. "There's fifty less pedophiles in this world," he said. Anderson, a father of nine, has preached that killing all gay men would give the world an AIDS-free Christmas. So when in September 2016 he attempted to go to South Africa on a revivalist crusade to 'win souls', it was hopeful to see the South African government deny him and his eighteen-man-strong entourage entry.

The South African Home Affairs Minister, Malusi Gigaba, examined Anderson's history and concluded to Parliament in Cape Town that Anderson is an undesirable person under the country's Immigration Act. "Steven Anderson will be advised that he is a prohibited person in South Africa." South Africa had again led the way, becoming the first African nation to expressly ban someone from entry because of his homophobia. "We have a duty to prevent harm and hatred in all forms against LGBTI, as any other person in a democratic state," Gigaba said.

That action gave me hope, gave me life.

On social media Anderson lamented that even before he left America, he'd been told at the airport that not only would he be denied entry into South Africa but he couldn't even transit through the United Kingdom. So he headed to Botswana instead and lambasted South Africa from there. But even in that conservative country, though it allowed him in, upon arrival he was greeted by protesters. He continued with his sermons of hate, and an elderly man who challenged his homophobia was manhandled at the church he was preaching in!

Such manhandling of an elder is anathema to most Africans, and Anderson's gleeful recounting of the event at a Gaborone radio station was just too much. In that interview he continued to advocate for the killing of gays and lesbians, and then proceeded to piss on his hosts by saying they had a drinking problem in the country, and that he'd seen many drunks. The president's patience wore thin, and he ordered Anderson arrested and deported even before the interview was over. Immigration agents were dispatched to the station to boot Anderson out of Botswana, and Africa.

"He was picked up at the radio station," President Ian Khama confirmed shortly afterwards. "I said they should pick him up and show him out of the country. We don't want hate speech in this country. Let him do it in his own country." Khama's leadership gives me hope.

That hope wavered a tiny bit in November 2016. At an international conference on Black portraiture, imagery and depiction in Johannesburg, South Africa, I gave a presentation about the state of LGBT rights across the continent. I told participants that I'd just come from New York, where, at the United Nations, the African bloc had spearheaded an effort to torpedo the work of the first-ever independent expert investigating violence and discrimination based on sexual orientation and gender identity. They wanted to halt the work of Vitit Muntarbhorn of Thailand, a human rights expert who had completed a tour of duty in Syria, and was appointed to the post of Special Raconteur in September. He had already begun his work, but the group objected to his mandate, which was to investigate abuses directed against LGBTI people. With so much state-sanctioned abuse on the continent this wasn't exactly a big surprise. However, the African nation bloc said it wanted a delay because "there is no international agreement on the definition of the concept of 'sexual orientation and gender identity'."

This assertion was so off the mark that the American ambassador at the time, Samantha Power, described it as patently false. She would later assert that violence and discrimination based on sexual orientation and gender identity are "well established", and have been referred to repeatedly in U.N. statements and resolutions, including in the General Assembly and Security Council. "In reality, this amendment has little to do with questions around the definition of sexual orientation and gender identity," she said. "Instead, this amendment is rooted in a real disagreement over whether people of a certain sexual orientation and gender identity are, in fact, entitled to equal rights."

During my presentation, I posed the same question to the scholars and participants in the room that Botswana, on behalf of the African group of nations, had posed to the U.N. General Assembly: "Should sexual orientation and gender identity be included in broader issues of human rights concerns?" Then I gave them the unsatisfying response that Botswana's ambassador, Charles Thembani Ntwaagae, gave to the U.N.: "Those two notions are not, and should not be, linked to existing international human rights instruments."

I told the audience that while the African bloc's response was totally unsurprising, what stung was South Africa not raising an objection. I said that being in South Africa, with its great constitution that outlaws discrimination, was bittersweet at the moment because they had not done anything to halt this, but instead had gone along with their reactionary neighbors.

A month later, at a second hearing, and in a second attempt to quash the appointment, the African bloc, with their supporters in the Organization of Islamic Cooperation, saw their efforts dashed for good as more nations rallied round to vote in favor of it, particularly countries from South America. The defeat was a clear sign that, while divisions remain, the world is coming to the view that discrimination has no place in the 21st century. And this time South Africa broke ranks with the African bloc and made its position very clear to the world. Jerry Matjila, the South African ambassador said, "We will fight discrimination, everywhere, every time. We cannot discriminate against people because of their own lifestyle or intention. That we cannot do in South Africa."

His words give me hope. And back home in Nigeria I am filled with hope when a leading Nigerian online publication, Pulse.ng, calls out Nollywood, our robust film industry, opining that the 'representation of homosexuality in most Nollywood movies is at best a caricature attempt at bad comedy.'

I have to admit that I used to be of the mindset that, even if it is a poor depiction, at least there is one, especially since many habitually say we gay people do not exist in Nigeria, and in all the years that Nollywood has been churning out films – movies that are sought after all over the continent – we have rarely been seen. But the depiction of Nigerian gay men as bearded effeminates sporting bright red lipstick and making exaggerated arm movements is not funny, nor is it remotely the norm, and I now feel that if Nollywood *is* going to depict us, then they had better do it right. We are not going to be the butt of their jokes. And clearly the editors at Pulse don't recognize the caricatures on screen either. Nigerian gay men and women may not be having pride marches, but their friends and neighbors are actually starting to see them, and see the quiet dignity many of us display in the face of constant onslaught. Pulse has seen fit to call out these directors for their lazy caricaturing, and I am heartened.

Judging by Nigerian gay Twitter usage, the baby steps of coming out are growing into purposeful strides. Google points out that Nigeria, Kenya and Ghana routinely top the lust list for searches online for gay porn, giving the lie to claims we don't exist. This too gives me hope.

I'm hopeful when my young male mentees in Ghana show up for my dinner parties with their boyfriends. They know it's a safe space, and that any others in attendance who are not gay will be nonjudgmental. Despite the charade these young men engage in in public, using the modern tactic of putting pictures of the many ladies who are their pals on their Facebook walls to create the impression they are lotharios, I'm hopeful. They are inching closer to living, if not out loud, at least openly. While they may say to office colleagues that the guy who calls them every day is "my cousin" rather than "my lover", I know their moment will come. I'm hopeful.

Though such things are still regrettably rare, I was very hopeful when I read a report of the Ghanaian police arresting several men in Accra for blackmailing and extorting two young gay men – men the criminals forced to strip naked, and used the photos they took of them to extort money. The gay guys reported what happened to the police, a rarity in these cases, and the police did in fact lie in wait for the blackmailers and promptly put them in handcuffs.

On the downside, in April 2017, in rural Nigeria, students were arrested and extorted for allegedly conspiring to attend a gay wedding – with the police in the northern Kaduna state dragging to jail fifty-three young people who their lawyers maintain were simply attending a birthday shindig. After keeping them in custody overnight, a judge set bail for these young people at 500,000 naira (about a thousand U.S. dollars), an extraordinarily high sum for students there. The judge further mandated that a blood relative must provide the cash, adding unnecessary hardship for those accused of the victim-less 'crime' of attending a party. This was another big step backward for my country.

A month earlier, during exam week at the esteemed University of Nigeria, Nsukka, at least five students, some of them friends, were brutally beaten and then robbed of their smart-phones, cash, computers and even generators by a marauding band of homophobes who had gone on a manhunt of suspected gays. All the while taunting them with chants of 'homo'. What was so shocking was that the four ringleaders were fellow students who felt they could beat up, steal from and blackmail their contemporaries with impunity. And they used the tactic of going through their victims' phones and WhatsApp contact lists to target others.

Their three-day rampage caused terror among their class-mates, yet even after beating one to a pulp and demanding he pony up fifty thousand naira, (about U.S. $170), what the thugs didn't expect was that some of their victims would not just report the assaults to the university authorities, but also to the police. And when several of the perpetrators were arrested, they immediately blamed their victims, saying they found out these guys were gay, and found evidence on their phones, so... One even told the police he saw no evidence, but simply was told they were gay so he joined the mob. Gay bashers bank on fear, on the victims being too scared to report violence for fear of being ridiculed or even being arrested themselves. And of course once one makes a report, one has outed oneself.

In this instance the Nigerian police in Nsukka gave me hope. They arrested the thieves and got them to return the phones and computers to their classmates. Though the assailants got out on bail, they are to make restitution for the items they could not return. It is unclear if the university will sanction them, expel them, or just graduate them.

At time of writing, the university authorities have done nothing to punish the offending students; one of the victims has successfully graduated. Is this premier institution of higher learning going to turn out rabid homophobes as alumni, or brilliant, open-minded world citizens? The police and the few university faculty members who responded to the students are to be commended, and in a bleak landscape they give me hope.

And in Lagos, gays aren't exactly all in hiding. As my girl Kainene points out to me, gays and lesbians will continue to gingerly step out. "I'm sure to the outside world it seems like, 'Oh my god, gays in danger here,' but in Lagos we will carry on as we always have. People will get over themselves. I am not going to be tar-and-feathered and driven out of Lagos. That's not going to happen. Nobody cares, but that would be so long as I don't go on TV and say, 'I'm gay'. But that applies to everything here. You just don't wear your heart on your sleeve here, and you don't fly your rainbow colors out in public. I don't feel the need to hide, but I don't feel the need to make a big statement either."

I have hope that one day even wearing your heart on your sleeve will be met with a shrug.

Of indifference.

About the Author

Growing up in Lagos, Nigeria, Chike Frankie Edozien learned to read from the newspapers his father brought home daily. He grew up to become an ink-stained scribbler telling the stories of others in service of a greater good. He is a contributor to the 2016 Commonwealth Writers anthology *Safe House: Explorations in Creative Nonfiction* and in 2017 his 'Last night in Asaba' was published by Jalada Africa/Transitions.

(photo: David Campbell Morrison)

Acknowledgments

So many people pushed for this work to be completed and I'm so thankful for all of them. It wouldn't have come to pass without the encouragement and assistance of my parents, Mary Edozien and Onia Gil Edozien, as well as their children Roy, Annette, Don, Gil, and Victor Edozien.

In addition, Chuks Gwam, Nii Obodai Provencal, David Krebs, Jacob Basboll, Mark Davies, Paul Bellman Nancy Trejos, Winnie Hu, Joe Chan, Gbugemi Okotieuro, Kinna Likimani, Zukiswa Wanner, Ted Conover, Ellis Henican, James Bill Adams, Sampson Akligoh, Christa Sanders, Bibi Bakare-Yusuf, Wanda Ibru and my lord Skido, Oskar Ibru, all provided material assistance.

To Sharon Bowers, my indefatigable agent extraordinaire, for believing and never wavering, and my editor John R. Gordon for patiently enduring draft after draft, after draft.

I will be forever grateful to my very dear Binyavanga Wainaina, who pushed me hard to hold up the mirror to myself and express fearlessly what I see. And to Lola Shoneyin, who told me long ago in New York City to "hurry up and finish." I'm also indebted to New York City for the gift of Maaza Mengiste, Kai Wright, Emmanuel Iduma, Albert Beroukhim and Mona El-tahawy.

My siblings from other parents, Eric Lipton, Nectarios Leoni-das, Elinor Tatum and Mohamad Bazzi, you all make me a better person every day. My brother Marcus Mabry is the friend that everybody deserves and I'm happy you never leave me; I love you. Awam Amkpa, Auntie Ama Ata Aidoo, and the amazing Ellah Wakatama Allfrey – I hope to make you proud one day.

And now, Scott Ikeda, you can give me 'lovings' as you have my attention again!